STREETWISE®

LOW-COST
WEB SITE
PROMOTION

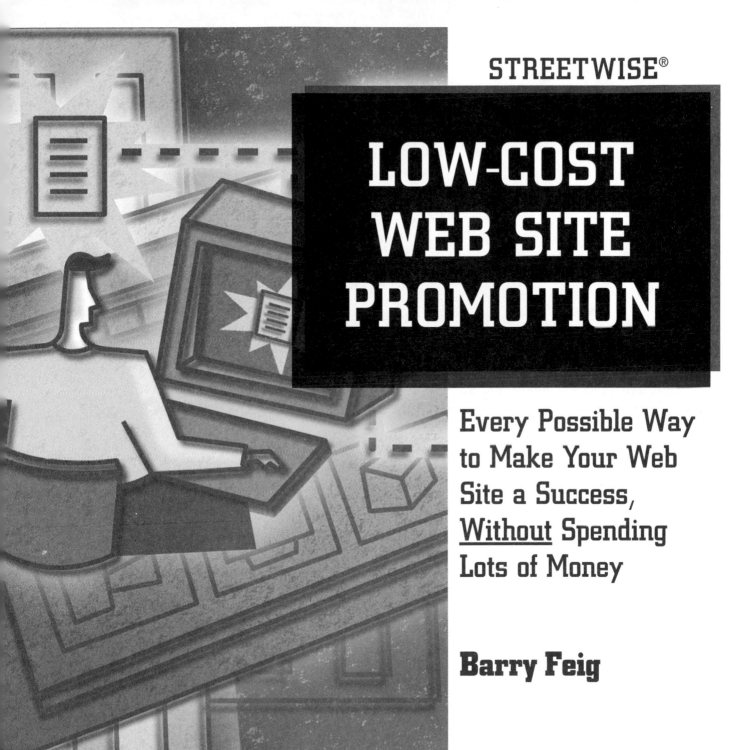

STREETWISE®

LOW-COST WEB SITE PROMOTION

Every Possible Way to Make Your Web Site a Success, <u>Without</u> Spending Lots of Money

Barry Feig

Adams Media Corporation
Avon, Massachusetts

A Streetwise® Publication.
Streetwise® is a registered trademark of F+W Publications, Inc.

Published by Adams Media, an F+W Publications Company
57 Littlefield Street, Avon, MA 02322. U.S.A.
www.adamsmedia.com

ISBN: 1-58062-501-0

Printed in the United States of America.

J I H G F E D

Library of Congress Cataloging-in-Publication Data
Feig, Barry.
Streetwise low-cost web site promotion / by Barry Feig.
p.   cm.
ISBN 1-58062-501-0
1. Computer network resources. 2. Web sites. I. Title.
HD30.37 .F44   2001
658.8'4-dc21   00-065018

This publication is designed to provide accurate and authoritative information with regard to the subject matter covered. It is sold with the understanding that the publisher is not engaged in rendering legal, accounting, or other professional advice. If legal advice or other expert assistance is required, the services of a competent professional person should be sought.

—From a *Declaration of Principles* jointly adopted by a Committee of the
American Bar Association and a Committee of Publishers and Associations

Many of the designations used by manufacturers and sellers to distinguish their products are claimed as trademarks. Where those designations appear in this book and Adams Media was aware of a trademark claim, the designations have been printed in initial capital letters.

Cover illustration by Eric Mueller.

This book is available at quantity discounts for bulk purchases.
For information, call 1-800-872-5627.

Dedication

To quote from the Mamas and the Papas:

This is dedicated to the ones I love.

(And thanks Jeremy for coming up with it.)

Acknowledgments

There are a great many things that go into the making of a book and many people in the background. I would especially like to thank Web Goddess, Joan-Marie Moss, (don't just call her Joan, or she gets very upset), who seriously helped me write this book and turn drivel into English. She also greatly helped me both through dry spells and with words of encouragement.

CONTENTS

SECTION 1: BUILDING YOUR GRAND SITE

SECTION 2: RESEARCH AND TACTICS

Contents

SECTION 3: BRINGING IN MIND-BOGGLING TRAFFIC

CONTENTS

SECTION 5: TOOLS YOU CAN USE RIGHT NOW

Contents

SECTION 6: KEEPING TRACK

Preface

So much to do, so little time—especially in the explosive world of the Internet. That's the mantra of the Internet marketer. Because of growing competition in every segment of the Internet, today's Web site owner has to be more knowledgeable and creative than ever before.

This book is meant to inspire you to create new promotion strategies and to give you the tools you need to compete—and win. One thing is constant: If your site doesn't promote regularly, it won't get traffic. But the Internet is also a fun way to make a living—even though spending hours in front of a monitor and typing in letters is sort of a perverse enjoyment. This is a how-to book on achieving your Internet goals, whatever they may be. It's a compendium of ideas.

Here are some of the problems this book will solve:

- How to take an idea and build a comprehensive Internet site around it.
- How to get research that really works without busting a budget.
- The hows and whys of marketing on the Internet—and all the latest traffic-building gizmos

The book is filled with ideas, strategies, and examples that you can mix and match for your particular situation. It can be subtitled "The Bible of Internet Promotion" because it offers the essential tools of building traffic.

This book includes the full arsenal of marketing weapons—how to's, tips, tactics, strategies—and all of them proven. It's a comprehensive blending of strategies that can be used instantly. It's as useful for the Internet newbie, who is in the formative stage of building a site, as it is for the experienced marketer, who is racking his or her head for the next *big* traffic-building idea.

Try to read this book from cover to cover because every section builds on a previous section. After you've done that, thumb through

> The book is filled with ideas, strategies, and examples that you can mix and match for your particular situation.

it randomly and adapt the ideas for your particular Internet situation. I've tried to keep the writing light and informal. I've eschewed the marketing jargon of most business books.

By the way, you can help me out by dropping me an e-mail. Let me know how you used the strategy or built one of your own from the ideas in this book.

Happy surfing.

—Barry Feig
feig@barryfeig.com

Building Your Grand Site

Summary of Section I

- Why you should create your own Web site
- How to plan your site
- Basics of graphic design and all the bells and whistles
- How to write text for your Web site

CHAPTER 1 CREATING INTERNET TRAFFIC **CHAPTER 2** TEN STEPS AND TOOLS FOR A NO-NONSENSE, TAKE-NO-PRISONERS PROMOTION PLAN
CHAPTER 3 FOUNDATIONS FOR WINNING WEB SITE PROMOTION **CHAPTER 4** HOW TO POSITION YOUR SITE TO ATTRACT TRAFFIC
CHAPTER 5 SITE SPECIFICS **CHAPTER 6** HOW TO WRITE FOR YOUR WEB SITE

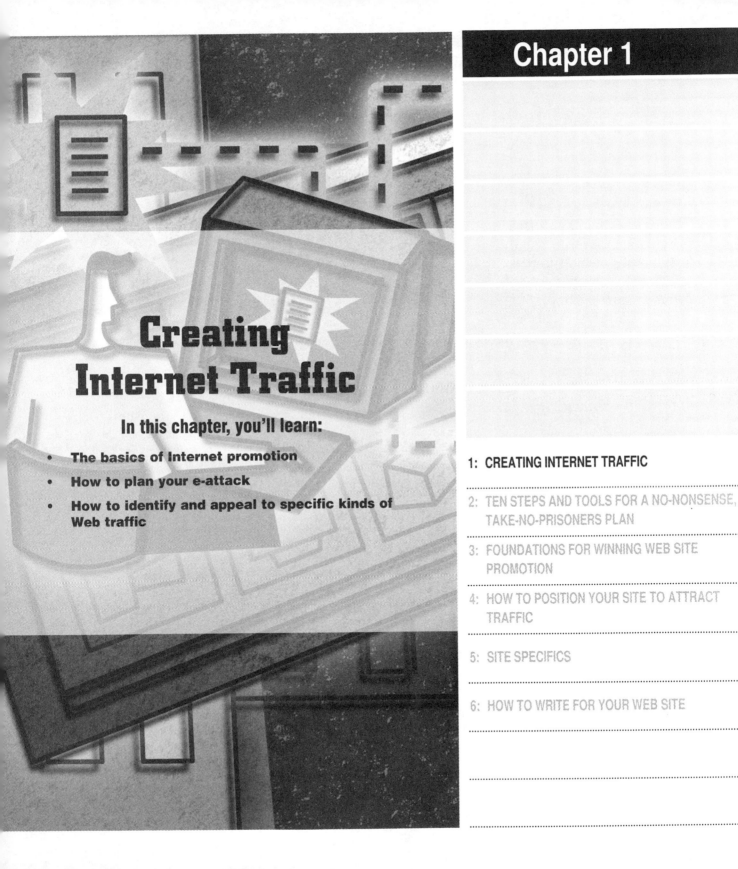

Chapter 1

Creating Internet Traffic

In this chapter, you'll learn:

- The basics of Internet promotion
- How to plan your e-attack
- How to identify and appeal to specific kinds of Web traffic

How big is the Internet, really? Imagine you've dropped out of the sky in a parachute, in the dead of night, in New York City. No one knows you're there. No one, but you, knows how you got there. Since you're new in town, no one knows who you are, or how to locate you. You don't know anyone either, but you're looking for a particular person, and you want that person to find you. You are surrounded by eight million people, yet you are, for all intents and purposes, anonymous. With over 12.5 million Internet names and over 30,000 new names being added daily (I added 3, myself, today), the new Web site owner faces quite a challenge.

> More than half of all U.S. adults are now online daily. Home use of the Internet has skyrocketed, and women now make up 50% of the online population.

If it's that difficult, why is the Internet so popular?

More than half of all U.S. adults are now online daily. Home use of the Internet has skyrocketed, and women now make up 50% of the online population, according to an Internet user trends report. Online shoppers more than doubled their spending in the past year, according to the report.

That's why you have spent enormous time and energy (and maybe money) planning and putting together a Web site. The Internet is a wonderful means of communication. It's a bit of an oddity, too. Suppose an alien came down to earth and you told him about this amazing feat of connecting most of the world through telephone lines. He'd probably ask what you're doing with this fascinating technology. And you might say, "We try to sell things to each other"—just as we did with the breakthrough new world (at one time) of television and radio.

But the Internet is a unique medium because it levels the playing field between tiny companies and big conglomerates since it allows anyone to reach out and talk to a potential audience of 100 million people. But just because the audience is there, it doesn't mean they will pay to hear what you have to sell . . . or say. Don't be fooled by the hype. Nothing will happen by magic or because of your strong will. While you can definitely succeed, and even make a little money, you're going to have to work hard. But it can be fun and even stimulating work. And it can be profitable.

A great many people point out the similarity of the Web to the introduction of television. But television was nowhere as democratic as the Internet is. If you wanted to promote a product on TV in its earliest days, you had to sponsor a program—or groups of programs. If you were really well off, you could buy a broadcast station. But today, with the Internet, every site is a mini-broadcast center where you can say or sell anything you want, provided you have visitors. It's your station. It's your show.

Promoting on the Internet is different from promoting in traditional media because you have total control of your budget. Spend as little as you want. Spend as much as you want. It's a station without geographic or demographic bounds. My site, *www.barryfeig.com,* was serviced by a Web provider in Finland. I used a company in India for some of my promotional work and research for this book.

> A great many people point out the similarity of the Web to the introduction of television. But television was nowhere as democratic as the Internet is.

Promotional opportunities

Look around you. Everything you see and hear provides an opportunity to promote your Web site. Even the parachute you used to drift to earth is an opportunity, if you write the words myplace.com on it (don't actually use myplace.com—someone already owns it). Yes, there are many promotional agencies that will do your work for you—for a fee—but you don't need a specialized promotion agency to publicize your Web site. I suggest you do it yourself—at the beginning stages anyway. The more time you spend doing your own promotion, the less you will have to spend in cold, hard cash. Besides the money savings, doing things yourself will create a learning curve for you. The Web has its own nomenclature and terms that sound mysterious. These words will become more and more familiar. Later on, should you decide to go to an outside source, you will be able to separate promises from performance and become a better, more knowledgeable Webbee.

Types of advertising

Your "advertising" can be national, regional, or even local in nature. You'll find that many special-interest sites sell advertising banners and other types of related advertising. These costs can range from *free* to tens of thousands of dollars each month. Most charge a fee and say they can reach specific demographics that cannot be reached by conventional media. For instance, it is possible to have your advertisement appear every time one of *your* search words is used on a particular search engine.

Okay, you are almost ready to sit back and let your Web page become your money machine, right? Well, here's a hard reality. Ninety-two percent of Web sites are not making enough money to cover their own expenses. Although some sites are so poorly conceived they will never make a go of it, many others suffer from lack of promotional expertise. Your investment in marketing your Web site is no less important than the cost of developing the site itself. It is a necessary marketing expense, not an optional one. You will never sell anything—even if your site is the greatest site in the world—if nobody knows about it. Without promotion there will be no prospects, and without prospects there will be no sales.

Budgeting

I'm going to assume that you probably don't have enough money in your budget to buy a commercial on the next Super Bowl (but there are some interesting statistics at the beginning of Chapter 25 if you decide to splurge). I'm also going to assume that you want to make the most of your contacts through the Web, and that you don't have a great deal of money to spend. That's a good idea, but like most good ideas, there's a catch. Although promoting on the Web can be a free ride, you might want to speed things up by using some kind of paid, traditional media. That's why you see so many ads for Internet companies on TV, the radio, and the other mass media. And that's why you'll see a section about it later in this book.

The purpose of this book is to bring visitors to your site, no matter what you want to do with the traffic. There are a great

Use Traditional Business Practices on the Web

The overnight millionaire who made a fortune by putting a site on the Internet is a myth. Sure there are some people who made money on the Internet by drumming up investor capital, but as of this writing, paper profits are turning to paper losses. A great many people build an Internet site, forget about all the things they learned about business and wait for the money to start rolling in. It doesn't happen that way. The sites that work best are those that adhere to traditional, successful business practices. The Internet is not a new business. It is new marketing channel.

many ways you spend your money on building traffic on the Web. Like any other business, you'll find charlatans and quacks trying to pare your bankroll down to the lowest common denominator. If this book saves you from tying in with even one of these people, it will have been well worth your money. It's also true that many startup Web companies have their pockets full of investor cash that will give them an instant presence. We'll save those tips for the hard-cover edition of this book with the gold-leaf pages. One of the wonderful things about the Internet is the number of "freebies" available.

Why are you on the Web anyway?
(Not a trick question)

There are many reasons to develop a Web site. For some people, a Web site is a form of communication. For others, it's a way of imparting knowledge about something. For some, it's a way for people to show their individuality. For many others, it's a "business through a computer monitor." If you're like most people, in any of these categories, you came up with the site—and the money or sweat equity—without a great deal of forethought about how you're going to bring in people once the site was completed. Don't be upset about this. That's the way most people do it. Creating and dreaming is fun. Selling is hard work.

This book will furnish you with the options, strategies, and Web resources you need to create successful marketing forays. But the book will work only if you keep an open mind and rid yourself of pre-conceived notions. There are two important keys to getting the most out of using this book: (1) adopt and (2) adapt.

Change is an essential element of a successful Web site—it must continually evolve or adapt. Adopt what has worked and adapt it for your particular product or marketing environment. Evolve your promotion to take advantage of new ideas, techniques, and technologies. This book is proactive. It suggests you take the initiative in your marketing excursions. I've boiled it down to the Ten Commandments of Web site propulsion.

Change is an essential element of a successful Web site—it must continually evolve or adapt. Adopt what has worked and adapt it for your particular product or marketing environment.

The Ten Commandments of Web site promotion

1. Thou shalt devote oneself fully to the task.
2. Thou shalt put thyself into the "shoes" of the visitor. Thou shalt immerse thyself in thy visitor's wants and needs and be beholden to those who land upon thy site, for the visitor is Heaven-sent.
3. Thou shalt be a sponge and soak up everything related to thy site.
4. Thou shalt steal from worthy competitors.
5. Thou shalt strive to be like Gumby, always and forever flexible.
6. Thou shalt change thy Web site in accordance with consumer learning, for it is made from computer blips and beeps, not gold.
7. Thou shalt honor thy search engines whether they be friend or foe.
8. Thou shalt take a hard-nosed approach and cast out forever pet ideas that don't bring in the masses, for they are false Gods.
9. Thou shalt take at least one hour per day to promote thy Web site.
10. Thou shalt not spam.

> Thou shalt put thyself into the "shoes" of the visitor.

Adopt and adapt

We've spent a lot of time learning what works and what doesn't work in running a business and in sales and marketing. Heck, marketing and demographics have been big business ever since market research positioned JFK as the darling of the American public and the president of the United States. Marketers have learned what makes the market—and the American consumer—tick. They have determined how colors make us react and what kinds of articles we'll read and how to create a buying frenzy for pet rocks.

However, 99.9% of that information just doesn't work anymore. In the cyberworld, it's essential to unlearn everything that was held as gospel. I'm talking about trashing everything that you believed to be true and relearning even the basics, like how to get acquainted with other people.

In this new world, you don't just go up and introduce yourself to others and tell them about your business, any more than you would use a bullhorn to shout to the residents of New York City that you're arriving. Even though you can send a single e-mail to 1,000 people all at once at no cost, you just can't do that. It's called "spamming," and you will get in a heck of a lot of trouble if you do that. In fact, you might be banned from the Internet. Likewise, you don't send e-mail promoting yourself and soliciting business unless you are very confident that the recipient wants to get that information from you. There again, your activities will be considered spamming and will win you only ostracism.

Cyberspace is a place where communication at lightning speed is possible, but caution is essential. Inhabitants on this new world are jaded. They are much more selective and critical of what they are willing to read. And they have the ability to delete your efforts to "sell"—or even let the computer filter it as just junk mail—without worrying about the clutter of discarded paper.

> Even though you can send a single e-mail to 1,000 people all at once at no cost, you just can't do that. It's called "spamming," and you will get in a heck of a lot of trouble if you do that.

Preplanning is key

Promoting your Web site is both a science and an art. And it can be frustrating. What worked for *www.goodstuffcards.com* (a site that specializes in collectible cards about the movies) may not work for *www.barryfeig.com*. Here's a good exercise: *www.goodstuffcards.com* is a consumer site; *www.barryfeig.com* is business to business. Go to each of these sites and compare their different goals.

The act of planning leads you through a process of evaluating the marketplace, identifying your competition, evaluating your strengths and weaknesses, and determining your goals. As with any business course of action, you need to scope out where you are going and how you plan to get there.

> As with any business course of action, you need to scope out where you are going and how you plan to get there.

The official Web site preplanner

Every decision you make about your Web site should be focused on what you want to achieve with it. This sounds easy, and there's nothing wrong with saying, "I want a Web site because I want a Web site." But if you are serious about developing a site that will attract more than friends and family you need to have a goal; otherwise, you will be spending money or time for services you don't need or want.

Janet Attard, owner of the company Business KnowHow (*www.businessknowhow.com*) which is also on America Online, was instrumental in helping draft this preplanning checklist.

- ❏ What do you expect to accomplish with your Web site?
- ❏ Whom do you expect to use it? Customers? Vendors? Employees?
- ❏ Who will do the marketing?
- ❏ If you're a business site, how many items will you include?
- ❏ How many sizes and colors or other variations will be involved?
- ❏ Where will the photography and copy come from?
- ❏ How often will you have to update the Web site?
- ❏ Who will do the updates?
- ❏ Who will design the Web site?
- ❏ What will it cost to design the Web site?
- ❏ What will it cost to make changes on your Web site?

❏ Will you have to hire employees to manage your Web site?

❏ How many sales or leads will you need to break even on costs?

❏ How soon do you need to reach your goals?

Quick tips

✓ Continually sift through the marketplace to make sure your great idea isn't already taken. If it is, build on it.

✓ Stay focused. Always be prepared to react to a changing market.

✓ Keep the Ten Commandments of Web site promotion in a place where you can refer to it often.

Summary

The planning and coordination of your promotional efforts is critical and continual. Since it will serve as your blueprint to success, you should have it written down on paper so you won't waste your time in taking mindless turns into fruitless avenues. What you do at the very beginning stages will affect you once the site is completed.

As an Internet marketer, your most valuable asset is time. And, yes, time is more valuable than money, so spend yours wisely. Because your time is a limited resource, you will need to learn to prioritize. Certain things are more important than others. For example, consider the amount of time you spend on various promotions and marketing activities. Do you actually know which is most productive for you? If you don't, you're wasting precious time. Test all of your advertising, and spend your time appropriately.

> The planning and coordination of your promotional efforts is critical and continual.

For more information on this topic, visit our Web site at www.businesstown.com

Chapter 2

Ten Steps and Tools for a No-Nonsense, Take-No-Prisoners Promotion Plan

In this chapter, you'll learn:

- A quick ten-step plan for meeting your objective
- Different kinds of surfer mentalities
- How to find out what your competitors are doing

D eveloping a working and traffic-building Web site takes a great many decisions. Many of these decisions you will have to make "on the fly" as an individual issue comes up. But there are a series of steps you can take early on to make sure you stay ahead of the game:

1. Define your objectives and your audience.

As a worthy Web site promoter, you should have at least an idea of the people you want to visit your site and why they will be visiting. For a startup Web site, you'll find that visitors will mimic ants feasting on a lollipop. There will be one or two initial explorers who accidentally stumble on your site. These ants will alert one or two additional ants, and pretty soon there will be many, many ants feasting.

Unlike ants, people may come looking for information, or they may find you because they need your company's product or service, but there can be many other reasons. They may want to buy something. They may want hard facts. Or they might just be bored and want to play.

> Define what categories of people you're seeking, and it will be easier to target your marketing efforts.

Mesh your goals with theirs. Define what categories of people you're seeking, and it will be easier to target your marketing efforts. Identify the common ground you share with your prospective visitors and why they should care about your site. If you are just running a fun site, you may be really pleased just to receive e-mail from like-minded people from around the world. If you are in charge of an e-commerce site, your sales will probably be the first thing you look at. Define how you want your customers to react when they navigate to your site. What do you want to accomplish—and, more important, what do you think your visitors want to accomplish?

Here is a brief questionnaire to help you refine and define your mission:

- Do you want to promote through traditional marketing channels?
- Are you selling a unique product or service?
- Are you selling the same product that other people are selling? If so, why should anyone come to your site?

- Are you providing information of some kind?
- Are you trying to reinforce a brand image?

All these questions will be expanded on in the next few chapters.

What category does your audience fit into?

Although every Web surfer has his or her own "style," it helps if you know the general categories of people who regularly use the net. They can be broken down into eight categories: simplifiers, surfers, newbies, bargainers, traditionalists, sportsters, information mavens, and gamesters and interaction seekers. Knowing these categories can help you decide on your promotion and site-building tactics.

Simplifiers

They use the Internet to make life easier in some way. They have a specific purpose in mind when they connect and log off immediately after finding what they want. An example of two companies that cater to these people are Expedia.com, a site that allows users to buy air travel online, and 123Greetings, a company that creates and sends greeting cards and postcards with a click of a mouse.

How to hook them: Sites must provide clean, uncluttered content. Ease of access and use are very important to simplifiers. The key is to make product information available and simple to access. Your return policies and customer service policies should be readily available and spelled out.

Surfers

At one time, surfers drove the net. Surfers leap quickly from site to site continually seeking new experiences. Surfers are stimuli junkies and are always looking for new bells and whistles, constantly downloading new gizmos and hi-tech features. Site examples include *www.comedycentral.com* and *www.magiceye.com*.

How to hook them: For these people, you need cutting-edge site design and gee-whiz effects. These people get bored and uninterested unless you update your site frequently. But beware; surfers

> Although every Web surfer has his or her own "style," it helps if you know the general categories of people who regularly use the net.

don't like to spend money. They consider Web entertainment free and feel that it is their entitlement for owning a computer and being on the forefront of new technology. Attracting surfers means cutting-edge site design and features, constant updates, a strong online brand, and an assortment of products and services.

Newbies

These are people new to the Internet and, often, new to computers in general. Their favorite features are e-mail and chat rooms. They tend to go after specific subject matter. Since they tend to return to sites they enjoy, it is relatively easy to keep them coming back to your site. Companies with a strong offline presence have a strong potential to reach these people since they readily stay with products they know and use. Newbies are often afraid of their computers and are unwilling to click on unfamiliar elements.

How to hook them: Keep your site simple. Guide newbies every step of the way. Make sure your keywords are both descriptive and clear for the search engines. Keep your site warm and novice friendly. If you want newbies to click on a link, then say clearly and unambiguously "Click here." It's easy to scare a Newbie off, but they will be incredibly loyal if you put them at ease.

Bargainers

Bargainers are devoted to the quest for deals. They love the adrenaline rush they get when they find the lowest price. The hunt is more exciting than the actual purchase. Examples are *www.shopper.com* and *www.amazon.com*.

How to hook them: Appeal on both their rational and emotional levels. Satisfy their need for the lowest price. Bargainers have an innate and uncontrollable urge to tell their friends how they got the lowest price. Use price comparisons to show them how much money they saved.

Traditionalists

These people tend to hang out at newsites, financial sites, and portals (logon to *www.go.com* for an example of a portal). Traditionalists spend twice as much time per page as the average

Whose Name? Whose Site?

There's a game going around in offices and bars that have Internet connections. People go to Register.com, which is an Internet Registration service. The object is to find names that are not already taken. You simply type in a name and see if someone has registered it. When played in a bar, the loser has to imbibe in his or her favorite beverage if the name is taken (maybe losing is not that bad an idea). It's a really fun way of killing a few hours. If you always meant to register goldengiraffe.com you're out of luck. You can settle for goldengiraffe.net, or goldengiraffe.org. Same thing with holymonkey.com.

user. Traditionalists want "all the news that will fit on a Web page." They want to feel they're getting something special for their time spent online. Examples are *www.go.com* and *www.netscape.com*.

How to hook them: Create your own portal, or gateway. Eschew fluff, and keep your material hard-hitting and to the point. Collect links to other hard-news sites.

Sportsters

These people act like traditionalists but focus on sports and entertainment sites. They are drawn to fresh, colorful, and offbeat sites. Examples are *www.jumptheshark.com* and *www.film.com*.

How to hook them: Keep your site fresh and colorful with reviews, current news, and gossip. Load your site with sound bytes and clever visual media.

Information mavens

These people want to know everything about anything. They fill their heads with minutiae and (to you) triviality. They are the kind of people whose secret wish is to be on *Who Wants to Be a Millionaire?* and *Jeopardy.* But information mavens may be your best friends. They may want inside information that only you can deliver.

How to hook them: Make it your mission to attract these people. Declare your leadership position as an expert in their field (whatever it happens to be). It doesn't always make a difference whether you are or aren't, as long as you sound authoritative. Every Web site does something better than anyone else's. At least every site should make that claim. Make your product stand out by being number one in some aspect of your category that consumers care about. If you've identified your consumers' mindset, you can create your Web site in a way that speaks to your customers personally. If you've identified your leadership position, you can plaster it on all of your sales materials—and broadcast it.

Gamesters and interaction seekers

Gamesters like to interact with their computer and seek out puzzles and interactive material.

> Keep your site fresh and colorful with reviews, current news, and gossip.

How to hook them: Even if your site is purely informational, make it fun by offering quizzes and games. Let gamesters compete against you. Examples are *www.pogo.com* and *www.emode.com*.

2. Target search engines in everything you do.

It is estimated that 85% of people employ a search engine to find information online. Unfortunately, only 1 "hit" out of 15 brings the surfer to any kind of useful site. Search engines are to be courted, catered to, and indulged. A top listing on the search engines is a "Holy Grail" for Web promoters, particularly for promoters without much of a budget for paid advertising.

Computers, not people, run most search engines (although some do use real people to index sites). These computers are trained to look for certain keywords or phrases. Since many pages on your site can be indexed with a search engine, the words you use become an important strategy in attracting visitors. The best plan of attack is to create keywords, simple phrases, and actual content with words that search engines can understand.

But here is where things get sort of tricky. It is imperative to use phrases that both computers and people can understand and that your target market will search for. We'll use goodstuffcards.com as an example. Let's pretend you wanted to buy a set of movie cards for your son's birthday and you don't know a great deal about the movie collectibles business. Since you are a doting mother, you launch the AltaVista (*www.altavista.com*) search engine. In the search box, you type "movie collectibles" and get 1,092 matches (I tried it). If you're like most people, after seeing the first 30 or so citations, you're going to get bored and give up. Neither you, your son, nor Good Stuff Cards is happy. And neither is AltaVista because they're in business to help you find goodstuffcards.com. If you don't, you might go to the other major search engines.

As a Web site promoter, it is up to you to develop the actual phrase that the surfer will look for, the search engine will index properly, and will lead to your site.

While we're on the subject of search engines, it is very important to understand what the page titles and metatags do since these

> As a Web site promoter, it is up to you to develop the actual phrase that the surfer will look for, the search engine will index properly, and will lead to your site.

play a very important role in how the search engines rank your site. If you're not sure of what metatags and page titles are, I suggest you take a quick look in the glossary because they are very important in the next section.

In these preplanning stages, examine your site and those of your competitors. Make a list and guess at the key phrases a surfer would use when searching for sites like yours. Before you identify your own key phrases, look at what your competitors are doing. If you are the only one in the world selling a hard-to-find object, it may not be too difficult to know what keywords to use. For example, suppose you are selling "purple elephant dolls." If this phrase is registered with Yahoo! and someone enters this keyword, your site may be number one on the results list. This is because you don't have much competition or there aren't a great many sites featuring purple elephant dolls.

But now, let's say, you have a product area that has a great deal of competition. Perhaps you are an orange juice broker. It would take extensive Web site promotion, marketing, and advertising to get to the top. Obviously, you're going to have to take drastic measures to get to the top. (There's more about keywords and metatags in Chapters 6 and 18.)

3. Create a short list of domain names and variances.

A domain name (or URL) should be the first matter of business to build traffic. The domain name is how people describe you and is usually (not always) the name of your Web site. As the Internet grows, names that were once generic are becoming Web site names. For instance, if your daughter wanted to open up an online lemonade stand—don't laugh, I've heard crazier ideas—she would be unable to use the name lemonade.com. It's already owned. If she wanted to be creative and change the spelling to lemonaid.com, she's also out of luck because it's owned by a consumer advocacy group in Michigan.

The name should be brief, so it can be easily typed. It should not contain any ampersands (the & character) because people tend to confuse it with the word *and*. There are thousands of

> The domain name is how people describe you and is usually (not always) the name of your Web site.

domain names taken every minute, so it's getting tougher and tougher to find the right one. If you have a catchy domain name, register it now—don't even wait until you hit Chapter 3, which includes everything you ever wanted to know about domain names.

4. Ferret out your competitors.

With millions of Web sites out there, there is bound to be competition. Let me rephrase that. With millions of Web sites out there, you will have competition. But the Web also makes spying easy—and I mean that only in the nicest way. With traditional media, you can only guess what the competition is doing. The Internet, however, offers built-in ways—all legal. And they're all ethical, especially when you put it under the context of market research.

Here are three ways to see what your competitors are doing:

> With millions of Web sites out there, you will have competition.

- Search for your competitors on the major search engines using their names and words that relate to their services. Sometimes the search engines will even identify what sites your competitors have their banners on.
- Logon to closely related newsgroups (Chapter 11) and see what people are saying about your competitors.
- Check your competitors' codes to learn what search words and metatags they are using. They won't always be 100% accurate, but you can pretty much see what the various search engines see. Here's how:

  1. Logon to your competitor's Web page using either Internet Explorer or Netscape.
  2. Click on View.
  3. Click on Source.

In that jumble of strange-looking words and symbols, you will see a section called "Description." You will also see metatags. These are the keywords that search engines are using to index your competitor's site.

5. Enlist the aid of your visitors.

Most every business wants word-of-mouth promotion because it's a free source of new customers. The Web is no different. In everything you say and do, you should be asking for referrals from your customers. Your very first visitors can be a gold mine for you if you court them and actually sell to them. Statistics show that 28 to 42% of the people who have bought something from you will buy again.

Think of the potential here. Let's say you design a new Web site to show off your family—and your new baby. At the baby's christening, you mention that the baby pictures will be on your new Web site. So when Uncle Bob checks out your site, he sees a little box that says "don't forget to tell our other relatives out in the Northwest." So Uncle Bob calls his Aunt Nell who sees your site, thinks your baby is the most adorable baby she's ever seen, and bequeaths your young son $1 million in her will. And it's all because of a referral. That's how your referrals can help your Web site grow.

Of course, it doesn't always happen like that, but word of mouth is the least expensive and most effective way to get new business. Build relationships with your visitors and ask them to share the relationships with others. (See the section on "Viral marketing" in Chapter 22.)

Collaboration with your visitors is one of the most important advantages being discovered on the Internet. It is very common for visitors to a site to have as much knowledge on a subject as the experts behind the site. Collaboration between visitors can add a lot of value to your visitor's experience. Information should be archived so it can be a good pool of data for future visitors. Discussion forums, polls, surveys, guestbooks, chat, and more can help you increase the value of your Web site for others. The concepts and reasons for using these components are well covered in later chapters.

> Word of mouth is the least expensive and most effective way to get new business.

6. Cultivate partners and relationships.

Associations, affiliations, and partnerships are of prime importance in driving traffic, unlike many other kinds of media promotion. As of this writing, portals are also big. These are gateways to many portions of the Web strung together in categories. Links can also play a big role in driving traffic. Words and phrases linking one site to another are really what brought the term *surfing* into use big time. Affiliate and link programs allow you to generate traffic from both larger and smaller sites.

Travelers cruise the Internet like a giant board game. On some squares, they jump to another and on others they stay for a while. The whole point of building an online presence is to create new relationships. Otherwise, you are stuck with your existing network, probably geographically confined to the area of the world you live in. New, online relationships are commonly triggered by visitors to your Web site. Humanclick (*www.humanclick.com*) is a company that created a program that allows companies to talk in real time. Their growth has been driven by allowing companies to link up with them for free.

Plan on getting links from companies that are partners with yours, sites with industry information, sites from associations and trade groups. These will keep your name in front of the people you are trying to reach. Another way to advertise online is through performance-based marketing, also known as an affiliate program. You can actually advertise your products and services across thousands of Web sites while paying only for results.

7. Talk up your site constantly.

Don't laugh. So many people get caught up in the sheer thrill of seeing their site online they forget to talk up the site. Put it on your letterhead, your business card, and all other promotional materials. Successful promotions start with you. If you aren't excited about your site, no one else will be either. Know your prospects and customers. Gather a list of your customers or potential prospects. Plan on contacting them about your Web site and ask them to spread the word. A good way to build a database is to send out frequent e-mails and ask people to respond.

8. Integrate your marketing.

This means that everything you do should convey the same message and represent what you stand for. All of your literature, and

> Travelers cruise the Internet like a giant board game. On some squares, they jump to another and on others they stay for a while.

even your office, should convey the same message. Integrated marketing is the practice of promoting by using several forms of media simultaneously with the goal of creating a singular brand or site image. It's been used by offline merchants and advertisers forever because it works and is a tried-and-true business strategy. Ziff-Davis, which owns magazines, trade shows, online and television properties, uses one integrated strategy to great success.

With the explosion of the Internet, integrated marketing has undergone a transformation. The Web lets offline companies deepen their relationship with customers because it is a one-to-one method for doing business.

9. Do everything regularly.

The main secret to a successful low-cost Web site is to get started and keep doing something on a regular basis. Your visitors and promotion partners should feel they are visiting an active site. When you're sitting in a doctor's waiting room and you see only old magazines, you might wonder about the compassion of the doctor. In the same way, visiting a site that was last updated in 1996 is a sure way to lose visitor trust. When designing your Web site, build in ways to keep it fresh.

10. Measure everything.

The way to build is to analyze all of your hits all the time. Most Web site owners have bundles of information at their beck and call. If you follow the hints in this book, you'll know everything about your site visitors—from the time they logon to your site and where they logged on from to the search engine that brought them to your site. Thoughtful study of this information should be planned into your attack so you can act accordingly. It's good to periodically step back and see what's working and what's not in any business. Then expand on what's working and either drop what's not or "tweak" it to see if it can be improved.

Keep updating and evaluating your site. All Web sites should always be in the process of being redesigned or renovated. This is

> The main secret to a successful low-cost Web site is to get started and keep doing something on a regular basis.

one of the beauties of the Internet. Change happens quickly. If you had a store, you would have to call design engineers, contractors, building inspectors, and the like. When you change your Web site for the better, it takes only a few minutes. One of the key aspects of promotion is to keep your site updated, and fresh and clean.

Quick tips

✓ Attracting new traffic is much more difficult than satisfying existing traffic. It easier and more profitable to make existing visitors "go further" rather than to chase new visitors. Until you fix up your site so that it works for the traffic you are already getting, why spend a lot of time, effort, and money chasing more visitors?

✓ A good ranking results when searchers enter words into a major search engine and their search results indicate a good match to your site. It is especially good if your site is listed in the top ten matches.

✓ Make your Web site fit your business, rather than the other way around.

> Attracting new traffic is much more difficult than satisfying existing traffic.

Summary

Plan your complete marketing process, complete with strategies and tactics, right from the start. And be prepared to implement your marketing plan with the launch of your Web site. You should have your messages clear; your target audiences defined; and various press releases, events, and possible advertising campaigns at the ready for the moment your site is introduced to the public.

For more information on this topic, visit our Web site at www.businesstown.com

Chapter 3

Foundations for Winning Web Site Promotion

In this chapter, you'll learn:

- How to plan for your Web site focus
- When to include bells and whistles on your Web site
- The six Cs of Web site communication
- The basics of segmentation and targeting

This morning I received a call from a client who was distressed about how her Web site was doing. She is a very successful merchant who sells children's behavioral modification products. We'll call her company "Kid Trainers" to save her from embarrassment. Her line includes toilet training aids, homework helpers, products for hyperactive kids, and other goods. Although she registered *www.kidtrainers.com* religiously with the search engines, she wasn't getting "hits," and people were not ordering her products. They weren't even requesting information. I looked at her Web site and became disturbed. It was a pretty site from a design standpoint, but nothing on the Web site called out "buy me." Nothing even said "visit me again." So I asked her some basic marketing questions.

"What is the purpose of the site?"
"To sell my products," she said.
"Which products?"
"All of them. I have fifty."
"Which ones are most important?"
"They all are."
"Which one are you focusing on?"
"All of them."

This was getting hard, and I was getting frustrated. Focusing on fifty products is very difficult to do. The woman is a brilliant marketer who did well with traditional marketing channels but had no clue about plying her trade on the Web. There's something about Web marketing that makes reasonably sane people do crazy things. I should admit here that my original site was terrible.

Her first page was loaded with words on how to modify a child's behavior, but none of her products were on the first page. Visitors had to keep clicking to find even one of her products. I kept plowing along with my questions.

"How are people going to find your products if they stumble onto your site?"
"They can click on the little tabs."

> There's something about Web marketing that makes reasonably sane people do crazy things.

"How do they know which tabs to click on?"
"If they have kids, they should know."

Her problem was in thinking that visitors want to hunt. They don't. Web travelers want everything easy. In creating her Web site, our entrepreneur forgot that her mission is to sell and to make it easy for people to buy.

Of course, selling is not everyone's mission. Every Web site is different. Some sites strive to be entertaining. Some are merely brochures on the Web. Every Web site owner, though, needs, and wants, to attract traffic of some kind. They also want repeat traffic. It is not enough to get 'em in the door. It is important to have a plan for what will happen when they get there so they will come back. It's much less expensive to resell, or up-sell existing visitors than it is to acquire new visitors.

> Web travelers want everything easy.

What are the benefits of repeat visitors?

There are many reasons to go after repeat visitors, for instance (1) you develop a relationship with your visitors, and (2) you get multiple chances to make the sale.

By providing info to your repeat visitors or by providing a valuable service for free, you can earn the trust of your visitors. If your visitors *trust* you and the advice you give, you will increase your chances of making the sale.

This book is not meant to be an all-encompassing tome about developing your Web site. But if you don't have a site that people want to come to, you're not going to get hits or return traffic.

The six Cs to generating repeat traffic

The Web has evolved since its early days. People now go to the Internet for a specific reason rather than out of curiosity. Since the early days of the Internet, people have learned what a site should offer them. Internet travelers today are purposeful and demanding. When they wade through a sea of information and find the site they want, they expect it to look professional. They also want to be informed. There are many ways to provide information, but all can be broken down to the six Cs (and an S).

Content

This is probably why most people come to your site. They come to view your content. You can't "drive" people to your Web site, but you can lure them with readable content that fits their needs. Give visitors information of value. Make sure that the information is clear and well written. If you sell too hard, you will be sent to marketing oblivion with a click. People aren't looking to be sold. They want to be informed. Provide content that your competitors aren't providing. Nothing will turn off your visitors faster than rehashed ideas (except for the aforementioned slow-loading doohickeys). All too many sites are playing copycat and offering nothing more than what can be found elsewhere.

Currency

Keep your site fresh. Update your content and your page monthly if possible. People go to the Web looking for up-to-the-minute information. You can meet this need by providing high-quality information that's topical and readable. It should engage your customers and give them reasons to come back.

Consistency

Don't use different elements on each page. Your entire Web site should have a unified look and feel. Changing formats merely confuses your visitor. Look at *www.goodstuffcards.com* again. There are few gimmicks. It's easy to navigate. Base all of your visuals on a theme and stick with it. After the first few times a visitor accesses your site, he or she will develop a mental image and expect it. On a similar note, don't use more than

Treat Your Customers Like Friends

Don't forget the power of relationship marketing. Like any other business, how you conduct relationships is the most important part of building your customer base. Make friends out of your customers instead of just asking them to send you money for one reason or another. The trick is to build steady relationships. There are many tips and ideas throughout the book to help you do this. It's easier to sell to steady customers than to acquire new customers.

a few different typefaces throughout your site. It gets confusing. Everything you do should convey the same message and represent what you stand for.

Credibility

You may be a one-person operation, but the beauty of the Web is that no one has to know that. Even though you may be working out of the basement of your home, the appearance of your site needs to be sharp, professional, and coherent. Become an expert in your field and stick with your area of expertise. Offer only a few related product lines. Save your diversification for new Web sites connected by links.

Convenience

Make sure your site is easy to get to and easy to use. Don't make life difficult for people. At one time, frames were in vogue, but people found them much too complicated. Frames technology allows you to have more than one Web page on your screen at the same time. Typically, sites with frames include a menu down the side or across the top with the main page (or contents) filling the rest of the screen. With a structure built on frames, a visitor to a site doesn't know where to focus his or her attention. Using frames became so complex that they were actually discouraging people from using the sites. Make it easy for visitors to get where you want them to go quickly and painlessly.

> Make sure your site is easy to get to and easy to use. Don't make life difficult for people.

Clarity

Once again, don't try to confuse your visitor. State your points clearly and succinctly. Your home page should tell the surfer, "I know what you want. Here's how to find it."

Simplicity

When people are surfing the Web, they generally don't want to spend more than a few seconds on any page until they've found exactly what they're looking for. Too much text on your home page will cause visitors to move on. If your site looks complex and confusing, they won't come back. If they feel comfortable and feel you have something worthwhile to offer, they'll likely come back again.

If you want only techies to visit your site and do business with you, then use the jargon they understand. If you want scientists, then use their unique language. Write in the language that your intended visitors use. Get to the point. Be specific. Invite dialogue. Apply the writing to the reader's interests—not your own. Keep it simple. And remember a confused reader won't buy what you have to offer—worse, they won't even take the time to ask you to explain.

Surprisingly, when most novice Web entrepreneurs—or even experienced entrepreneurs—develop a new site or business, promotion is the last thing they think of. They simply get caught up in the excitement of getting on the Web. The common thinking is if you build a product that makes the earth move for someone, buyers will come knocking at your door. But in reality it works the opposite way—you'll get a swollen brain trying to figure out why your site isn't attracting traffic or selling your goods.

> Surprisingly, when most novice Web entrepreneurs—or even experienced entrepreneurs—develop a new site or business, promotion is the last thing they think of.

Build promotion into your site

I know you're going to say that building the site is the fun part. Promoting is not. I agree. But, later, when you realize the importance of promotion, you're going to say, "Darn it (or worse), I should have thought about it earlier" because then you're going to have to change everything—from the metatags to the graphic elements to the words. It's not human nature to want to change a finished product.

Here's an e-mail I just received from the Kid Trainers:

We are in process of cleaning up our act. We took your advice. We've cleaned up a few sections (a very slow process when you have a catalog of 50 products), but we are going to submit each major section with its own URL. I wish we had done it right from the beginning. I'll keep you posted.

This chapter will help you design or redesign your Web site according to your audience's needs. It will show you how to demand their attention—and that of the search engines.

Bells and whistles

You can do some really fun things on your site. You can play intense animations. You can add sound. You can add streaming videos. You can make the colors of your site change continually and make your banners blink on and off.

Don't. If you have these attractions on your site, get rid of them. If you don't have them, don't add them.

Cybergizmos are fun the first time a visitor happens on your site, but like a movie, they get boring the second time around. Multimedia gadgets can even be frustrating—and downright annoying—the first time a surfer hits your Web site because fancy graphics take time to load. It might be apropos to look back to our second commandment from the last chapter, "Thou shalt put thyself into the shoes of the visitor." Many features can be imported into your Web site. Each feature must be looked at to see how it furthers your goals. If you're not sure about making the feature work or whether it will enhance your site for visitors, leave it out. Consumers will be more upset about having a feature that doesn't work than they will be if you don't include them at all.

> Cybergizmos are fun the first time a visitor happens on your site, but like a movie, they get boring the second time around.

Customers don't complain—they just leave

When designing your site, you should remember that complicated graphics take a long time to load. A study released by Boston Consulting Group cites slow page download times as the leading cause (48%) for online customer bailout. Speed is of the essence for Web surfers. And to make things even more difficult, not everyone has a superfast modem, especially outside the United States. Only so much information can travel through a tiny phone wire. This is what limits the size of pictures, the amount of sound, and many other aspects of the Internet. So, use bells and whistles only when your site, your targeted market, and your mission call for them.

Animations and clever videos can have a purpose beyond stoking the curiosity fire. Use gimmicks when your product or service needs to be demonstrated and there is no other way. A good rule of thumb is if it doesn't bring enhanced informational value to your Web site, get rid of it. Keep your site uncluttered, clean, and focused.

If you're going to cram everything into your front page, you're going to scare off an awful lot of people. Clutter and too much variety on a page confuse people. We all know that confused people do not buy, don't we? If you can be very clear up front about what you're offering, and if you can clearly lead your visitors through your presentation, you stand a better chance of holding their attention. Giving them a department store or library-sized selection and expecting them to dig around until they find what interests them isn't going to cut it—at least until the general surfer is much more adept at getting around in cyberspace.

A site that got it right

Coleman Vision (*www.colemanvision.com*) uses a video to great success on their Web site. I had decided to get more information on LASIK surgery to improve my vision. To say that I was apprehensive is putting it mildly. I was terrified. My optometrist suggested I check out the Web site of a Dr. Coleman, who is in my area. I checked the site, and it was a good one. It answered all of my questions and had two videos explaining the procedure. The site was informative and professional. After the surgery, which was a huge success, I gave out Dr. Coleman's site address to almost everyone I met who wore glasses.

Subsequent to this, I received a call from Nebraska's Hand & Shoulder Institute about developing a Web site. They were pioneering a new treatment for carpal tunnel syndrome. I suggested they put a video on their site along with other information to allay patient's fears.

> If you're going to cram everything into your front page, you're going to scare off an awful lot of people. Clutter and too much variety on a page confuse people.

Here are five traffic-building times to add a video, sound, or other gimmicks to your site:

1. When you absolutely must have a product demo and there is no other way
2. When the bells and whistles offer added value to consumers
3. When there is no other way to disseminate the information
4. When you want to have fun—but not at the expense of your communications
5. When your mission is to entertain

How Web travelers journey

People on the Web usually want more than just a good time. In the early days of the Web, surfers would go from site to site just to see what everyone was talking about. But times change quickly in Internet-land. Surfers now want to accomplish something, whether it's to find the lowest airfare or to find that hot new music track to download.

The mindset of the "typical" surfer

People on the Web want information, and they want it fast. The term *surfer* is really a misnomer. Surfers don't really surf. They frantically leap from one site to another in search of their goals. They'll give your site about 30 seconds, and if they don't find what they want, they're gone forever. And that 30 seconds includes the time it takes to load your page. Fancy gizmos can take precious minutes to download. Surfers get frustrated quickly. If they don't find what they want instantly, they're gone. If they take the time to watch your doohicky perform, they'll say, "That's cute, but where's the content?" and they'll probably never come back again. In fact, a good portion of surfers turn off the graphic options in their browsers. Sounds can also be an unexpected annoyance to Web travelers. That song you loved so much that you had to have it on your Web site? It's probably a disruption to visitors.

Determining Your Site's Keywords

When searching for keywords for your site, logon to *www.wordtracker.com/trial.* They'll help you find keywords that apply directly to your business and that people are searching for. Try the free trial and see how it works for you.

Quick tips

✓ Don't use bells and whistles unless absolutely necessary. If you use them, make sure they work.

✓ Surfers don't want to wait a long time for a page to load.

✓ Multimedia can be fun if used correctly. Experiment in-house with your Web-authoring program to see how much time it takes to load. Keep in mind that most bells and whistles irritate rather than motivate your customers.

> Build your site up through the point of view of your prospective customers.

Summary

Build your site up through the point of view of your prospective customers. Adhere closely to the six Cs of Web site promotion. Most people on the Web don't want to search. They want to find. They should get a feeling of satisfaction for finding your site and accomplishing something. Keep your site highly focused and targeted.

For more information on this topic, visit our Web site at www.businesstown.com

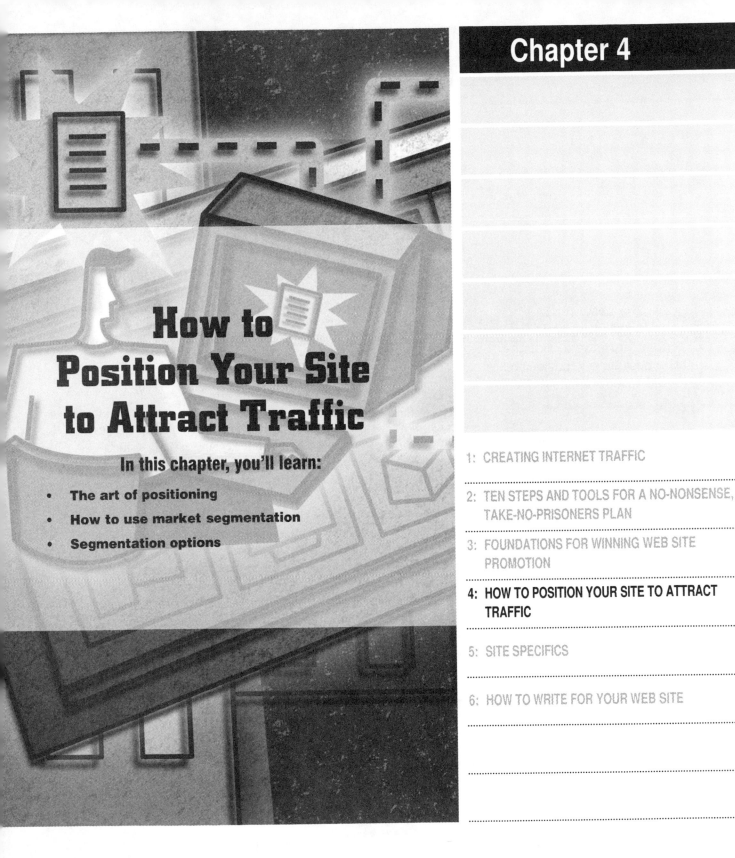

Chapter 4

How to Position Your Site to Attract Traffic

In this chapter, you'll learn:

- The art of positioning
- How to use market segmentation
- Segmentation options

A s I began writing this chapter, I received a frantic Instant Message (live chat over the Internet) from a student. He was on my site and needed information on selling architectural services for a report he had to turn in the next day. I told him that the best way to sell was through relationship marketing and there was a great deal of information and free articles on my site about selling professional services. "But," he said, "it doesn't specifically say HOW TO SELL ARCHITECTURAL SERVICES."

While I helped him choose the right articles for his report and suggested he take a Valium, the conversation brought up an interesting point. The increasing demands for personalized content and relevance put more pressure on Web site owners to have a coherent, well-defined positioning strategy. Many Web site developers struggle with the basics of structuring and organizing a site because they are speculating on what their prospective traffic really wants. It's simple, really. The traffic-building mantra is "ME! ME! ME" (meaning the surfers), not "YOU! YOU! YOU!" Visitors want you to be specific in solving their needs of the moment. Positioning is important because it targets new visitors for your site while keeping existing visitors coming back for more.

> The first step in developing your positioning is to isolate the best target market for your product or service.

The first step in developing your positioning is to isolate the best target market for your product or service. Your efforts will be most effective if you focus on a group of prospects with common characteristics and similar problems. Start by defining on paper your ideal customer or client. List all the characteristics you expect to find in good customers or clients. Be sure to include characteristics that make your product or service valuable to them. Now, narrow down this list by making lists of characteristics and people who should not go to your site. Use both lists to identify your positioning and your target market. Put it in writing and either frame it or make a screensaver out of it.

Positioning and focus

You should be able to describe your entire site and your key positioning in a sentence or less. Focus your site in a single-minded way. Become an expert in your field and stick with your area of expertise.

Offer only a few related product lines, and save your diversification for new Web sites connected by links. Focusing means doing one thing and doing it well. Having five mediocre site benefits is not nearly as effective as having one strong one. An all-purpose cooking sauce, no matter how good it tastes, is not nearly as powerful a seller as a spaghetti sauce. Do you go to the store looking for an all-purpose sauce or one that makes baked ziti taste good?

How to determine your focus and positioning

Remember working on the school newspaper when you were taught the five Ws and the H? How brevity and conciseness and intensity of the lead were the key ingredients to winning the hearts and minds of prospective readers? If you never had journalism, the five Ws and the H are not a rock group—or even the defensive alignment of the Washington Redskins—but a one-sentence solution to getting to the thought processes of your prospects. It's your positioning and focusing statements on the head of a pin. The five Ws and the H are the keys to winning the hearts and minds of Web travelers. The sentence that contains the five Ws and the H should determine all the aspects of your site because it will determine how your site will bond with travelers.

> Having five mediocre site benefits is not nearly as effective as having one strong one.

❑ Who is the site for?

❑ What will the site do for the surfer?

❑ Why would the surfer want to land on your site? Why should the surfer seek you out?

❑ Where can a surfer find you, and upon whose recommendations?

❑ When is the optimal time to reach your target market?

❑ How will it affect the surfer's life?

The five Ws and the H function as the heart of your traffic-building strategy and provide an ongoing checklist to ensure your new site stays focused. The five Ws and the H should control all the traffic-building promotional tools you use. Write your sentence containing the five Ws and the H down, and put it next to your target market statement.

Take this self-test before you publish your Web site:

Why are you building this Web site?

What action do you want the visitor to take?

What do you want this person to get out of your site?

How is it going to advance this person's goals?

How do you want the reader to feel after viewing your site?

Compare your answers with the information you just wrote down about the five Ws and the H, and your target market statement. If they jive, you're well on your way to a focused and profitable Web site.

The visitor or sales cycle

Rarely does a sale occur on a first visit. Surfers usually want to date first and watch how you court them. No matter how your visitors found your site, you have to work at keeping them loyal and an active participant in your Web site. Many startup companies think of their Web site as "a place to sell our products." It's an admirable goal, but in order to sell your products, your prospects have to:

- Find you

- Read through your materials

- Trust you

- Find your competitors to compare wares and prices

- Hunt up their credit card

- Figure out how to order

> Rarely does a sale occur on a first visit. Surfers usually want to date first and watch how you court them.

Much of the time, visitors to your site are thinking, "Is this company for real?" Can I trust them with my credit card number? It usually takes four visits for a prospect to get up the nerve and security to buy something from you. Who are these people (meaning you) anyway? Bringing in people who have never been to your site is more difficult than attracting people who have been there already, but repeat visitors are essential to maintaining a profitable Web site. The key is to sell these people on the Web site itself, and keep them coming back to that site until they're ready to make a purchase. When they do make a purchase, they'll be loyal and happy—and they'll spread the word.

A well-visited site should also cater to people who are just "kicking the tires" and looking for information on a general type of product. They may want to buy eventually, but aren't sure whom they'd like to buy from. The most successful sites create trust first and sell in subsequent visits. Reach people who don't know they need your product—until you tell them about their need.

Targeting, segmentation, and niche marketing

Big businesses like Yahoo! and Wal-Mart have the money to appeal to all people. Since you probably don't, one of the keys to your success will be to go after a niche. Targeting and segmenting are two of those buzzwords that pop up now and again in marketing. Niche marketing is how you feast upon those words.

Web markets are divided into targeted opportunities. The depth of these opportunities will help you make decisions about the quantity and the quality of your marketing efforts. Successful niche marketing is the product of segmentation. Here's a formula for how it works:

Your target divided by your segmentation = Your niche market

A key part of segmenting is defining a broad, targetable base of consumers whose latent needs are not satisfied by existing sites. We did that a page or so back. Don't try to be everything to everyone.

> Web markets are divided into targeted opportunities. The depth of these opportunities will help you make decisions about the quantity and the quality of your marketing efforts.

Just as customers screen you, you should decide whom you want to serve. There are bucketloads of opportunities out there if you look with an open, creative mind.

There are only two basic segmenting options, and both work:

1. Attract people who need the information or products on your Web site.
2. Develop or change your Web site to appeal to certain groups.

The primary mission of segmentation is to satisfy those customers in a concentrated way that you can afford. Your product should be special for some reason. The trick is to find your leadership position and appeal to a consolidated audience that shares similar interests. The ultimate segmentation goal is to reach and sell to a concentrated number of people that are already disposed to your site and your product. Here are some ways to segment that may stir your creative traffic-building juices.

Sex

Just as there are different products that appeal to men or to women, so there are sites that appeal to men or to women. Though this is really too broad a strategy, it may help you narrow down your thinking. Focus your content and your visuals to appeal to one of the sexes. For instance, *http://wwwomen.com* is a site that provides a guided tour of some great women's sites.

Age

Age is our largest affinity group. People gravitate to people of similar ages. Sites can be targeted and positioned to children, teenagers, young singles, or the middle-aged.

The Mature Market

This category is not lumped into age segmentation because it is large, growing, and full of subsegments. This group is growing faster

Filling a Niche

JustBalls.com (*www.justballs.com*) saw an unfilled niche in selling sports equipment. Instead of selling a the whole range of sports equipment, they looked for a single slice—balls—and set up "The Biggest Ball Store on Earth." You name it, they have it. You'll find baseballs, softballs, footballs, tetherballs, fitness balls, toy balls, and all sorts of balls.

than the overall population. This market can be broken down into four subcategories, each of which has different needs:

- Age 50–64 (older)
- Age 65–74 (elderly)
- Age 75–84 (aged)
- Age 85 plus (very old)

Contrary to a common misconception, mature households have more money to spend than any other demographic. Disposable income (that is, income after taxes) per capita is higher among mature households than among groups having a head of household under 50. Retirees with an abundance of time and money appear to have found a new entertainment vehicle—the computer. This group represents a strong market for financial services and recreational sites alike. Senior citizens 65 and older are more influenced by outside forces than those in the 55–64 year-old group, who tend to make choices based on a desire to reduce risk. One site that targets this market is *www.aarp.com*.

Occupations

If you ask people to tell you something about themselves, they'll usually mention their job connection first. It is what defines them. In advertising, it helps to market to an occupational aspiration. For instance, if a person works on an assembly line, place him in situations where he can become a foreman.

Computer usage

One of the most obvious categories of Internet users, however, is the segment of people who use the Internet both at home and at work. This is a truly elite segment. A Strategis Group study pointed out that home-and-work Internet users have a median income of about $67,000, compared with $51,000 for work-only users and $48,000 for home-only users. Home-and-work users don't like television and spend far greater time on the Internet.

> If you ask people to tell you something about themselves, they'll usually mention their job connection first.

The bottom line about segmentation

There are a great many ways to segment your audience. A variety of other demographic, behavioral, and psychographic factors also have an impact. There's no substitute for doing proper market research so you can predict the reaction to your traffic-building program. Chapter 4 has the down-and-dirty about finding out about your market.

Freebies to reinforce your niche

What are you planning to give away for free at your Web site? Nothing? Every site needs a "hook" to get people to visit in the first place, and that "hook" needs to get those people to return to the site regularly. A successful freebie will show your travelers that you know what they want. It will show how your product or service will fit their possible needs. If a visitor takes advantage of a small free service or product once, it will give him or her more reason to learn about you—and it will provide incentive for the visitor to return. This could be the perfect opportunity to form a relationship with an individual interested in your target market. You're going to find ideas for freebies in many chapters in this book.

Whatever you give away, though, should have a definite goal. Giving away something free should increase the value of your site to your visitors and get your name in front of a new audience, which is what you should continually be thinking about. Freebies should encompass your brand and your expertise, and reinforce your niche or your target market. A key ingredient to a successful freebie is making sure it is representative of your site's strengths.

Give away free information:

As an expert in your field, create informative reports that will be of value to your visitors and help them do something faster, better, cheaper.

- Create a series of how-to articles. Don't give everything away in your first article. Create a teasing synopsis on what is to come in your next issue or your next update. Write

> There's no substitute for doing proper market research so you can predict the reaction to your traffic-building program.

something to show off your expertise and that positions you and your site as a primary, authoritative source.

- Give a taste of your product or a free quote. Many insurance companies are offering a limited edition of their services for a very small fee. Progressive Insurance offers you a chance to get quotes from their competitors. Travelocity.com will give you a quote on any airline ticket, but they are counting on your buying your ticket from them. Use your Web site to get a small sample of your product into the hands of your prospective customers.

- Give away a free piece of software. Web Site Estates offers free PowerPoint templates and e-business resources. Several printers offer free, downloadable fonts. By updating these periodically, both companies keep visitors coming back and position themselves as site owners who want to help their visitors succeed. To reinforce the positioning of their Dayrunner Appointment books, AnyDay gives away a free online "Dayplanner."

More ideas and concepts

1. The four key words of a successful Web site are educate, invigorate, advertise, and sell. If you bore customers or sell too hard, you're only a mouse click away from oblivion.

2. Content is king. Visitors want to be entertained, or at least informed. Provide content that your competitors aren't providing. Give visitors information of value.

3. Know what people will and won't buy on the Internet. It's ludicrous to think a visitor would buy a box of Cheer when he or she can run down to the local supermarket. Web sites generate more leads than actual sales. Follow up leads through e-mail. Although people may check out a particular Web site once or twice a week at most, they always check their e-mail.

4. Customers rarely buy anything on their initial visit. Keep them coming back for more by continually adding value to

Use Gimmicks Only When Possible

Don't let the fun stuff over-whelm your content. In the '50s, 3D movies became the rage. And we're not even going to mention Smell-O-Vision (really . . . it's as bad as it sounds). People ran to see the new technology and to wear the funny glasses. However, most never came back a second time. Producers found that if they were going to have a 3D movie that people would come to see, the plot had to pretty darn good.

your site. The Internet is a different kind of medium. People have to come to you.

5. Reinforce your positioning cross-promotions by adding links to the companies that you are participating with. Try to work out reciprocal Web relationships with your participants. For instance, they advertise on your Web site, and you advertise on theirs. Plan this from the start. There's much more about this in Chapter 17.

Quick tips

✓ Build promotion into your site; don't add it as an afterthought.

✓ In order to segment your site for your audience, explore similar sites to learn the buzzwords and graphics they are using for your target market.

✓ You'll get bored with your site long before your traffic will. Consumers often like the comfort of familiarity.

Summary

Without a marketing strategy, you are going to lose your Web marketing battle. While adopting current marketing strategies, you will share the Web market with others. By reshaping your own marketing strategies, you are going to dominate the market! Build your site up through the point of view of your prospective customers. Adhere closely to the six Cs of Web site promotion.

Be Proud of Your Name!

Show people that you are serious with your business name. Everything that has your business name on it needs to carry a little mark next to it—TM. The intent is to show that you plan to register your business name and a notice to others that you consider the name to be your own. Use it on every piece of stationery, in every letter that carries the name. Declare your name on absolutely everything.

For more information on this topic, visit our Web site at www.businesstown.com

Site Specifics

In this chapter, you'll learn:

- The basics of setting up a site that will attract traffic
- The importance of first impressions
- How to use titles effectively
- All about using keywords to promote your site from the start

My friend Marc called today. He had stumbled upon a Web site that he loved but forgot to put a bookmark for the site into his favorite places. A bookmark is a shortcut that people place in their browsers so they can easily get back to a site. Marc, who is not particularly computer savvy—like most people—loved the graphics and the content but couldn't find it again. We tried spelling the site different ways, but apparently, the Webmaster had registered only one name with no alternative spellings. We ran a search on AltaVista for keywords describing the content in the site, but it was to no avail. Thus, because of poor Web site planning, the site owner lost a customer and the referrals that customer might have given.

Don't let this happen to you. Make every aspect of your site work both independently and synergistically with other elements to create and keep traffic. Consider this chapter a toolkit for Web site design. But this is a toolkit with a difference. It's all about generating and keeping traffic. No matter how exciting your Web site looks to you, it's of no value unless hordes of people see it. This toolkit will also help you prepare for the search engines. Search engines are a picky lot. We're going to go into great detail about search engines in Section 4, but preparation is key. What you don't do now, you're going to pay for later. And since this book is called *Low-Cost Web Site Promotion*, we want to save you money.

> Make every aspect of your site work both independently and synergistically with other elements to create and keep traffic.

Everything starts with the title

Even before we get into the content of your site, we need to talk about the most important elements of your site. The title and domain name. Your domain name is the "brand name" you give to your Web site. It is your Web address, or URL. It consists of your brand name, followed by two or three letters, like .com or .net (pronounced "dotcom" or "dotnet"). Once upon a time, almost every commercial Web establishment used .com, but a great many .com names have been taken. Now, new suffixes are becoming popular, like .net.

The title and domain names are the most important source of information for any search engine. The title is a great place to be creative, but not tricky. Tricky titles will backfire because only you will get the joke. If someone is looking for wholesale seafood, a name like Wholsaleseafood.net or Wholesaleseafood.com will get better results than FloundersRus.Com.

Your title should give advance notice of your Web site benefits. Don't make your visitors guess what your site will do for them. Credibility and traffic start with your name. Make it easy to type, easy to remember, and easy to spell. I have a friend who started a business selling natural products that supposedly delay the aging process. The name of the site was Juvination (*www.juvination.com*). But it was simply too hard to read and too hard to spell. If your URL is not descriptive enough, register additional names and redirect them to your key site. Your server will have explicit instructions. Finding just the right domain name can be a challenge. I've been told that 90% of the English dictionary has been used in registering Internet domain names. Even more amazing is the fact that some 60,000 names are registered every day—and that's just for the three biggies, .com, .net, and .org. Names are so scarce that people are paying huge sums of cash ($7.5 million in one case) to acquire them.

If you can't come up with a good name or a variant that describes your services, there's a free site that will do this for you at *http://bizweb2000.com/wizard*. Try it out and play with it. Register a group of names rather than just one. Get a few friends together and ask them how they would spell your domain name. Write down the answers and register as many as you can afford.

Neil Cohen is a specialist in these kinds of things. He points out the differences between .com and .net: "We tell them the same thing every time . . . if you are only using a .net address and not a .com address, you are losing your hard-earned visitors. Everyone remembers .com before .net; it's that simple. Even most Web browsers, if the extension is not

> Credibility and traffic start with your name. Make it easy to type, easy to remember, and easy to spell.

Register Alternative Names, Too

When you register your name, pay the extra money on extensions like .com, .net, .org. A new one is .wa. It will prevent people from using your name and trying to copy your business. For instance, besides Barryfeig.com, I have registered Newproductsworkshop.org, New productsworkshop.net, and Newproductsworkshop.com. The theory is that more people will be looking for my services (which the name expresses), rather than just my name.

entered, will default to .com." His advice is to think of all the keywords and key phrases for your product/service and Web site, and put them in your URL. Load the domain name with your best keywords to get ranked higher in the search engines. Then submit that URL to the search engines, and have it redirect to your main site or use it as a "doorway" page (which we'll be getting into later in Section 4) to forward traffic to you.

You have a great many options when choosing a domain name. Unfortunately, all but one or two of them are negative. For instance, you might use the name of the Internet service provider (ISP) that is hosting your site.

Perhaps your Web site URL is something like *http://www.barrys/ internethosting.com/wholesaleseafood*. But that is hard to type. Another negative is that you can't move your site easily if you want to choose a better or cheaper Internet host. You can use suffixes like .net, but most people when looking at a site will guess .com first. Dotcom is also used globally, so if you expect to attract any international traffic, .com is almost mandatory.

If you have a traditional business name, always try to use it for your name by putting .com after it. People will usually try www.yourcompanyname.com when they search for your site. Search engines will also gravitate to a site that has a name with a good selling benefit.

There is also a theory that you should use names that are loaded with keywords. I just registered newproductsworkshop.com (the old name of my company) because I wanted the search engines to associate my company name with my keywords. Allegedly, this little tactic will skyrocket my search engine rankings! That's what the ad said anyway.

> If you have a traditional business name, always try to use it for your name by putting .com after it.

Make every page title unique

You should also give every one of your pages a unique title. These pages identify your page content. It should reflect an accurate description of your page as well as the site in general. The title is what you see in that little rectangular box on the top of your browser when you log onto a page (Figure 5.1). It gives both search engines and your visitors help in identifying your page. When someone bookmarks your page, the title is what your browser sees and indexes. For instance if someone wanted to refer to an article on my Web site, the title of that article would stay in the browser. Make sure that the site name will load even if the prospect doesn't type the www. This is a small matter that many site owners overlook—even the big site owners. It should take you about a minute to fix this problem.

Figure 5.1: Distinctive Title Bar

First impressions and a captive surfer

First impressions are critical on the Web. Surfers will start making a judgment about your site, even before it is finished loading. No, surfers are not very patient. Quickly describe your site's main areas, content, and any freebies or special offers you'll provide your Web visitors. Special offers might include savings from ordering online, giveaways to guestbook registrants, or special offers such as my recent favorite: a free ISP (Internet service provider) account.

Theme and look and feel

Gotcha. You're reading my words. Something about the theme of this book caught your attention. It could have been the title. Or the fact that it had the same format as the other books in the *Streetwise* series. Or maybe it was something in the advertising. But in any event, the book caught your attention. Something is urging you to read the next sentence. You've been hooked. It's my job to keep you interested and excited and to follow the theme that attracted you.

> First impressions are critical on the Web. Surfers will start making a judgment about your site, even before it is finished loading.

As I mentioned in the last two chapters, consumers will give your site about 30 seconds before they get bored, so visitors need to know what you're trying to communicate instantly. Your entire design should communicate a mood and a tempo that is consistently conveyed by harmonizing your graphics, your copy, your colors, and your typeface. Obviously, if you were trying to develop a page on sexually transmitted diseases, you wouldn't want bold, blaring music, and manic graphics. You would instantly lose your credibility. If you are doing a page selling custom-baked dog food, use a picture of a dog to announce your intentions.

Over the past few years, many graphic designers have shifted from creating various print media to developing Web sites for the online medium. In the process, they have applied proven print design techniques, creating sites that look very similar to print media documents. This is great for maintaining a brand image across media; however, a recent study conducted by the Poynter Institute showed that this is not an optimum way to design a site.

What is the mood or emotion that you want to elicit in your viewers? Write three adjectives to describe the way you want your site to feel.

> Help out your visitors by using color and layout schemes to define different sections of your Web site.

Graphics

Help out your visitors by using color and layout schemes to define different sections of your Web site. Site layout should be homogeneous enough to make each section recognizable as part of the same site. Variances in colors, backgrounds, and shapes may be used to differentiate each Web site section or subtopic, but keep colors consistent and balanced. Don't overdo the colors. Subtle differences are enough to be perceived and acted on. Make sure your graphics load quickly.

Choose your graphic format carefully. JPEG is great for photos and other color-rich images. JPEG art compresses in a big way. On the Web, you can afford to lose a bit of detail in order to save space and download time. Typically, a 30 to 40% compression level will retain enough detail to keep the image usable. GIFS are another strong format. Though the details and colors aren't usually as crisp as a JPEG, file sizes are small and they load quickly.

Writing for the Internet

In some circles, there's a massive debate going on about how to write for the Internet. Some say "chunk it," that is, create lots of very short, boxed concepts and very short pages so that readers doesn't have to scroll down your page to see what you want them to read. Others say that's not important and that people will read what interests them just as long as it interests them. Who's right? Both.

Joan-Marie Moss of the company Creative Options (*www.creativeoptions.com*) has been studying this in great detail for six years now. Here's her response:

> It depends. Everyone is different. Everyone has different goals and expectations. Those who enjoy reading and who are out there to find information will read everything. Those who are uncomfortable with the computer or who are simply surfing for a quick fix won't read more than a few words. You have to know your market. What do they want? What do they like?

Navigation issues

Well-structured Web sites make it easier to provide clear navigation. Prioritize content and organize your Web site into major areas, then, if necessary, into subtopics. Provide links and menus throughout your site. The larger the site, the more need for easy links between sections. Section tabs, buttons, or links should be available on each lower-level page.

Wherever possible, provide navigation choices. Studies show that most Internet users develop personal navigation habits quickly. Some users prefer using menus; others prefer site-specific search engines. Offer your visitors a choice of navigation methods. Every

> Prioritize content and organize your Web site into major areas, then, if necessary, into subtopics.

page should show every link to every other page. For instance, if a fish lover probing a hypothetical *www.wholesaleseafood.com* found a special flounder recipe on page three, she should be able to link back to the home page and any other page easily and flawlessly.

Navigational elements

Offer navigation help in the form of captions that pop up when a mouse moves over a link. All navigational links should be clear and helpful. Provide an indication of what users will find when a link is selected. Helpful navigation elements can be buttons, arrows, text, or more complex sitemap graphics.

Since many visitors will find pages that link off from your home page, include a link back to your home page on every single page. Links should appear to previous and next pages. If you don't, people who found an inside page in your site from a search engine will often jump to a secondary page but will not find your home page. Surfers, being as antsy as they are, will leap to someone else's Web site!

Content

This is probably why most people come to your site. They come to read your content. You can't "drive" people to your Web site, but you can lure them with readable content when it fits their needs. Although it goes without saying that all of your content should be clear and well written, many Web sites provide poorly written material with spelling and grammatical errors. On a Web page, a misspelled word stands out like a Manx cat at the Westminster dog show. Spell check everything, and never publish a page without letting it sit overnight so that you can read through it again the next day. I once found a misspelling in a brochure for a spell check program. I didn't buy the product. Use a spell checking program every time you make a change. Have your copy read out loud before you post it. Before I send out anything—be it an e-mail or a complex proposal—I use a speech-to-text program to read it out loud to me as I read along. You'll be amazed at how many changes you'll make when

> You can't "drive" people to your Web site, but you can lure them with readable content when it fits their needs.

you hear what you've written out loud. Two great speech-to-text programs are Talk to Me and Monologue. Both are shareware programs and can be found at ZDNet.com (*www.zdnet.com*) as well as at online shareware sites. Either one is mandatory, especially if you write your own copy.

Quick tips

✓ Make everything easy for your target customer.

✓ Search engines place a great deal of emphasis on the title of your Web site pages.

Summary

Consistency is the key. Navigational elements should be placed consistently throughout your Web site. Place menus in the same location on each page and organize the menu choices in a standardized manner. Each menu should reflect the most likely choices of one point to another. It isn't necessary to list every single site page on every single menu. Some items, such as linking or Web site policies, generally need to be on only the first page the surfer sees.

> Navigational elements should be placed consistently throughout your Web site.

For more information on this topic, visit our Web site at www.businesstown.com

Chapter 6

How to Write for Your Web Site

In this chapter, you'll learn:

- How writing for your Web site is different from writing for an ad
- The importance of keywords and how to use them
- How to make the best use of graphics
- Why you should be promoting your Web site even at the beginning stages

When I mentioned in the previous chapter that you should be promoting your Web site as soon as you create your Web site, I wasn't kidding. Just like your visitors, search engines will be looking for certain words in your headlines and text, as well as your keywords. They will also be looking at subheads and body copy.

In the online world, words are your biggest lever—both behind the scenes in your HTML code and metatags, and in the all-important text on your Web pages. Words lead to new and repeat traffic. Your site visitors want to understand, *now*, exactly what your product or service can do for them. Don't use long sentences when short ones will work, and don't use long words when short ones will do. Write for results rather than to impress. According to Joan-Marie Moss:

> Good writing will get you started. Great writing will captivate the online community. Your words have got to grab your visitors by the throat and speak to them with a passion that creates interest and desire. The words you use on your Web site must build on your visitors' inner drives and haunt them long after they've gone on to other sites.

Keywords

Keywords are words that are specific to you and your business. They describe the contents of your site. They're the words that you can expect your prospects to use when they try to find you on the Internet. Coincidentally, they are the same words that you will use frequently on your Web site. (Take a look at the end of this chapter for a list of keywords that will stimulate your thought processes.)

Since the majority of Web site travels begin with one of the major search engines, visibility on search engines has become crucial for most businesses. The content and keyword layout of your pages will be the overriding factor that most search engines use in determining how high you'll rank. Although I will be talking about

In the online world, words are your biggest lever—both behind the scenes in your HTML code and metatags, and in the all-important text on your Web pages.

submissions in Chapter 18, submitting is not enough. You should prepare your keywords in advance and use them often. You will increase your ranking by using the same keywords and phrases relevant to your site in your visible content as well as in your search engine submission strategy. Emphasize the keywords and topics that apply to your site. This methodology ensures targeted traffic to your site and enhances the search experience for the end user.

Create keywords you think people would type in the search engines to find the types of products or services you offer. Don't just use nouns. Use phrases rather than a single word. Use descriptions also. For instance, if you were developing a site for a baseball card collection, you might use phrases like "baseball memories," "Tom Seaver collection," "Tom Seaver photos," "baseball collectibles," "sports investment opportunities." Pretend you were searching for your site. What words would you use to find your site?

Check out the Web sites of your competitors. What kinds of keywords are they using? Now try to integrate their keywords into your headlines and subheads. You'll get listed in the same places as they are, only in a higher rank because you used their keywords even better than they did. If you can't think of good words, there's a site that will generate keywords for you: *www.wordtracker.com/trial.* It will generate keywords directly related to your business and tell you how many sites are using the keywords on a major search engine.

> Create keywords you think people would type in the search engines to find the types of products or services you offer.

Using words effectively

1. Use multiple, specific headlines. Headlines and subheadlines create immediate context when a visitor is exploring your site. There should be a headline on your screen at all times. Your headlines should grab the surfer with the drama of the crazy tabloids at the supermarket checkout counter (Don't tell me you don't read them—everyone does.) Your headlines should summarize what's inside your Web site.

   People scan headlines to grasp meaning and often to summarize an entire block of text. That's why being overly fancy is counterproductive and a waste of time. Be as clear as you can. Site readers want information immediately, and their attention shifts fast. This is why short copy blocks will serve you well, especially if they're highlighted by bullets, keyword-rich links, and subheadlines.

2. Use the same words in your headlines that you will use as keywords for you search engines. You can make these headlines specific by using your keywords. Most search engines love seeing keywords over and over.

3. Start every page in your Web site with a summary or selling proposition describing the content on the rest of the page. This will help you get better search engine rankings, and it makes your pages easier to scan. Try to use your keywords in this summary also.

4. Make your copy brief. Get rid of unnecessary adjectives. Good text is concise and easy to understand. Pare your writing down to the bare minimum. Go easy on the adjectives and adverbs—they slow down the reader. Once you have all of your copy just the way you like it, cut it down by half. A wall of text scares Web surfers away. Stick to the point.

5. Use bullets. A bullet is a character, like a period or a small diamond, that sets off a line or two. Bullets attract the eye and help the reader find what he or she is looking for much quicker that reading a whole paragraph. Bullets break up text and serve as mini-headlines. The ideal length for a bulleted list is three to five items, which is probably the most readers scanning can grasp. If your bulleted list is too long, combine several bullets into one.

6. Keep it simple. Buzzwords and jargon can be important, but they make for slow reading. Remember that most of your visitors will be reading from a computer screen, which is a great deal more difficult than reading a sheet of paper.

7. Use combinations of short and long sentences and paragraphs. Intermingle long and short sentences. Short sentences invite the reader to read more. The reader doesn't have to work too hard. Vary the paragraph lengths. Long

Use the same words in your headlines that you will use as keywords for you search engines.

paragraphs look, and are, daunting to the reader. An ideal paragraph should have about four sentences of varying lengths. The perfect mix is a ratio of three short sentences (of 8 words or fewer) to one longer sentence (of 8 to 20 words). People can read only one screen of information at a time, and a wall of text looks as if it will take too much effort. If a screen shot of text on your Web page shows one continuous paragraph without a headline or graphic, it's too long.

8. Avoid generalities. Visitors are looking for a specific piece of information. Anything else is superfluous. Generalities bore readers to tears. Specifics give people the ammunition they need to make a decision. If you say a certain piece of info can help the reader, explain how. If you point out a specific feature of a product, give the benefit. Don't say, "this new product can save you money"; say, "this product can save you x amount over a competing product."

9. Write your links as headlines. Because of how easy it is to use a mouse, people jump from one link to another. Make your links look like headlines, and deliver your primary message. Be sure to use your keywords here as well.

The first fold—your conduit to traffic

The first fold is the first third of your page. Assuming your page loads quickly—you're not slowing them down with any fancy graphics or gimmicks, are you?—surfers will stick around until the first fold loads. It must immediately provide information that surfers want. The first fold is your visitor's welcome mat to the rest of the site.

In the first fold, you should be answering the question that every surfer wants to know: "What am I doing here?" In this regard, the appearance of the first fold is critical. A garish or cluttered page destroys any credibility that might flow from the content.

It works like a newspaper. The top fold of the first page is what attracts your interest to buy and read further. How many newspapers

> In the first fold, you should be answering the question that every surfer wants to know: "What am I doing here?"

have you bought because the headline in the first fold grabbed you? Of those who click off a site never to return, it is estimated that 90% click off because the first fold didn't grab their interest well enough.

Three words that lead to new and repeat traffic

When I went to advertising school many years ago, I was told that the most important words were "free," "new," and "you." They're even more important on the Internet.

- Free. The experts are always advising Web owners to offer visitors something for free–and rightly so. It's fast, widely accessible, and almost ridiculously inexpensive when you consider the technology involved. If you visit ten Web sites at random, you'll find more than half will have a link to free material. Use the word *free* in the first fold.
- New. People are looking for new and current information on the Web. Update your content and your page monthly if possible, and use *new* in the first fold.
- You. There is no greater interest than self-interest. Every time the word *you* is used, you are targeting a person's self-interest. There are many ways to personalize your Web site. If possible, include the reader's name also. You can do this by using cookies (Chapter 20). Personalize your page for the user's interest as much as possible.

Content and readability

The more of the following that you can include, the better the reader will understand and accept your messages.

1. Information. Include facts with authoritative resources. Be careful about offering complex facts that the surfer may or may not understand or agree with. Surfers aren't going to

Learn to Write By Writing

I just finished the new Steven King book, *On Writing,* and he says (and this has been my mantra for years) that the best way to write is to keep writing and reading. Keep writing drafts of your Web site and set aside the best ones. Now, after letting the idea sit for a week, edit, edit, edit. With each draft delete 10% of your words and some of your hyperlinks. You'll find that it makes your site easier to read and navigate. Take out EVERYTHING that is not meaty. Remember, no matter how good your site looks, surfers are going to spend only seconds on it, and if it doesn't meet their immediate needs, they are going to click you to oblivion.

take a leap of faith just because you said it's so. You need to support your statements.

2. Balance. If you're presenting your personal opinions, clearly distinguish them from the universal facts. Recognize that not everyone thinks the same way you do, and acknowledge that there are other ways to look at what you're saying. Encourage your reader to judge the reliability of your information.

3. Originality. Make sure your site and the information you present is fresh, innovative, and insightful. Keep that same interesting approach throughout. If you really know your subject and your readers, your writing will show it.

4. Color and tone. Use conversational but intelligent expressions. Use an active voice and strong nouns, and minimize adjectives and adverbs. Look for ways to include examples, anecdotes, contrast, irony, and wit when appropriate. Be sincere and be yourself. Let your personality show through. Keep the reader focused on your unique message.

Make sure your site and the information you present is fresh, innovative, and insightful. Keep that same interesting approach throughout.

Hidden parts of your Web site

This is the section that confuses Web site novices as well as some experienced hands. It is the source code (HTML) of your site and is not usually seen by anyone but the Web site developer. It is the underpinnings of the site that create the actual Web page your visitors will see.

Search engines read certain segments of your HTML code (as well as some visible pages) and index them in a great big database that is referenced when a user (searcher) performs a search. If the word that the searcher enters into his or her query isn't in your HTML code, there will be no match and your page will not be listed.

Although we will be discussing search engines in a good deal more depth in the section on "Search Engine Frenzy," it will help if you get familiar with the parts of the page.

The header is the area of the page that contains all the key information about your site. This is ordinarily hidden from view but is readily available for you to see. The hidden material looks something like this (every one of your pages should have its own headers):

```
<HEAD>
<TITLE>Page Title Goes Here</TITLE>
<META name="keywords" content="My keywords here">
<META name="description" content="My description here">
</HEAD>
```

Let's go over the main sections.

The <TITLE> tag of your page is one of the most important elements on it. Many search engines start with your title. All the search engines look at the keywords in your title and give those keywords a lot of importance in their ranking system. Use some of your most relevant keywords in your title. Take time in choosing your title because often that is what the search engines see. The actual words in your title will display on the search page in response to the searcher's query. If the title is weak, search engines may ignore you completely. Longer <TITLE>s can be stronger than short titles are because more words allow you to build a more compelling reason to visit a page.

<META name="keywords" content="My keywords here"> are the words used to tell the search engines what your site is about so it can be indexed. All the major search engines use somewhat different methods, but you should choose the best 15 or so words as the cornerstone of your search engine strategy. All keywords should be plural because that's how searchers will look for you page. For instance, people will look for soup kitchens, rather than a particular soup kitchen. Do not list any keyword more than five times because search engines may think you're trying to fool them and may ignore your site completely. Use the keywords you consider most important first and limit your total word character count (all the letters and spaces in the keyword section) to 200.

> You should choose the best 15 or so words as the cornerstone of your search engine strategy.

Frames

Some search engines ignore frames (when the screen is split into quadrants, all acting independently). They will not follow links that are in frames. This means that if your opening page is created with frames, the search engines will find absolutely nothing else on your site. Stay away from frames.

Bookmarking

If people like your site, they will want to come back again and again. Make it easy for them. Every browser, including AOL, MSN, and CompuServe, has a feature that enables people to go back to a site. On some it's called "Favorite Places"; on others it's called a bookmark. People often forget to place sites that they like in their bookmark lists. Make sure to remind them with a copy line like "Bookmark Me Now."

Make sure your site is running

Nothing can be more destructive to a Web site than broken links and being unavailable to surfers. If your site goes down, you may not even know about it. For this reason, it would be wise to sign up with Netwhistle.com. This service provides free Web site monitoring. If your Web site ever becomes unavailable, Netwhistle.com will send an e-mail to you or your pager gateway with detailed error information. It's worth using.

Tactics that lead to surefire traffic

Value is not something you put into or tack onto a Web site; it's what travelers take out of a Web site. Obviously, you have something of value to share with travelers or you wouldn't be putting up a site at all. Here are some tactics that give extra value to your site and have been used to great success as traffic builders.

> People often forget to place sites that they like in their bookmark lists. Make sure to remind them with a copy line like "Bookmark Me Now."

Make your pictures and graphics available to download. Many people love to hoard graphics and illustrations.

- Pump up your site with free, downloadable information. People are on the Web for information. Write compelling, informative reports or how-to guides that will be of value to your visitors. But go easy on the "sell." Your visitors know the difference between hype and reality. Submit this new info to the search engines, and they may index it along with your site. It will create additional means for a consumer to hit your site. Though you may (or may not) want to copyright the article, at the top of it mention that the reader can use or distribute the article freely providing he or she secures permission from you and makes prominent use of your URL. You can also include a footer on the article that allows readers to e-mail the article to anyone they want.

- Make your pictures and graphics available to download. Many people love to hoard graphics and illustrations. Create graphics or screen savers that people can use for their own sales or to decorate their computer. They're simple and fun. Make sure you add your URL so other people can find you if the graphics are mailed around.

- Give away inexpensive things like mouse pads and calendars. This is sort of a tricky traffic builder because many people will log onto your Web site just to get whatever you are offering. If you're going to go this route, tie it into a survey and always include your URL so people can find your site. The people at *www.mywebkey.com* are offering free keyboards that tie into advertisers and bring them directly to a Web site. Go to *www.justfreestuff.com* to get a feeling of what people are offering.

- Give away a free service that your visitors actually need, for example, a free Web-based e-mail service to entice your visitors to come back again. The return traffic you can receive from offering this type of service may astound you. If you have a free Web-based e-mail account that you use on a daily basis, for personal or business use, you already know that this free service keeps you coming back.

- Offer advice to your customers about specific products and services. For instance, if you are a promotion agency, give visitors a clear-cut answer to their problems without telling them outright to call you. People love the accessibility and clarity of Q&As.
- Sweepstakes, contests, and scavenger hunts are great traffic builders. Hold contest and scavenger hunts weekly or monthly. Scavenger hunts are especially motivating to visitors. Have visitors hunt for a word, a phrase, or an item on your site. Don't just offer one prize though. Offer a multitude of smaller prizes so people feel like they have a chance to win.
- Set up a chat room. Chat rooms are similar to newsgroups and discussion forums. Chat rooms also come in thousands of different topics. Conversation scrolls by the screen, and participants can immediately respond to one another. In addition to posting messages, chat rooms can be used as a great market research tool. Observing conversations in chat rooms can provide valuable information about your customers. Make sure the chat room relates to your particular industry or that visitors share a commonality of circumstance. Chats can be real time, or you can set up a forum that allows people to respond whenever they feel like it. There's more on setting up a chat room in Chapter 21.
- Let people talk to a real, live person. Many people know that Webbing can be a very impersonal experience. There are now programs that can change all that. One is called Humanclick (*www.humanclick.com*), and it's free. It's a program that allows surfers to talk (using text) to site operators in real time. People can contact you whenever you want and you can see who is on your Web site.

> Sweepstakes, contests, and scavenger hunts are great traffic builders. Hold contest and scavenger hunts weekly or monthly.

A checklist to make sure your site is on target

Janet Attard, who owns the Business Know How section on AOL (also businessknow-how.com), offers these tips for making sure your site is traffic friendly:

> Are the most important elements of your site visible without scrolling up and down or from side to side on screens set to 600 × 800 size?

- ❏ Can visitors find information easily?
- ❏ Is the navigation clear and consistent throughout the site?
- ❏ Does the back button always take visitors back to the preceding page?
- ❏ Can visitors bookmark individual pages?
- ❏ Do the pages load quickly (10 to 20 seconds) on standard modem connections?
- ❏ Can visitors easily find out who runs the site?
- ❏ Can visitors easily find an e-mail address to contact if they have difficulties using the site?
- ❏ Are the most important elements of your site visible without scrolling up and down or from side to side on screens set to 600 × 800 size?
- ❏ Does the site look good and work from both Netscape and IE browsers (version 4.0 and up)?
- ❏ Do you have alternative text tags under graphics (to allow visitors who have graphics turned off to find important links)?

And for e-commerce sites:

- ❏ Can visitors tell immediately what you sell?
- ❏ Can they quickly find products and product descriptions?
- ❏ Are there links to related products (accessories to wear with a ladies suit, for instance)?
- ❏ Can they tell what to click on to place an order?
- ❏ Can they find your phone number from every page in case they have a question?
- ❏ Can they find your name, address, and fax number?
- ❏ Can they find price information?

❑ Can they find information about the company and its management?

❑ Can they find any other important information you want them to have?

Quick tips

✓ Make it a point to submit each and every page in your Web site. If you don't, you will seriously limit your exposure to people doing searches for you.

✓ You should also make sure that the www prefix is not an integral part of your name.

✓ Create a strong, powerful, easy-to-remember, easy-to-type Web site address (URL). Just one incorrectly typed hyphen means your prospect won't be able to find your site.

✓ Use testimonials. Encourage people to tell you what they think; better yet, give them a place, like a guestbook or a forum, where they can share positive feedback.

Summary

Think of your Web site as your storefront. Dress it up, but be careful not to get carried away with all the bells and whistles. Too many Web sites drive people off before they come in by using a lot of Java and Flash and heavy graphics that don't load worth a darn except on the most state-of-the-art computer systems—which the vast majority of surfers don't have yet. Cable and high-speed access to the Internet is still a dream in many parts of the country and is still cost-prohibitive for the average surfer. So remember to keep it simple.

Create a strong, powerful, easy-to-remember, easy-to-type Web site address (URL). Just one incorrectly typed hyphen means your prospect won't be able to find your site.

For more information on this topic, visit our Web site at www.businesstown.com

Research and Tactics

Summary of Section II

- **How to build your Web site on a strong foundation**
- **How to create a one-of-a-kind promotional message**
- **Getting press coverage**
- **The basics of newsgroups**
- **Announcing your Web site**

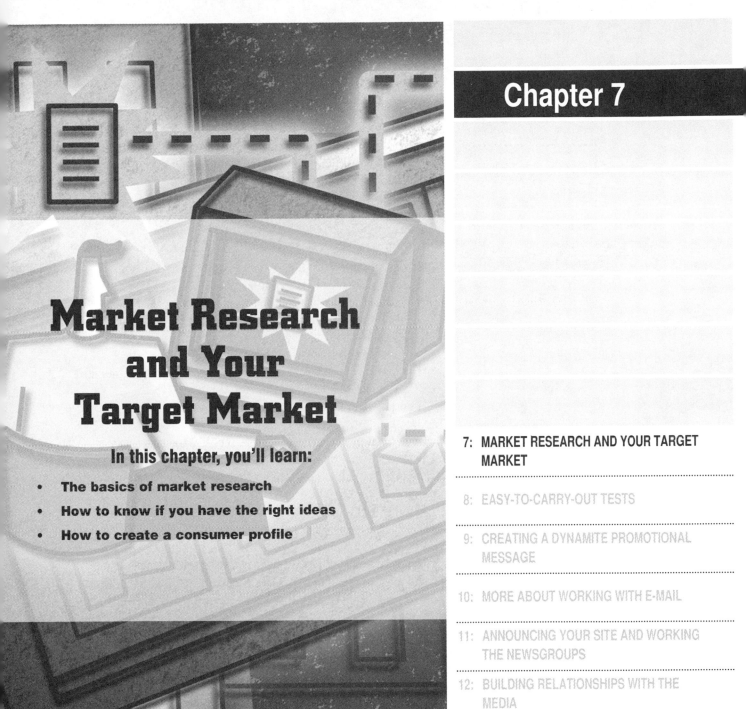

Market Research and Your Target Market

In this chapter, you'll learn:

- The basics of market research
- How to know if you have the right ideas
- How to create a consumer profile

The poorest view of a market is from your office or your home. Research is the art of making the unseen, seen. Well-planned research will tell you everything you need to know about your market, dramatically increasing the odds of success. Strategically planned research encourages your customers to tell you their inner secrets—what makes them buy what they buy.

> **Research is the art of making the unseen, seen.**

"Hi Bill, what did you think of my Web site?"

"It was, uh, interesting."

"Glad you like it. What did you like best?"

"I liked the dolphin eating the fish. I liked the naked people and the way you made them dance. Yeah, the animation was definitely cool. But what does that have to do with the lawn mowers you're trying to sell?"

"How about the clown. Did you like the way his nose lights up whenever you clicked the mouse button?"

"I gotta go get lunch. The clown was a nice touch."

Unfortunately, a great deal of research is carried on that way. You create a site and then wait for people to stroke your ego. Don't feel bad. I did the same thing when I first did my Web site. Although I now know it was terrible, everyone said it was really nice.

You just spent four weeks creating a Web site, and you have earmarked a few dollars more to promote it. But are you sure the site is getting the right message across? How will you know?

Although you should have built your site through market research, most people don't. Market research is learning what drives people to your Web site and what keeps them there. It tells you what's hot and what's not. It tells you what products people will buy on your Web site and what they won't buy.

Market research is easy to conduct, and if you use the tools available on the Internet, not expensive at all. But it is crucial to success.

Targeting your marketing audience

It's easy to look at your Web site and say, "I'm going to sell everything to everyone." Or, "everyone will want to see my Web site."

Everyone won't buy anything. "People" don't surf Web sites. Individuals do. It is very important in the world of advertising to market your products or services to the prospects most likely to buy what you are offering.

Many Web sites fail because they don't have the knowledge or direction in their marketing efforts. These companies think that they have the best product and everyone is a potential client. They spend millions on their Web sites and billions more on advertising. When traffic is low or sales are not up to expectations, they shut down, thinking that this wonderful product was not so great after all.

I assume you're reading this chapter because you are in business for the long haul. You'll do anything possible to be successful, but without the knowledge of a true marketing guru, one's success is likely very limited.

Focus more on the benefits of your products or services and who could benefit from using them. Then you can narrow down your promotional efforts to attract your desired clientele. Your products or services may benefit a certain age group, gender, income bracket, or geographical location. By knowing who to target and which medium to use for your products or services, you have a better chance of success.

> "People" don't surf Web sites. Individuals do.

Studying your market audience

Get involved in the things your audience does. Think of as many questions as you can about your audience and find the answers from their point of view.

- What Web sites do they visit? How do they benefit?
- What newsletters do they read? Why are they reading them?
- Which forums do they participate in, and why?
- Which print magazines do they read, and why?

Asking yourself these sorts of questions will allow you to personalize your Web site for your target market. You will narrow your targeted audience, and you will have a better idea who your ideal customer would be. With this new knowledge, you can choose the best ways to market and promote.

What market research should tell you

- Which products you can sell over the Internet, and which are unlikely to achieve great demand
- How to improve your marketing structure so people will come back time and time again
- How to appeal to your typical prospect
- How to tell who your typical prospect is so you can target him or her often
- What your customers like or dislike about your site, and whether they would refer other people
- What your customers like or dislike about your site, and whether the will come back again
- How strong your promotional message is

Research is a dynamic discipline that is always evolving and not static at all. When used correctly, it drives the entire marketing cycle. It can be as simple as asking questions of your site visitors or as complicated as doing a psychographic study of zip codes. Ad hoc research is much less effective than research planned to play a role at every stage of the marketing and product development cycle.

In most businesses, when you do research, it is abstract. It's hard to get to know which kind of people to talk to because you can't actually see the people buying your product. This isn't a problem on the Web because you can see the people entering your site in real time. They leave a trail that you can follow. You can see what they're interested in; what they ignore; what products, services, and techniques work and what don't; what level of technology they use; what they're confused about; and what they like. The Internet is really an ideal research tool.

And there are a great many more uses than just fine-tuning your site. In theory, every site's visitor-count can yield valuable market data. You can extrapolate trends by looking at what links people jump to and come from. And you can see what topics new or popular Web sites are covering.

Research is a dynamic discipline that is always evolving and not static at all. When used correctly, it drives the entire marketing cycle.

You Can't Research Enough

An oddity of the Internet is that everything is out there for you to see. You can spy on similar businesses and do a check (through your Web statistics) on who is hitting your site. I can't say this enough—research, research, research. If a company has a banner space you want, discover how to outmaneuver it or even outbid it for the placement.

Building your visitor profile

One of the most important things to build—up front—is a visitor profile. These are your visitors' attributes, and include such personal information as:

- Sex
- Age
- Interests
- Income level
- Zip code

- Web habits
- Buying habits
- Marital status
- Customer satisfaction
- And anything else they're interested in

The really nice thing about doing customer profiling is that people are more than happy to give you the information you want if you can tailor their Web experiences to their particular preferences.

Lands' End's Web site (*www.landsend.com*) offers a good example of how to ask your customers for additional useful information:

Sign up to receive your very own Newsletter from Lands' End. We'll send you news via e-mail at the interval you request (weekly, twice-monthly, monthly).

Use the checkboxes below to customize the contents of your Newsletter.

You may also use this page to modify the Newsletter you're already receiving or to cancel your subscription.

> The really nice thing about doing customer profiling is that people are more than happy to give you the information you want if you can tailor their Web experiences to their particular preferences.

Getting user opinions

I've been running focus groups and doing research for a while. My experience shows that the following is a good way to phrase a question seeking help on making a site better: "If there were one thing about our product or service (or whatever) you could change, what would that be?" This simple question can tell you where and why visitors are unsatisfied, and what you have to do keep visitors coming back.

A funny thing happens when you ask people their opinions—provided you don't go overboard: people respect you more. Customers suddenly feel enfranchised. They become part of your site. They are not just dollar bills anymore because you asked for their opinion.

The Internet changes frequently and so do your customer's expectations. With every change, the standards rise a little more. The research you conducted last week may no longer be valid and your customer may have moved beyond what she told you a few weeks ago. So you should be continually revising your knowledge base.

Your best customers should be your guide

Your research doesn't have to be fancy. You don't need an expensive knowledge management system, or even a fancy customized database. But you do need to know about the Pareto principle. In many product categories, a phenomenon called the Pareto principle exists (named after the heretofore obscure 19th-century economist Vilfredo Pareto).

The Pareto principle states that just 20% of your customers will account for 80% of your sales. You need to identify those customers and make sure you contact them whenever an important event happens in your industry or you want to make changes. Do this at least once a quarter.

You're not sure if your site visitors want to see a new chat room? Ask them. Put a quick one-question survey on the front page of your Web site with three or four answers to pick from. ESPN, AOL, and numerous other media companies do these just for fun. No, it's not scientific, but it can be extremely helpful. Just watching the response rate to your "down and dirty" can tell you if your users engaged enough with the site to take a few seconds to answer the survey and more: What percentage of your traffic took the time to compete your form? What time or day of the week did you get the strongest response?

These survey responders may or may not be a statistically sound cross-section of the audience you ultimately want to hit. But they are an active part of your market. And if something doesn't work with them, odds are it won't fare well in the broader market.

> Your research doesn't have to be fancy. You don't need an expensive knowledge management system, or even a fancy customized database.

Create research groups

If you can identify your best customers, create an online research group and query them often. You can set up a chat room, message center, or bulletin board and ask them questions that are important to your Web site and your product line. It's important to develop a thick skin and to heed what they say.

These are benefits that traditional research won't provide. And it's all there for the taking, if you'll just ask.

Other testing media

Although it's tempting to try to get all of your information online, you should explore other media also. Your customers don't live on the Internet (most don't anyway). You need to use various media to reach your customers and to make it easy for them to respond. Put your message out via e-mail, telephone, regular mail, fax, or on your Web site. And allow your customers to respond in any way they choose.

Here's the customer profile that Lands' End uses:

If your e-mail address has changed and you are no longer receiving your Newsletter, enter your new address below to subscribe afresh.
   What's New Newsletter E-mail Address
   ❏ *Subscribe*   ❏ *Unsubscribe*

What kinds of product news would you like your Newsletter to include?
   ❏ *Men's*   ❏ *Kids'*   ❏ *Overstocks*
   ❏ *Women's*   ❏ *For the Home*

How often would you like to receive your Newsletter?
Send my e-mail as text only.

> You need to use various media to reach your customers and to make it easy for them to respond.

Plan your research

It all starts with planning. As the huge failure rate of Web sites suggests, many attempts to build or promote a business online have failed because there was no up-front research, and thus no defined strategy.

Research is key to helping identify:

- The market
- Segmentation of the customer base
- Predicting ROI (return on investment).

Primary market research, consumer data, and an incisive competitive analysis are crucial building blocks that play a key role in the planning phase.

As the huge failure rate of Web sites suggests, many attempts to build or promote a business online have failed because there was no up-front research, and thus no defined strategy.

Concept testing your Web site idea

Concept testing gets a reaction from a group of people. By using this type of testing, you gain a clearer picture of how your potential customers perceive your concept. You can discover how easy your site is to navigate and find out if you're promoting something of worth to consumers. Concept testing is a method of getting reactions from groups of real people about a Web site, ad, product brand, and so on. Online concept testing is fairly cheap and is a very fast method of getting information that can help you make or validate decisions.

Concept testing can help when:

- You are about to launch a new Web site
- You need a perception test
- You want to find out what product you should add to your product line (if you have a new product idea, do a feasibility test)
- You are trying to decide between three alternative ads

Let's say, for example, you have a Web site that targets senior citizens. Here's how to do it. You will need two things:

1. A Web-based survey system: The survey system is the mechanism for recording responses from your testers. It generates responses and provides reports of the results. At its simplest, software creates a form containing your questions and returns answers to a database.

   More complex surveys might require additional functionality. Your survey form can record demographic criteria of potential respondents and allow only specific target groups to respond. Some studies consist of staged tests where respondents can continue only if they have completed a previous survey. The list of research studies that are going on can boggle the mind.

2. A group of online respondents: Online testers, the second piece of the research puzzle, must be acquired, screened, and motivated to participate in the test. This is probably the most controversial piece of the equation because the goal is to find testers who are generally representative of your potential target audience. To perform classic "probability sampling" would require a great deal of time and skilled professionals, and would cost a great deal of money.

But, of course, since we're dealing with the Web, we can cut corners. We can get very good information for much less by simply being smart about the testers we use. For a basic Web site test, we can use respondents who are representative of the Internet community in general. For more sophisticated testing, it makes sense to use respondents who match specific demographic or psychographic criteria.

You can attempt to attract individual respondents, purchase a list of respondents, or hire a firm that already maintains an online panel. Since everything happens online and communication between the different groups is easy, an online concept test with 100 respondents can often be completed in less than 24 hours. The bottom line is that nothing spells competitive advantage like a good concept that has been validated by effective testing.

> Nothing spells competitive advantage like a good concept that has been validated by effective testing.

Here are some questions you need to answer while promoting your Web sites:

1. Which products are most appealing to online prospects?
2. Which headlines generate the greatest response?
3. Who are your best prospects?

Quick tips

✓ Make sure your surveys are brief and to the point.

✓ Rely on people who frequent your site often to give you ideas on improving your site.

Summary

In traditional marketing, the primary investment is money. When doing research, the primary investments are time, energy, and know-how. The more of these you invest, the less money you will need. There are hundreds of ways to gather data from the market, from consumers, and from business activity. They require careful planning and a commitment to follow through.

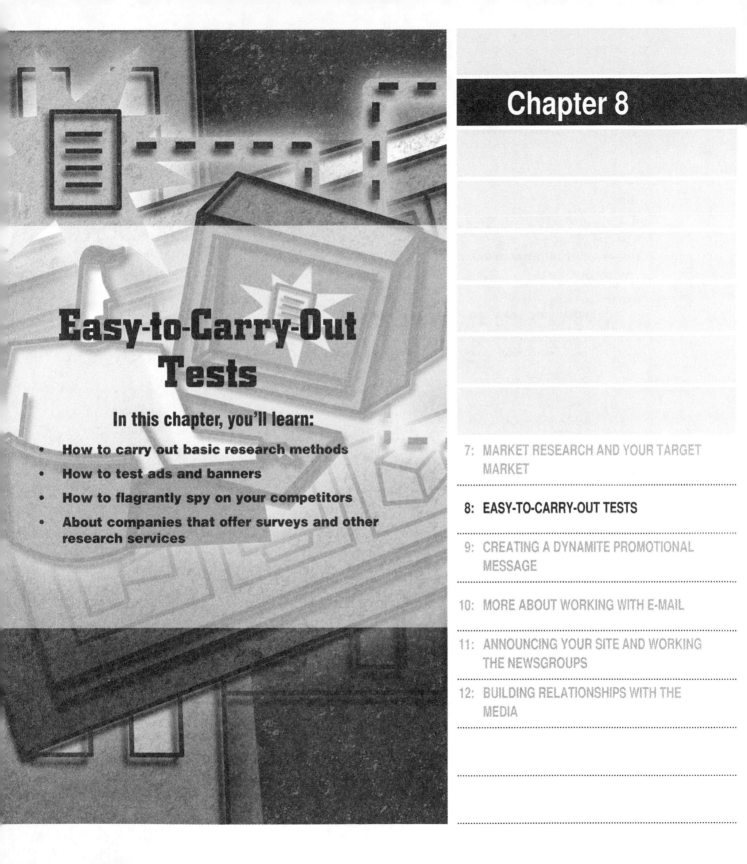

Easy-to-Carry-Out Tests

In this chapter, you'll learn:

- **How to carry out basic research methods**
- **How to test ads and banners**
- **How to flagrantly spy on your competitors**
- **About companies that offer surveys and other research services**

Chapter 8

You don't have to be a
research genius or a
numbers cruncher to
carry out tests.

You don't have to be a research genius or a numbers cruncher to carry out tests. The first test that we're going to talk about is very similar to the ones run by big newspaper and magazine organizations, but on a much smaller, more interactive scale. Here's how it works. Marketers buy split run advertising in magazines. Half the general circulation will get ad A. The other half will get ad B. The only difference in the magazine is that each will have a different ad. Each ad might have a different phone number or box number so it can be determined which ad generated which response.

Response is calculated for each ad, and the results are compared to determine which yielded the better response.

You can implement the same types of tests quickly and cheaply. Here's how.

Select Usenet newsgroups whose readers are most likely to be interested in the benefits of your Web site. Your ads or messages should be completely identical except for one variable. The variable could be the headline, a banner, a business proposition, your SIG (signature line), or even the body copy. The conditions should be as identical as possible for each half of the test. Run each headline (or any variable you choose) several days each, or run one headline one day and another the next.

Here's what you're going to be trying to achieve:

- To learn the pulling power of each headline: The headline that generated the greatest response should be used throughout all of your communications, except, of course, if you think of a better one that wins in another test.
- To compare the popularity of one product over another: The results would reveal which products should be given more prominence in your marketing efforts and help you add additional services to your site.

Guestbooks

You can use your guestbook to conduct continuous market research. The beauty of using a guestbook is that once it's set up, it generates free information continuously. I have a friend who builds his whole marketing program around guestbook data. He has a guestbook form that allows visitors to get their choice of any one of his many reports free, just for filling out a survey. They input information and submit it. It's an excellent way to get feedback from your site visitors. It reveals what is really interesting about your Web site and what your visitors want.

As a variant on this, you can have two guestbooks. My friend also rotates different guestbooks each day with a different free report offered and tracks which guestbook gets the most "signatures."

Other ways to conduct market research

- Analyze site records to see which parts of your site are pulling best. Your service provider will tell you how to do this since each host has a different way of tracking traffic. There's more about this in Chapter 28.
- Logon to your competitor's Web site and see how they have updated their site. Look for any changes in their keywords and descriptors.
- Look closely at the e-mails you get from your visitors. You might also send these people letters asking them how you could improve your site. If you decide to query prospects about site improvements, use multiple-choice questions to help them focus their responses.

Spying on your competitors

You can stay one step ahead of the competition by gathering information about their ways of doing business. To stay ahead on the Internet, you have to know what your competition is up to. This section will show you how to check out your competitors' products and marketing schemes without them even knowing it.

Assuming you are not inundated with competitors, go to their Web sites and buy their products to determine their sales process and Web tactics. An added benefit is that you will get on

Don't Forget Your Guestbook

When I put in my guestbook, I had no idea who would sign it. Then, within a week, I got 50 signees. Where did they come from? A marketing newsletter that published my site. I found this out by calling everyone on my guestbook. Were these people annoyed? Hardly. They were thrilled that I paid attention to them. It was a great way to sell my services and find out where all the hits were coming from. Guestbooks are a great research tool—if you use it wisely and follow up on responses.

their mailing list and e-mail list so you can see future promotions. If your competitors sell cars, don't go out and buy one, but be prepared to spend some money in the name of research. You'll get your money back in full—with interest—in hands-on knowledge.

Since some of your competitors may recognize your name, use an employee name or even a fictitious name. By doing this covert operation, you'll find out exactly what your competitors are doing, whom they are dealing with, and how they are doing it. Further, by purchasing their products, you will be able to experience exactly what a regular customer would go through. You can then judge their product, service, and operations against yours. You'll learn the ins and outs, their good points and their bad points so you can more effectively sell your product or service.

Finding your competitors with search engines

Make a list of all the keywords and phrases related to your own products or services. Type in a keyword or phrase in the search engines. This should give you a long list of competitors.

Look closely at the site while keeping in mind the following:

- How user friendly is the site? Do they provide enough information about the products or services? What links are they using that can help you?
- Does everything look professional? Is their site up to your standards? Is your site up to their standards?
- If they have a frequently asked questions page, what are their visitors asking? This will keep you a step ahead of your competitor by already addressing these issues about your products or services. Remember that you want to find out what made each of your competitors successful so that you can apply it to your own success.
- How much are they charging for their products? Can you sell yours for less? What payment methods do they offer?

> If your competitors sell cars, don't go out and buy one, but be prepared to spend some money in the name of research. You'll get your money back in full—with interest—in hands-on knowledge.

Do they provide secure online credit card transactions? If they are accepting credit cards, they may be moving volume. If they except only cash or money order purchases, you can be pretty sure it is not a substantial operation.

- Look for ideas they may have that you can use in your site.
- In what other ways do they attract their audience? What types of content do they use to get visitors to their Web site other than their products or services? Are they giving away things? Are they running contests or newsletters?

Keeping a steady watch on your competitors' movements

The site *www.netmind.com/html/url-minder.html* offers a free service that tracks any changes or updates that have been made on your competitor's Web site. This saves you some time and keeps you informed each time your competitor makes a move. Be specific in your request. You may want to know only when your competitor updates his or her price list. Give NetMind the URL of that page, and you will be notified every time updates are made to that page.

Here's another way. Some search engines give you a higher ranking based on link popularity. Do you want to know which Web sites your competitors are marketing on or how may other sites link to their site? Just go to *www.altavista.com* and in the search box, type in link: *www.mycompetitorsurl.com*.

How do you start spying?

For a really deep look into your competitors' moves and Internet presence, start with netWatch at *www.net-sleuth.com*. They offer search and monitoring services for over 280,000 newsgroups, e-mail lists, and Web discussion forums, as well as millions of Web sites. They provide immediate and crucial feedback in areas that can impact your business. They keep you apprised of how your

> Some search engines give you a higher ranking based on link popularity.

name and reputation are being used online. They also monitor the actions of your competition through public opinion (newsgroups, forums) and online news sources. They will search for specific key-words (for instance, your personal name, company name, product name, or your competitor's personal name, company name, product name) in over 280,000 newsgroups. All this can be fairly expensive, but they offer a free trial. You can even go to the extent of having netWatch search for all of your competitors' e-mail addresses on newsgroups. That way anytime your competitors are promoting their products or services or saying *anything* online, you will know about it.

You can also use Deja.com (*www.deja.com*). You can perform a search for keywords in specified newsgroups to find out if your name, or any other information about your company, is being used without your prior knowledge or permission. It can also pick up mentions of your competitors' products.

Do your surveys right

Most surveys on the Web are poorly done. From the respondent's point of view, they can be annoying, time consuming, and down-right misleading. Poorly written surveys yield low response rates, unrepresentative samples, and incomplete questionnaires. This is a shame because Web site owners and researchers are realizing that Web surveys can be a great way to learn about their customers. But they have to be built right. Whether you are building a survey to improve your site or querying a response panel through an established research company, there are some general guidelines that will help ensure that the survey is a success.

- Questionnaires should be like elephants sculpted out of marble. Just chisel away anything that doesn't look like an elephant. Include everything that needs to be there and nothing that doesn't. Keep your questionnaire short, sweet, and to the point.

> Poorly written surveys yield low response rates, unrepresentative samples, and incomplete questionnaires.

- Keep your surveys brief. People get bored quickly, and after the first few questions, most people can't wait for it to be over. Remember, people are doing you a favor by answering your questions.
- They should be easy to fill out. Test your surveys for usability with your online friends. I'm asked to look at surveys constantly. Keep your writing on an eighth-grade reading level. Think about the questions from the respondent's point of view.
- Flatter and motivate your respondents. Tell participants they are helping themselves or someone they care about. Offering an incentive (say, a discount on a product) is usually a good motivator.
- Keep your questions free of bias. Make sure they are unambiguous. Don't use jargon, business-speak, or humor—people might take them the wrong way. Each question should contain only one variable.
- Elicit precise answers to your questions. Know exactly what you want to accomplish in the survey, and take care that the questions fit those objectives. Don't be afraid to use open-ended or essay questions. They take longer to tabulate but can yield incredible insights.

> Keep your surveys brief. People get bored quickly, and after the first few questions, most people can't wait for it to be over.

Online focus groups

Marketers have used focus groups offline for years. Essentially, a focus group is a selected group of people with similar purchase habits or demographics gathered in a conference room to discuss your product. Right now there is a strong trend toward conducting online focus groups. In some respects, they are even better than their offline version because there are no geographic barriers, much lower costs (about half as much), faster turnaround time, and intangibles such as respondents being more open without an interviewer staring them in the face.

"I think [the panelists] were more definite about things they didn't like [on a new Web site] than they'd be in front of a moderator," said Lisa Crane, VP-Sales and Marketing for Universal Studios Online, according to a *New York Times* article. Crane used the online focus group to test a redesigned site that was being developed for Captain Morgan Original Spiced Rum.

One company's online focus group

A research company sent out a questionnaire to 6,000 Internet homes and received 2,700 responses within one day of sending out screener e-mail. They then formed two groups of eight panelists each for the client, who required that respondents be over 21 and have certain drinking preferences. The company rescreened panelists just before the focus group began, and had alternates lined up should anyone not qualify.

The groups were held in a private chat room on the research company's site. A moderator fielded questions and answers on one side of a split screen. Proponents of online focus groups say the only limitation, aside from the lack of face-to-face contact with panelists, is the quality of graphic presentation.

Research tools to help you learn what you want to know

There are many do-it-yourself tools in Internet-land. Three of them—Click To Market, MarketTools, and NFO Worldwide—help online marketers take a quick pulse of viewership, the market at large, or both.

Creating your own survey may sound intimidating, but Zoomerang (*www.zommerang.com*) makes it simple. Choose from more than 100 survey ideas—each one contains sample questions in a ready-to-send template. If you have particular needs or are just feeling creative, you may build your own survey from scratch. Up to 20 questions in a variety of formats can be incorporated into a custom questionnaire, which can be e-mailed to respondents or accessed

> There are many do-it-yourself tools in Internet-land. Three of them—Click To Market, MarketTools, and NFO Worldwide—help online marketers take a quick pulse of viewership, the market at large, or both.

from a site. The real-time data collection mechanics and reporting reside on Zoomerang.

Click To Market (*www.clicktomarket.com*) claims to capture and analyze opinions, intentions, and preferences; provide instant feedback; and take action against key business objectives. Click To Market gives you private, 24-hour access to real-time survey results. You can also choose to show your respondents up-to-the-second results with Insta-Results. This feature is extremely popular because it gives respondents an instant reward—people love to see how their opinions compare with others. The site says it's free to try for the first time. Results are e-mailed to you.

Expensive but helpful tools

InsightExpress costs about $1,000 per survey, based on the number of completed responses. It will help you draw up a questionnaire and pick a demographic target from among its 700,000-member panel. Big guns like Kraft and AT&T have used online surveys for product screening and concept testing. Online researchers usually obtain results from two response pools: samplings of site visitors (via e-mail or intercept) or market samples. Research firms, including MarketTools, NFO Worldwide, Harris Interactive, and others, all maintain their own huge panels—captive consumers who contributed detailed demographic information and expressed willingness to participate in surveys. They also have access to thousands of lists that can be refined to a perfect fit.

> Online researchers usually obtain results from two response pools: samplings of site visitors (via e-mail or intercept) or market samples.

Quick tips

✓ There is a free spying service called Spyonit.com. Check it out and use it often.

✓ Start your own FAQ based on your customers' inquiries and update it often.

✓ Use Newsgroups to build a mailing list and send e-mails to your customers, asking them to review some aspect of your site.

Summary

Many people use research for support rather than enlightenment. Research should function like a prism, reflecting truths that are important to a Web site. A research plan needs to be a mosaic of prism reflections, forming a complete picture. The tools available to us are getting more and more powerful every day. But nothing will ever replace the painstaking work of drawing the pieces together to make your site what visitors want.

A research plan needs to be a mosaic of prism reflections, forming a complete picture.

For more information on this topic, visit our Web site at www.businesstown.com

Creating a Dynamite Promotional Message

In this chapter, you'll learn:

- **How to create your promotional message**
- **Why and how to use power words in your writing**
- **The master promotional plan called AIDA**

Focus on your promotion

A strong promotional plan should be highly focused. The most important asset you will have for your promotion attack is time. It can take a month or more to begin getting links on other people's Web sites and even more time to get placement on the major search engines. It can take up to a couple of months to begin getting substantial amounts of reciprocal links from other related sites and to get good placement on search engines.

Once you have submitted your site to the search engines and started to communicate with other sites, focus your time on:

- E-mail
- Discussion lists
- E-zines
- Newsgroups
- Bulletin boards
- Classified ads
- Mailing lists
- Commercial online services

These are important traffic builders that will literally generate traffic within a few days and allow you to test ads, slogans, sales letters, and your Web site design. Make sure you have a winning combination before you start to get traffic from reciprocal links and search engine listings. This chapter will furnish you with the information you need to start your promotional campaign. It will give you the tools you need to start instantly.

How to create a dynamite promotional message

Usually, I don't recommend writing from formulas. People see through that. You need to put your soul into your promotional writing. Remember that people buy from people, not Web sites. I think it's fair to assume that you're not the head of General Motors and

> A strong promotional plan should be highly focused. The most important asset you will have for your promotion attack is time.

the name that's on your Web site is not as well known as Amazon.com. Thus, your promotional campaign will have to exude faith and trust. This is communicated by both your Web site and your promotional campaign. Solutions and benefits are why people buy things and why they logon and stay on a particular site. That's the thread that's common to all successful Web sites and why the following mantra should be the core of your promotional campaign:

People don't buy products.
People don't buy features.
People buy benefits.

Certain promotional basics are musts for every business. If you set those up from the very beginning, you'll save countless hours of work, avoid unnecessary errors, and speed up the creation of other less common materials that you may need at various times.

> Solutions and benefits are why people buy things and why they logon and stay on a particular site.

AIDA is not an opera—it's a key promotional tool

Years ago, someone devised what is called the AIDA formula. It worked then because it was based on solid marketing and psychological concepts. It's a way of getting to the heart of the prospect. It works now on the Internet, too. AIDA stands for:

- Attention: Use strong, emotion-packed words.
- Interest: To gain interest, answer these two basic questions: What's in it for me? Why should I care? Or, more simply put, so what?
- Desire: If your market doesn't have a burning desire for what you have to offer, you will never be able to get them to act.
- Act: Act means causing a person to commit an action, such as getting in touch with you and buying from you.

But it's equally important that you remember that you have to grab the reader's attention fast and get right to the point. In the world of the Internet, time is measured in lightning speed. Make your message just as short as you can while telling the readers what they want to hear.

What's important is that you get to the point and offer concrete information. Forget the outlandish promises. No one believes them anyway. Keep luring them in by appealing and focusing to their self-interests.

Tip for getting audience attention: Show immediately what the individual will gain by reading his or her e-mail or visiting your Web site. You might consider beginning with a question, a challenging statement, or a promise that the visitor will benefit by reading what you have to say.

Whether you're creating a Web site or a promotional message, remember that it's important to provide surfers with an easy-to-follow roadmap of where you're going to take them and why.

> Get to the point and offer concrete information.

Share of heart—the ultimate emotional sell

Share of heart could actually be a part of AIDA, but it's more of an enhancement. Share of heart is how consumers emotionally (as opposed to intellectually) respond to your promotion and your Web site. It's the connection you make with your consumers—an emotional state where consumers respond through feelings rather than through cold, hard facts. It's where you put all the elements of your promotion together and create a product that's more than the sum of its parts. You achieve share of heart when you instill your promotional words and graphics with something of great emotional and personal value to the individual consumer. It's the vital right-brained message you send to consumers that causes them to make a commitment to your product. Share of heart answers the two key questions that are part of almost every purchase:

How is this product going to reach out and touch the respondent?

How is it going to improve the buyer's life?

It's about adding a touch of salesmanship to your product through subtle cues. Despite what a great deal of research suggests, consumers want to believe your Web site will satisfy their needs the way you say it will.

Six steps to a powerful promotional message

1. Research. Read everything you can get your hands on. That includes really studying the Web sites you visit and the e-mails you receive. What words do you see used? How are they used? What is significant about the subject lines on the e-mails you find most interesting? What about the message inside?

   Make lists of those words that grab your attention, especially those that apply to your products and services. You're going to be using those words to assemble powerful messages.

   Get inside your own skin. Identify the most important thing that makes you and your products or services unique. Decide on the most important message you need to give your potential customers that will create the synergy that will bond you and them.

2. Gather all this research together. First, create a list of focus words—words specific to you and your business. They're the words that you can expect your prospects to use when they try to find you on the Internet and, coincidentally, are also the words that you will use frequently on your Web site. These words may transform themselves into keywords for search engines. (Take a look for a list of keywords in the sidebars on pages 107 and 108 that will stimulate your thought processes.)

   Second, make a list of the benefits you offer your prospects. If you're like most, you can rattle off the features you offer, but you forget the benefits that you're offering. Benefits, not features, are what people buy. And don't

> Read everything you can get your hands on. That includes really studying the Web sites you visit and the e-mails you receive.

forget to instill emotions into your benefits to create a share of heart.

Next, create a 10- to 15-word mission statement—your purpose for being. A clear customer-based mission statement is vital to a focused Web site and promotional strategy. The key is to find out what your visitors want and to build your mission statement around satisfying their needs. A mission statement is a brief proclamation of your business's intent—your Web site plan written on the head of a pin. It's as brief and pithy as a classified ad. The mission statement functions as the heart and soul of your promotional strategy and produces a vivid checkpoint to make sure your product or service stays focused. If you don't have one, you're building your house without a blueprint.

Here's the mission statement for Wal-Mart:

> *To provide a range of products*
> *that deliver value to Middle America.*

This brief sentence says everything. It offers emotional and practical benefits to consumers. On the emotional side, people are comfortable in knowing they're getting a good deal. On the practical side, Wal-Mart's execution of the mission statement means that consumers really are getting a good deal. The statement also targets the customers—Middle America.

Finally, create a 5- to 6-word grabber, a 10- to 12-word grabber, a 25-word description of what you offer the world and what makes you truly unique, a 50-word description of what you offer the world and what makes you truly unique, and a 100-word description of what you offer the world and what makes you truly unique.

3. Write. Sure everyone can write. But if you want to write exceptional messages, you've got to practice. You might write and rewrite the same message a hundred times, experimenting with different word combinations and different approaches and different focus. Rewrite. Writers know it. Editors know it. Direct marketing experts know it. There are

> A clear customer-based mission statement is vital to a focused Web site and promotional strategy.

no writers—only rewriters. Keep looking for ways to improve your work. I can tell you for a fact that the biggest complaint of people on the Internet right now is sloppy use of the language.

4. Test. Create and send an e-mail to a select handful of people. Invite people you respect and trust to be honest with you (preferably not personal friends and family). Get their honest reaction. Join newsgroups in your industry and request that members review your e-mail messages.

5. Rewrite. Go back to the drawing board. And, by the way, be absolutely sure that you proofread every word, every letter. When you're completely satisfied that you have the best possible written components for your promotional campaign, save them in a convenient place so that you can cut and paste them as needed. There is no reason to reinvent the wheel every time you need a promotional message if you have all the key promotional components readily accessible. And an added benefit of taking this approach is that you will minimize the possibility of spelling and typographical errors that will reflect very poorly on you.

6. Repeat, repeat, repeat. When you finally achieve copy that does the job—gets the response you're looking for and leads your readers to do exactly what you want them to do—use it often as your core promotional message. Resist, at all costs, the urge to change it. Find all the various ways you can use your message over and over again. Your Web site, your press releases, your brochures, your direct e-mail and traditional mail campaigns, traditional media, your everyday e-mail, every written communication between you and the public must carry that same message.

> Repeat, repeat, repeat. When you finally achieve copy that does the job—gets the response you're looking for and leads your readers to do exactly what you want them to do—use it often as your core promotional message.

Premade Promotions

This is a canned approach—meaning that you used material you prepared in advance. It works pretty much like a brochure that you have printed up. You might personalize a printed brochure with a

Reply to Your E-mail

E-mail response: It is crucial that you make an attempt to respond to most, if not all e-mail. My rule of thumb is to respond to all mail with suggestions or comments, but to ignore mail that shows the writer has clearly not even looked at your site or your Frequently Asked Questions list (if you have one). I also ignore any e-mail connected to multilevel marketing or pyramid marketing, and any mail promising me I will get rich quick if I follow the enclosed advice.

The subject line is one of the most important parts of your e-mail campaign. Begin with the subject lines in your e-mails and the headings on your Web pages.

cover letter. You can personalize your promotion over the Internet with phrases that target your specific audience. With a variety of messages, you can respond to inquiries speedily without having to create a new message each time. People on the Internet want speed. If you don't answer a query quickly, the customer will probably forget he even wrote it. This happened to me quite often before I learned to anticipate the results of my promotional requests. At the very least, add the customer's name in the salutation.

Promoting through e-mail

In every e-mail communication that you send out, you should be promoting your site. After you sign your name, make sure to add a hot link to your site. A short ad or SIG file can also help bring people to your site.

Currently, there is no better way to bring large numbers of previous visitors back to your site than to stay in touch with them via e-mail. Your Web site and your mailing list can work together. Include announcements of new Web site features in the mailings, and provide a way for visitors to the site to sign up for the mailing list. Web information can be more visual, is easier for the reader to navigate, and is speaking to readers who are in a receptive mood since they came to you.

E-mail formats

The subject line is one of the most important parts of your e-mail campaign. Begin with the subject lines in your e-mails and the headings on your Web pages. It's a noisy world out there. People on the Internet today receive about 35% more reading materials today than they did a year ago. Some receive 100, 200, 300 e-mails a day. (We've been told that there are numbers of surfers who consistently get in excess of 1,000 e-mails a day.) There's no telling how many sites the average surfer visits each day, but I can tell you that on a good day I might hit 50 to 75.

Do people read all those e-mails and Web sites? Well, yes and no. They read what grabs their attention and whatever promises to fill an immediate personal need. The sheer volume of information, though, is becoming more of a challenge every day. People are learning to be a lot more selective about what they'll spend their time reading. They keep their fingers poised over the delete key and use it frequently. They use software that sifts through their mail and sorts it into folders, and automatically deletes anything they have no interest in seeing.

How programs sort and display e-mail

Most e-mail programs sort by two criteria: subject (keywords) and individual (e-mail address). So it's imperative that you get those subject lines right. And it's imperative that you avoid, at all cost, the image of one who sends out junk mail.

The two things that are always displayed are the "From" line and the "Subject" line.

These two seemingly inconsequential lines will make all the difference in whether your mail will be read or deleted. They work exactly the same way as snail mail when you look at the envelope and the return address before you decide to throw it away. To make matters worse, some e-mail programs condense the subject and the sender's name to just a few characters. Obviously, you have to make your point quickly. Put the important words up front, in case they get deleted, and make sure you capture the person's interest. Use the copywriting tricks we discussed at the beginning of the chapter.

> Most e-mail programs sort by two criteria: subject (keywords) and individual (e-mail address).

Tease before you deliver

If you can't make people want to find out more in the first five or six words they see in the subject line, they're gone, and chances of getting them back are slim to none. Worse, if you mishandle those words and come across as someone who has nothing but a self-serving, bald-faced promo to offer, you can bet that they'll never purposely give you a second chance. Remember those 50 to 75 Web sites I told you I might visit on any given day? Well, of those, I *might* bookmark one, maybe even two, that I think are worth going back to again. The rest are history and forgotten within the first 30 seconds after I leave the site.

So it's up to you to create the most powerful text you possibly can. Summarize it in the subject line in five or six words. Then write a powerful message in the body of your e-mail that delivers on your promises, and you've got a winner!

> The key to building your promotion is to do it in a well-planned manner, using AIDA as your starting point.

Quick tips

✓ When writing anything, don't send it out until you've reread it the next day.

✓ E-mails can be potent tools for garnering traffic when used correctly.

Summary

The key to building your promotion is to do it in a well-planned manner, using AIDA as your starting point. Use well-planned emotional words in your promotion, and gear it to your consumer's needs and wants.

For more information on this topic, visit our Web site at www.businesstown.com

More About Working with E-mail

In this chapter, you'll learn:

- The five-step way to write your e-mails
- A self-test that will make sure your e-mail is on target
- Motion packed, power words

The five steps to writing e-mail

There are five parts to every sales letter and most memos. Although the order of the parts is not always constant, this guide can help you build your letter. Every letter should consist of a lead, a benefits statement, the deal, a credibility statement, and a call to action. By the way, you should format your e-mail copy so that it is no longer than 65 characters. That's what most people use for their e-mail. If you make it longer than 65 characters, it will look weird when it's displayed on-screen.

The lead

Begin your communication in an interesting way. Your lead must be interesting or catchy. The lead must captivate the reader personally. Even the longest e-mail begins with a lead. The lead will make or break your letter because if you don't motivate the reader to read on, the letter probably won't get read.

The benefits statement

These are the benefits that people will get out of using your product or visiting your Web site. Make the benefits clear and relate them to the prospect as specifically as you can. Use bullets, if possible, and back up the benefits more fully in the body of the letter.

The deal

This is the offer you want to make in your communication. Explain what you are trying to sell to the reader. It could be your site. Or it could be a product. Make your points clearly and succinctly. Again, using bullets makes it easy for the reader to assess what he or she is getting.

The credibility statement

Tell your reader why you (or your product) are qualified to do the task you are writing about. Explain yourself in terms of clients and know-how. Use testimonials and link them to the sites that gave you them.

> Every letter should consist of a lead, a benefits statement, the deal, a credibility statement, and a call to action.

The call to action

The call to action is the key part of your letter. Without a specific call to action, you might as well just toss the e-mail into the recycle bin. Remember that you must ask for only one action—whether it's to make a phone call or to return a reply card—in every letter.

Take this self-test before you write anything:

- Why are you writing this e-mail?
- What action do you want this person to take?
- What do you want this person to get out of this letter?
- How is it going to advance your goals?
- How do you want the reader to feel after receiving your missive?

Here are some e-mail subjects that made me want to read the letters:

- Joe Smith (a friend) suggested I write
- Let's go, Barry, up and at 'em
- Words that are magnets for money (for a newsletter)
- New domain names available
- Top ten Web site tips
- There's an e-card waiting for you
- An opportunity to freelance
- Will your site survive the crash test?
- Our bathrobe referral program just got better

> Remember that you must ask for only one action— whether it's to make a phone call or to return a reply card—in every letter.

Let your customers create your promotional message and e-mail

Now, here's a powerful concept. Think about it. At no time in the history of marketing has it been easier to give the customer what he or she wants. To do it, ask questions and do surveys.

People today are happy to tell you what they want and what they will buy. They'll tell you what they like and what they don't like. They'll tell you what turns them on and what motivates them. All you have to do is ask. This is another reason it's important that you get out there on the Usenet newsgroups and on the mailing lists where people share information with each other.

It is crucial that you make an attempt to respond to most, if not all e-mail. Respond to all mail with suggestions or comments, but ignore mail that shows the writer has clearly not even looked at your site. I also ignore any e-mail connected with multilevel marketing or pyramid marketing, and any mail promising me I will get rich quick if I follow the enclosed advice.

The response you send to any e-mail doesn't have to be much—a couple of lines will do—but it shows the person who sent the e-mail that someone actually read the message. The *worst* thing you can do is automatically send a reply saying, "Sorry, but we can't respond to individual e-mail"; give me silence any day over such an impersonal response!

I hope that this feature will help you take the first steps toward building a community around your site rather than simply a restroom on the info-highway.

I've been amazed at how willing people are to answer questions. Some lists devoted explicitly to marketing and various types of businesses are veritable universities and libraries of information. It's not uncommon for someone to write a scenario and ask for opinions or feedback and suggestions on where to go for information and how to approach the situation. People love helping others—even their own competitors.

> Think of using your Web site as a source of information for yourself as well as for your customers. Set up a forum and ask questions relative to your topic or your business.

Think of using your Web site as a source of information for yourself as well as for your customers. Set up a forum and ask questions relative to your topic or your business. Encourage your visitors to contribute to your success. Ask, for example, how they like your site, does it load quickly, does it offer them what they were looking for? You can ask them for examples of how they've used your services or products in their own lives—these can become endorsements and testimonials for your promotion. You can use them on your Web site, too. And you don't even have to work at it. Or you can ask what they would like to see you do differently.

If you really pay attention to what your visitors are saying, they'll actually tell you what they want, what would make them happy, and how you can talk to them in a meaningful way. They'll tell you what will get them motivated to buy from you, if you let them. And if you ask, they may even give you permission to put them on your mailing list.

Ah, but there's the rub. They might tell you what you don't want to hear. They may tell you that they're already happily involved with someone else. What are you going to do with that? Use it, I hope, to refine and shore up your promotional approach.

Messages that work while you're having fun

OK, you've followed me this far and I've given you a lot of information and work to do. Now it's a matter of kicking back and having some fun. You can do that on the Internet. You can't ignore your business. But once you have the key communications pieces in place, you can have fun.

We're going to be talking about e-mail lists and newsgroups more fully in the following chapters. If you like to hunt and fish or if you are passionate about handicrafts, you can—and should—start frequenting newsgroups and lists where people who share your interests hang out. You don't even need to broadcast to the members what a great product or service you offer—in fact, you shouldn't in most cases.

Start participating in the discussions. Have fun. Don't even discuss business. Same with your e-mails. Write e-mails to people, friends, new acquaintances, Webmasters of other sites that interest you. Talk about anything and everything except business. Ask for advice and information, offer suggestions, compliment them.

Say what? Don't talk about business? How is that going to stimulate interest?

Easy. Make sure that every piece of communication that leaves your computer carries a signature. It should be like a shadow tagging along right behind your e-mail messages.

> Make sure that every piece of communication that leaves your computer carries a signature.

Signatures

It's a four- to six-line personal promo. It includes your name and the name of your company, your e-mail and URL addresses, and your phone number. It also includes a short grabber or statement designed to tell what you do. Remember that five- to six-word promotional grabber I suggested you create? And the 10- to 12-word promotional grabber? And the 10- to 15-word mission statement? Here's where you put them to work.

This signature should go everywhere your e-mail goes, keeping you in front of the public and calling on them to get acquainted and involved with you.

In order to ensure that the signature does stick with you and that it isn't snipped by some of the lists and the newsgroups that are adamantly against promotions, you need to keep your signature to fewer than six lines—four lines is the ideal. Any more can be a problem in most circles.

Keep to this format, and you don't ever have to hard sell or promote your business or your Web site. Your signature will do the work. Focus on getting acquainted with the people in the group and sharing valuable, interesting information and ideas. Send messages that demonstrate that you are a fun person and that you're an expert in your field. Your signature sits there at the end of your e-mail reminding them of who you are and what you do. As they get more comfortable with you and see that you are a real person who enjoys the same things they do, they will also be reminded that you are in business and they will always have a way to reach you easily! Make sure you save all your e-mail addresses for a mailing list.

> Keep to this format, and you don't ever have to hard sell or promote your business or your Web site. Your signature will do the work.

Use a mini-promo

Let's talk, again, about the subject lines in your e-mails and in newsletters that you're going to develop. In most e-mail programs, the amount of space you have for a subject line is limited. Figure 10.1 shows the format of e-mail on America Online.

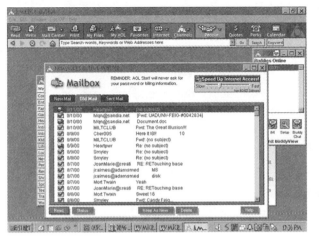

Figure 10.1: America Online e-mail account

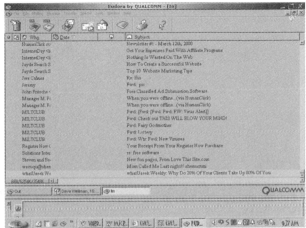

Figure 10.2: Eudora e-mail account

And Figure 10.2 shows the format for Eudora, one of the most popular e-mail programs. At least 17 characters are wasted on most e-mail and newsletter headers. They start with meaningless words like "the," "issue," and "newsletter," and other words that generally are of no real use to anyone. All these unnecessary characters could be applied to other more exciting or curiosity-building words. Replace this "word trash" with another selling word or another emotion-packed word that will grab the reader.

Renee Hopkins, Web editor and writer, who writes a regular e-mail newsletter for a retail natural foods store (Whole Foods Market's Arlington, Texas, location) contributed the following insight into her specific promotional approach to her newsletter.

Here's the format of her newsletter's subject line and how she arrived at it. The subject line:

FABULOUS FRUITS:
The Whole Story from Whole Foods Market,
Arlington, Texas, 5-31-00

The Most Powerful Words in the English Language

you	comfort
love	results
discovery	passion
today	sleek
good	unique
great	urge
proven	savvy
profit	free
guarantee	convenient
safe	

More Powerful Words

Here are more words with strong emotional appeal, listed in no particular order. How many can you use for your business?

scientific	home
amusement	courtesy
durable	growth
hospitality	hunting
clean	status
efficient	enormous
youth	low-cost
time-saving	genuine
affectionate	progress
appetizing	thinking
value	excel
fun	civic pride
ambition	patriotism
reputation	recommended
genuine	sociable
stimulating	stylish
save	royalty
popular	admired
economical	beauty
mother	personality
modern	independent
health	successful
quality	up-to-date
elegant	tested
bargain	expressive
sympathy	relief
necessary	tasteful

List compiled by psychologist H. L. Hollingwort.

Here's her explanation of how she arrived at it:

The elements always go in this order:

- The "hook" phrase (FABULOUS FRUITS)
- The newsletter's name ("Whole Story")
- The ID of the store and its location (necessary because there are more than 100 Whole Foods stores in the country, and this newsletter only covers this one store)

Previously I was including issue and volume numbers in the subject line, but was advised that this was not the best way to get people to open this e-mail. That information now appears in the SIG area at the bottom of the newsletter.

I realize that the first two words are the only thing most people see in their e-mail lists, and I made a conscious decision to make those words be descriptive of the particular issue's content, even though that may seem like a spam technique. The newsletter comes from *my* Whole Foods domain address and not from an auto-responder, which may help a little in the perception that this e-mail isn't spam. (Plus, the newsletter's only sent to those who sign up in person at the store.)

What would happen if you approached all of your promotional copy from this kind of reasoning? Do you think others would see your messages as something they'd want to read? Heck, yeah. This approach, especially if applied to everything you write, cuts to the chase, tells the readers that you value their time, and allows you to pack a lot more valuable information and motivation into your writing.

Impact writing for your Web site

1. Enlighten but don't preach. Work toward making your message emotionally and intellectually stimulating to the reader. When they've seen what you have to offer, readers should

feel uplifted and inspired to action. Give readers a sense of real personal benefit.

2. Persuade and offer authoritative information but avoid heavy-handedness. Let your intensity and strength of logic show through. Show that you are aware of trends, but keep your own message durable. What you put on the Internet may be around a lot longer than you will. You want it to reflect well on you.

3. Remain focused on what is directly related to the current or enduring interests of your specific readers.

A twelve-point creative checklist

1. Do you know where you fit in your universe and what your sphere of influence is?

2. Do you know *exactly* what your market is and how to play to it? You can't please everyone—especially on the Internet. But you can position yourself so that others will be able to seek you out and find you.

3. Do you position yourself as the guru, the expert in your area of expertise? Position yourself to fit and serve your targeted audience.

4. Have you checked and rechecked the perception, interests, understanding level, and concerns of your intended visitors? Remember, perception is reality! If they think it's so, it is so.

5. Have you included your correct address, phone number, e-mail address, and URL (where appropriate)? Check them! A simple typo here (it happens more frequently than you think) is a killer.

6. Is your spelling correct? Is your grammar correct? Have several people proofread your work. Put it away for several days and then reread it.

7. Did you make it very clear what you want your visitor to do next? Should they e-mail you, pick up the phone and call, or come back again?

> Have you checked and rechecked the perception, interests, understanding level, and concerns of your intended visitors?

Mission Statements

Here's a note about a mission statement that attracted 10,000,000 subscribers. America Online started as a simple online message service, but its strict adherence to making online communications accessible to the "technologically challenged" gave it license to venture into new areas.

America Online was seen as cutting edge while Prodigy was considered old, dull, and stale. The difference is in how both services were positioned in their formative stages and how strong the AOL mission statement was. Prodigy was conceived of as an information service, AOL as a communications facilitator. AOL was a new medium where people could meet other people, stay informed, buy products, and learn new things. They were the first in making their service user friendly—where people with no knowledge of computers could communicate freely and easily. Steve Case, CEO of AOL, talks about his company as a community rather than an online service. People meet online, talk online and even get married. (You exactly can't do that online. Yet.) They console each other via computer and congratulate each other through the same medium.

8. Did you include an offer or coupon? You'll find information on these powerful ways to appeal to your visitors elsewhere in this book. Pay special attention to them. They work.
9. Did you include testimonials, a success story? People *love* to read about other people's successes.
10. Did you include a location map and store hours (if you have a storefront)? This may be very important if you're appealing to a wide range of visitors, some of whom might elect to drop in for a visit.
11. Are all of your promotional efforts *you* focused, *not* me oriented?
12. Have you attended to all the details? Little things make the difference. Any inaccuracy will defeat your efforts.

Review this checklist again and come back to it frequently.

Using auto-responders

Auto-responders are a quick and convenient way for your prospective customers to get information about your products or services sent directly to them by e-mail 24 hours a day, 365 days a week. More important, they show you care.

Many Web-hosting packages offer free auto-responders when you sign up for their services. Some companies sell auto-responders with various features. Visitors to your site who read your ads may click on your e-mail hyperlink to request more information. Either an e-mail message window appears or your prospective customer's e-mail program opens. Within a few seconds of their clicking Send, they will receive your information by e-mail.

Your auto-response message can be about your products or services, price list, newsletter subscription, order forms, or anything you want your prospective customers to know immediately. When a customer sends an e-mail message to the e-mail address you have assigned to the auto-responder, he or she will immediately receive your message.

Another helpful benefit of auto-responders is that when a prospective customer requests information, his or her e-mail address is collected and can be forwarded to your e-mail address. With all the collected e-mail addresses, you can manually send follow-up e-mails.

Personalize your follow-ups. People respond better when their names are mentioned. Most experts agree that it often takes seven or more exposures to your ad before your prospects will purchase from you. You can set automatic auto-responders to follow up after a certain number of days, weeks, or months.

Quick tips

✓ Typos, spelling errors, and such are death to a promotional message.

✓ Promotional pieces all need to let the reader know the next step to take. Don't let your visitors get away without some action. If you do, your paths may never cross again.

✓ Make sure your messages are always consistent. Does every piece of your promotional package—Web site, e-mail, letterheads, brochures, flyers, radio, TV, adult education, newspaper features and press releases, magazines—carry your unique promotional message? People don't buy when they're confused. If they see on your Web site that you're a custom designer but on your brochures that you're the fastest "draw" in the West, they're just not going to buy it.

> Most experts agree that it often takes seven or more exposures to your ad before your prospects will purchase from you.

Summary

There's an abundance of ways that people who are fed up with in-your-face marketing can cut you out of the loop. Most e-mail programs now offer an option for presorting e-mail and deleting unwanted junk e-mail on receipt. And savvy surfers have a tendency to keep their fingers poised over the delete key—they're not the least hesitant to use it. So it's important that you think carefully about what you're sending people and how you're approaching your marketing efforts.

For more information on this topic, visit our Web site at www.businesstown.com

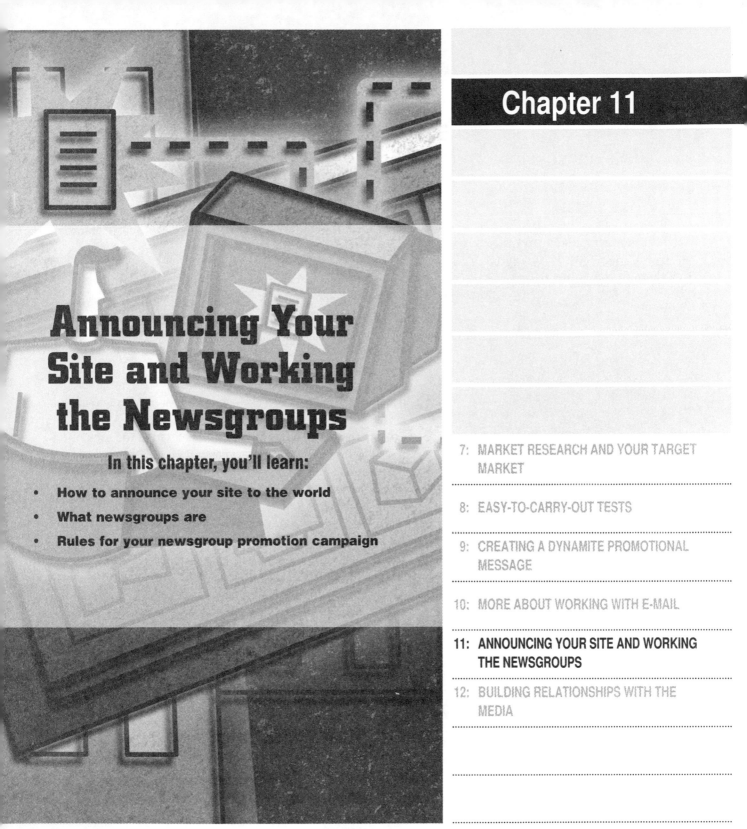

Announcing Your Site and Working the Newsgroups

In this chapter, you'll learn:

- How to announce your site to the world
- What newsgroups are
- Rules for your newsgroup promotion campaign

Chapter 11

Basic rules for announcing your site

Once your site is up and fine-tuned, you're ready to have your grand opening. It's time to unveil your site to the world. You're the Grand Poobah of your field. Don't get shy—you'll want to tell everyone in cyberspace that you've arrived. Now is the time to execute any promotion and public relations strategy you have developed. Here are some basic rules for announcing your site:

1. Start registering with Internet directories. (We're not up to the search engines yet. Section 4 gives you a thorough game plan.) Major directories are listed in the back of this book.
2. Make sure that every component of your site works absolutely perfectly. Nothing is more irritating than a hyperlink or gizmo that doesn't work.
3. Recheck your keywords by running a basic search in the major search engines to make sure they bring back sites similar to yours—even your competitors.
4. Contact the free announcement services listed in the back of this book. Follow their instructions to the letter. Sometimes they are called "What's New," "What's Hot," or similar names. Their sole purpose in life is to announce new sites. They work, and you should use them.
5. Call or e-mail all of your friends and business colleagues. Ask them to circulate your e-mail to others. When you network this way, make sure that your friends include their names in the e-mails, so it doesn't give the impression of spam.
6. All of your materials should clearly identify your URL. That means your advertising, your letterhead, your business card, your promotional giveaways—everything. If you can find a way to print your URL on your car in big black letters, do it. (Actually, magnetic signs are sold for that purpose.)

Creating relations with newsgroups

Newsgroups—or discussion forums—are places on the Internet where people go to discuss a particular topic that interests them. It is the

> Once your site is up and fine-tuned, you're ready to have your grand opening.

soapbox of the 21st century where people can express any idea they want about anything they want, no matter how off-the-wall their opinion is. Under the umbrella name, Usenet, it's a gathering place where people with specific interests post messages to a board for everyone to read and respond to. Newsgroups are different from chat rooms because they are not held in real time. It might take an hour or even a few days before a post is answered. Estimates vary as to the quantity of newsgroups, but it is fair to say that there are over 70 million running at any given time, covering absolutely anything and everything from aardvarks to zygotes.

Many smaller Web sites also have forums that follow the newsgroup format. Their participants may be much fewer than traditional newsgroups, but they are generally highly focused and should be considered in your marketing mix.

Promoting through newsgroups has a great many benefits, making your time spent worthwhile. It will ultimately drive a great deal of traffic to your Web site. Here's why they're so good:

- Newsgroups let you target your message to the exact audience—even the precise person—you want.
- You can reach thousands of prospects with a limited number of postings.
- Reading the newsgroups religiously lets you research your target market and learn about its needs, wants, and desires.
- By helping newsgroup members answer their questions, you gain recognition as an expert in your field.
- The ads and signatures you use in your postings are outstanding passive promotions that create excellent visibility for your site—if you use them correctly.

Promoting through newsgroups has a great many benefits, making your time spent worthwhile. It will ultimately drive a great deal of traffic to your Web site.

How newsgroups work

Each newsgroup contains a number of postings called articles. An article is an e-mail message from an individual. A newsgroup may contain as few as one or two messages or hundreds of messages. Each message looks very much like an e-mail you might receive from a friend. Each article has the name of the person who submitted it, and a "subject." Sometimes a moderator reviews the articles before they are posted to the list. The moderator may be an expert on the topic under discussion, or simply an interested party who started the newsgroup. It's his (or her) responsibility to make sure all articles are on target, are truly informative, and adhere to the rules set forth for the newsgroup. Each topic is connected by a thread, which is a linear string to a conversation.

Here is an example of a newsgroup posting where the person is thinking of undergoing a LASIK procedure to correct his vision. He's inquiring about risks and benefits. Several people responded with their opinions. I'm using this as an example because this is the actual board I went to when I was deciding whether or not to have the procedure done on myself.

Rob—Wednesday, 23 May 2000, at 8:30 A.M.
Should I do the LASIK Procedure?
Brenda—Wednesday, 24 May 2000, at 9:15 A.M.
NEW: Re: Should I do it?

And here is a one of the responses:

Make sure your Dr. is board certified, done thousands of procedures and make sure you are a perfect candidate all around. I have found you learn a lot more about LASIK AFTER you have it.

> As you become more familiar with the newsgroup, you will learn to recognize those who are the experts. Those who offer valuable information and knowledgeable responses are highly respected members of the group.

Generally the first article states the topic and subsequent responses to that article. You can scan through the articles and select any that look interesting. As you become more familiar with the newsgroup, you will learn to recognize those who are the experts. Those who offer valuable information and knowledgeable responses are highly respected members of the group. That's what you are going to be after you read and implement this section.

Most newsgroups also have archives of past postings. You'll find out where those archives are kept in the newsgroup's FAQ, which is typically posted to the list at least once a month. The archives breathe longevity into articles. Articles that were posted to newsgroups five or six years ago are still available today and will be open to the public for many years to come.

Originally, there was controversy about using newsgroups for promotional messages. The prejudice is mostly gone now. Announcement of professional products or services on Usenet is allowed, but only if you do it right and follow the rules. Some newsgroups allow you to post advertising messages. Some don't. But be careful. Many newsgroups still forbid such use. The best way to be sure is to check out the newsgroup's FAQ. (Ask for it if you don't see it posted.) It's also good practice to "lurk" awhile. Just read the posts a couple days until you get a feel for the personality of the newsgroup and to be sure that you don't inadvertently step on toes.

> Originally, there was controversy about using newsgroups for promotional messages. The prejudice is mostly gone now.

Before we start, a caveat

Why am I placing so much emphasis on following the rules? Because newsgroups can be pretty quirky and as irritable as rhinos in heat. If the members of a newsgroup—or a moderator—think you're being blatant about your ads, they will flame you (sending mean or threatening messages in all capitals letters) or mailbomb you. They will ban your postings forever. They may even try to get you thrown off your Internet host. So, for the good of your Web site and your very self-worth as a human being, follow the rules. Remember, someone else is paying the phone bills. A good guideline to follow is that your message should be of overall benefit to readers. The best way to do this is to involve yourself in the day-to-day chatter and workings of the group.

Think of it this way, a newsgroup offers you all the benefits available for one who wants to network at a cocktail party. You don't simply charge in and start selling. If you do and you antagonize the group, you'll bring the wrath of the group on your head. Once your words are printed, they will be out there for all the world to judge you. They won't fade away out of memory.

Scan through the articles and select any that look interesting. You can post advertising messages in applicable forums, or you can interact on a one-on-one basis with members of the group by answering their questions.

Basic rules for newsgroup promotion

1. Get intimately involved in the subject matter. Don't post anything until you get the look and feel of the discussion forum.
2. Make sure what you say is on topic. Visit the newsgroup for a week or two and read the articles without posting anything. (This is called "lurking.") Find out what the discussion is all about. That way, when you're ready to post your article you don't have to worry that it will be off-topic or not in the right format.
3. Read and reread the FAQ if the newsgroup has one.
4. Be helpful. Answer questions and give advice. Your postings will be appreciated and even anticipated.
5. Never type in all capital letters. It looks like you're yelling. And you will get flamed back.
6. Never post blatant ads. The object of newsgroups is to inform, not to sell.
7. Post only in groups that relate to your business or interests. Find, or create, a common bond with the others on the list.

> Get intimately involved in the subject matter. Don't post anything until you get the look and feel of the discussion forum.

The ultimate newsgroup strategy

Think of your newsgroup strategy as a collection of piano keys. You can plunk a few keys at random, and eventually you may come up with a tune. But if you plunk the keys in a predetermined order, you'll come up with the tune you want—maybe even a masterpiece—much faster and with a lot fewer errors.

The identify key

Find the newsgroups that are right for you. The toughest part of newsgroup promotion is finding the groups that are truly relevant. You must sift through a great deal of slag to find the ore you want to mine. Newsgroups are grouped into similar subjects called hierarchies. The major hierarchies are (as taken from Deja.com):

alt. (alternative)—Anything-goes type discussions covering every conceivable topic from aliens to Zen.

news. (news)—Information regarding the Usenet news network and software, including news servers and newsreaders.

rec. (recreation)—Discussions about arts, games, hobbies, music, sports, etc. If it's recreational, it's being discussed here.

biz. (business)—Discussions about business products and services, including product debuts, upgrades, enhancements, and reviews.

comp. (computers)—Discussions about hardware, software, languages, systems—you name it. Also, valuable consumer advice.

k12. (k through 12)—Education discussions covering such topics as using technology, curriculum, and classroom-to-classroom projects.

soc. (society)—Discussions of social issues and cultures around the world, as well as a place to socialize.

humanities. (humanities)—Literature, fine arts, and other humanities, for both professionals and amateurs.

misc. (miscellaneous)—Miscellaneous discussions covering such diverse topics as employment, children, health, and consumer issues.

talk. (talk)—Discussions and debates about current issues and more.

sci. (science)—Pure- and applied-sciences discussions for both professionals and laypeople.

Regional.—Discussions specifically about a country or a U.S. state.

> Newsgroups are grouped into similar subjects called hierarchies.

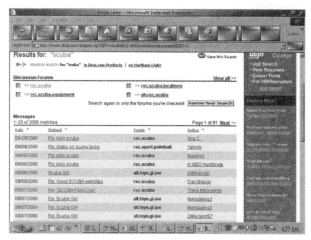

Figure 11.1: Searching by Topic

Forum rec.scuba

Post Message or Subscribe to rec.scuba

Discussions			Next >>
Last Msg.	Name	# of Msgs.	Latest Post by
08/09/2000	Seattle outlaws night diving and restricts diving	15	Jerome O'Neil
08/09/2000	Black	200	Jerome O'Neil
08/09/2000	From Scott: Get a life. Then, commit suicide.	167	Brian Wagner
08/09/2000	DIR Anthem	8	mjblackmd
08/09/2000	Brockville accident	6	Stroke Diver
08/09/2000	O2 Cleaning...	27	Popeye
08/09/2000	Close calls...near misses	33	Popeye
08/09/2000	Stuart Cove Feeder gets bit in head by 6' Reef Sha	22	Manaul Zia Marchen
08/09/2000	Cool experience	7	Uwe Hercksen
08/09/2000	tobermory death	2	Robert Wood
08/09/2000	Scuba diving in Vietnam?	26	SE
08/09/2000	Molikini & Lanii	4	Steve Gilchrist
08/09/2000	log book pages	1	Steve Gilchrist
08/09/2000	zvrtec	1	Zeke

Figure 11.2: Inside a Forum

Browse through each discussion group in a hierarchy to see if you're interested in its offerings. Then, search for the articles and threads that you can contribute to meaningfully. Look at Figures 11.1 and 11.2. Another way is by searching for newsgroups on the Web using search engines like Dogpile or Yahoo! or AltaVista. One of the best tools for identifying your target is *www.deja.com*. Search for specific topics or threads that fit your needs. For instance, if you run a site about underwater diving, you could try typing scuba into the DejaNews search box. But don't limit yourself to the "all-to-obvious" queries. Think of what people with similar interests might like. For instance, if you were a sporting goods retailer, instead of just searching for a sporting goods forum, you could explore racquet stringing, hockey forums, and tennis clubs, or scuba.

Another way to find appropriate newsgroups is through your e-mail software or newsgroup reader. There are many out there, including Outlook, Outlook Express, Trumpet, and others. Each one of these offers a search option that will allow you to enter your topic or keyword and will search for the newsgroups that fit those parameters.

The target key

Target your newsgroups and your threads carefully. Pick the newsgroup that is exactly tuned to your message. Find a thread that looks interesting or promising by reading down through the "Subject" list until something catches your eye.

The identify yourself key

The best way to identify yourself and promote your business is with a good signature line, called a signature (or SIG). The SIG should be attached to the end of every e-mail that you send out from your computer, but it is particularly vital to your newsgroup postings. The signature serves as a somewhat subtle statement that you are in business to serve the members of the group. The best ones, five or six lines in length, include your name, your company name, your URL, your contact info, and a brief description that summarizes what your business or site offers.

A signature is very easy to create. Simply type it into your word processor and save it as a .txt file (your word processor has good instructions if you're unclear about file formats and names). Here's a particularly effective one:

Bob Esposito
Good Stuff Cards
www.goodstuffcards.com
e-mail: info@goodstuffcards.com
Katonah, NY 10536   (914) 666-7693   (914) 241-8270 (Fax)
BORIS KARLOFF BEYOND THE MONSTER SERIES "II."
HERE NOW!

Keep your signature short. Don't used visuals or graphics unless you are willing to risk the antagonism of the recipient because it will look too much like an ad. Your object is to blend in seamlessly with the ebb and flow of a group. This kind of signature is acceptable as an attachment to your articles even in groups that do not allow advertising. Just remember that each online service has it's own special formatting rules for including a signature file. Check out the rules and be prepared to create and use several formats if necessary.

Develop several kinds of signature files to use for different newsgroups. That way you can make sure all of your information is right on target. You can create a short blurb to announce a sale, your Web site introduction, or even a special award. If your press release has been

> Keep your signature short. Don't used visuals or graphics unless you are willing to risk the antagonism of the recipient because it will look too much like an ad.

picked up by major publications, you can say "as seen in *The New York Times*" or "recognized on *ABC News*."

Here's a posting I read about SIGS on an e-business forum:

. . . very important: my signature line. It changes as I gain insight and inspiration. Right now it is:
Using words & images to clearly portray clients
Copyediting, Web Site Coordination, Translation Corrections
Office Support Services, 623-876-8168
10439 W Royal Palm, Peoria AZ 85345
http://www.ossWeb.com
mail to: *Oss@ossWeb.com*

Part of this is for information, part for providing credibility. A reasonable number of people interested in my services may read my SIG line in a newsgroup posting, pick up the phone, and call me. This also shows my geographical location, and that I do have a physical address rather than a post office box. Small clues that point to the fact that they have several ways to reach me.

The phrases explain my services, and I have made some excellent contacts and gotten some business as a direct and indirect result of putting this information in a signature line.

Having an informative SIG line is very important, and people serious about being good communicators will usually find something that fits and use it regularly.

Judy Vorfeld—Office Support Services
Polished Presentations
http://www.ossWeb.com
Oss@ossWeb.com

> You can search for particular groups each time you logon to the Internet, but the faster way is to subscribe to each group you want to target.

The subscribe key

You can search for particular groups each time you logon to the Internet, but the faster way is to subscribe to each group you want to target. Subscribing is a simple process of becoming a member of the group so that every time you open your newsgroup reader, posts from that group are delivered to your computer.

You may need a newsgroup reader program to read and post messages in newsgroups. A browser, e-mail software, or software specifically designed for handling newsgroups will work. You'll find free programs by searching for "newsgroups" or "newsgroup readers" on *www.zdnet.com*. Every time you open your newsreader in Netscape, AOL, MSN, Explorer, Outlook Express, or whichever one you are most comfortable with, you will automatically see a list of only your subscribed groups. If you are an AOL user, you can type "newsgroup" as a keyword, and AOL will take you to the newsgroup window.

The read, or examine, key

Once you've selected your key newsgroups, read all the relevant topics. Particularly focus on threads that you may be interested in responding to. The object is to look for a spot where you can contribute a relevant comment. Your responses, coupled with your signature, will bring you traffic by way of hits to your Web site and e-mail from potential clients.

Click on the Subject of that thread, and you will be able to read the whole message. Read and absorb the information it contains. Before you respond, click on View Thread. Read every message in that particular thread. Don't skip messages or rush along too quickly.

Here's a sample posting on AOL from someone interested in racquetball jewelry:

> Read every message in that particular thread. Don't skip messages or rush along too quickly.

Subject: Racquetball Jewelry
From: joeny1141@aol.comantispam (Joe Schmidt)
Date: 5/24/00 10:17 AM Mountain Daylight Time

I am thinking of buying some jewelry for my girlfriend and the racquetball jewelry I've seen some players wearing would fit the bill perfectly. I've noticed one supplier on the Web called First Coast Promotions in Jacksonville, FL, which advertises racquetball jewelry. Has anyone had experience ordering from them? Are they reputable and reliable? Any other suppliers out there to choose from? Thanks for your replies.

Joe Smith

And here's a response:

> Subject: Re: Racquetball Jewelry
> From: nel6464@aol.com (NEL6945)
> Date: 5/24/00 8:28 PM Mountain Daylight Time
>
> hey Joe
> My wife and I have both ordered from First Coast. They seem
> to be very reliable. We didn't have any problems.
>
> Nelson

And another response:

> Subject: Re: Racquetball Jewelry
> From: Racquetball Central Webmaster@racquetballcentral.com
> Date: 5/25/00 7:19 AM Mountain Daylight Time
>
> Kersten Hallander. I think she's ranked 3 or 4 in the women's
> open draw, also makes and sells racquetball
> jewelry . . . at least she did a couple years ago.
>
> John Fromdy
> Fromdy Sports, 555-222-7777
> P.O. Box 262787
> San Diego, CA 92196
> Sportwear and Sports Jewelry

And a response to the response. If you sold racquetball jewelry, it would be a great place to respond with your SIG and recommendations.

Subject: Re: Racquetball Jewelry
From: wccrup@aol.com
Date: 5/25/00 7:19 AM Mountain Daylight Time

And she still does, she was selling some at the U.S. Open.

Chuck

The post key

When you're sure you're up to speed in the discussion, prepare your article. Now find something inspiring or worthy to say. Believe it or not, after all the preliminary work, this is the easiest part. Craft your response simply, without using fancy adjectives.

Remember, you're the expert—you must be—you have a new Web site that proves it! Answer somebody's question in a polite, well-reasoned, and meaningful way. And don't forget your SIG because that's why you're there in the first place. The goal is to get people to your Web site.

But be careful. If you repeat what someone already said, you will not only lose your credibility, you may get a strong rebuke from the moderator and flames from other members. Yes, newsgroups can be a jungle.

> Craft your response simply, without using fancy adjectives.

Tips on posting

- Do not use all caps.
- Make your replies short and relevant.
- Always be polite and show a spirit of helpfulness and camaraderie. Remember you're providing a service (ostensibly), not an ad, to the newsgroup members.
- Post messages that are on the topic, and don't ever post blatant ads.
- Check back often and wait a sufficient period (say, a month) before posting the same message. If you keep repeating things, the regular members will find you pushy and obnoxious. That's a no-no.

Using newsgroups regularly and properly

The results you get from your newsgroup strategy—like all other activities on the Internet—are directly proportionate to the time and effort you invest. Remember, hundreds of people can read the exact posting you submit. The more you post, the more exposure you will get, and the more traffic you will draw to your site.

Plan on posting three to five messages a day each week. Cover a variety of subjects. Put your knowledge to use, and don't stray from the subject matter. You should start seeing visitors from the very first week. Here are some ideas for your posts. Make sure they don't take up more than a line or two.

- Announce a sale
- Announce a new business alliance (see if you can get your new partner to announce it in a separate article)
- Announce a new line of products
- Announce a contest
- Announce a special award or event

> Plan on posting three to five messages a day each week. Cover a variety of subjects.

Quick tips

✓ Venture into newsgroups slowly until you have built up a relationship with the members.

✓ It's good form to end your comment with the following: "Hope this helped."

✓ When working with newsgroups, make sure your messages are right on target. Make sure you use your SIG on everything you do.

✓ If your newsgroup postings are especially appealing and your reputation is good, you can build your own mailing list. You'll find several shareware programs at *www.zdnet.com* that will help you build your list. You can also subscribe to one or more of the list management groups mentioned in the back of this book.

Summary

Once you are a Web presence, the world should know it. All of your materials must clearly identify your Web address or URL. Announcing your new Web site involves the most time-consuming tasks, but sets the framework for attaining success. Your announcement program should be launched as soon as your site is ready. Directory listings, newsgroup contacts, and a formal press campaign should begin as early as possible. This will be a great source of traffic. Check and recheck your keywords carefully, and know how to take advantage of each of the opportunities in this chapter.

> Your announcement program should be launched as soon as your site is ready.

For more information on this topic, visit our Web site at www.businesstown.com

Building Relationships with the Media

In this chapter, you'll learn:

- How to write a press release
- How to build ongoing relationships with the media
- How to make sure your press material is newsworthy and will be published

anaging the news media through press releases and personal contact can be a full-time, frustrating job, but it can be vital to low-cost Web promotion. Although the newsworthiness of new Web sites has fallen off a bit as this book was being written, the Internet is still getting a tremendous amount of attention. A story about your Web site, or even a brief mention about your Web site in the press, can have a major impact on your traffic. A well-executed media strategy can gain your site *free* regional, national, and international exposure.

The media can provide your site with instant credibility because, to readers, this will be seen as an unpaid story geared to their interest. Good press widely circulates through relevant newsgroups, making you an instant expert in your field. When you tie in automatic links to your Web site, newsgroups can distribute them in a geometric manner beyond your wildest imagination.

> Don't forget, your target audience is not the swarming hordes dying to find out what your Web site is about, but the editors of publications that are targeted to the swarming hordes.

Press releases

If you don't include your time and effort, press releases are free. But before we get into the nuts and bolts of writing effective press releases, let's look at the issues the media deal with every day. Don't forget, your target audience is not the swarming hordes dying to find out what your Web site is about, but the editors of publications that are targeted to the swarming hordes.

Editors have several missions that they have to deal with. One is to fill the space they oversee. The other is to keep their sections fresh with articles and information that provide news and value to their readers. The big PR firms employ many people whose job is building relationships with the media. Since you don't have the resources or manpower of the giants, you're going to have to create excitement that stops editors in their tracks. And the editors I know are a pretty jaded bunch.

Your key tool will be the press release. The purpose of the press release is to connect with the media. It is the expected first communication with a media outlet. Whether you're looking for a story, interview, a TV appearance, or just a brief mention about your Web site—the press release is the right place to start.

Format and content

How you write your release in terms of format and content will play an important role in the success of your news release. Editors are bombarded with releases. When they get to their offices in the morning their fax machines, e-mail boxes, and inboxes are overflowing with press releases. Every release shouts "Read Me," "Publish Me," "Make Me Famous." I have a lot of friends in the media. They say they give a press release about 15 to 30 seconds before they decide to print it, file it, or use it. That leaves you only a tiny window of opportunity. But the good news is that the media is on your side, even if it doesn't seem as if they are. They need a constant flow of news releases to keep their publications useful and relevant to their readers.

How to start working on your release

Before we start, grab a sheet of paper or open your word processing program and answer the following:

1. What is unique about your Web site or what you're doing on your Web site? What are you saying to the editors that's so important? Why are you writing this release?
2. What is the focus of your Web site? What problems are you solving?
3. How will your ultimate audience (your prospects) respond to what you're telling them? How will it *benefit* them?
4. What are the facts and statistics you will use to support your focus, or premise? Most editors are sticklers for facts, so back up every factual statement with a source. I can't stress this enough. A boastful press release without hard numbers rolls the eyes of every editor I know.

What is unique about your Web site or what you're doing on your Web site?

Create the ultimate press kit

A press kit is basically a complex press release turned into a nice package that tells more about you and your company, and is all pulled together into a nice neat folder. Send your press kit when an editor, publisher, or producer wants to know more about you.

Your press kit should contain:

- An introductory letter
- One or two press releases
- A fact sheet containing the facts about you or your business
- A biography of you and your accomplishments
- Copies of published articles
- Your company literature and brochures
- Your business card

A press kit is basically a complex press release turned into a nice package that tells more about you and your company.

Story ideas

Here are some story lines for your first release:

- Launch of your Web site or newsletter. Say something newsworthy or even shocking about your Web site. Editors are rather bored of getting one press release after another about this or that Web site. How is yours different? What benefits can you claim that no other Web site offers?
- Web sites that bring together two well-known companies. This can be very interesting to the media, especially when both companies can offer more than either can singly. What about your alliance benefits the reader or visitors to your Web site?
- Publicize a contest or sweepstakes. But don't end your promotion when the contest is over. Highlight the winners. Winners are big news, especially in small towns.
- Giving part of your proceeds to charity or launching a charity funded by Web site visitors.

- Adding a new employee. Mention where, on your Web site, the person's bio and photo can be found.
- Receiving a major contract, grant, or award. Mention where, on your Web site, the details can be found.
- Release findings of a special report, survey, or poll. Polls are big news, especially when the results affect your readers, or they can say, "I didn't know that!"
- Give away something for free to Web visitors. One site I know received great press when they gave away free keyboards. The site never mentioned, however, nor did the media pick up on, the fact that pressing certain keys on the keyboard would bring the surfer to an advertiser's Web site. No matter, "free" is still a big, effective word.
- Launch a new service that you can offer exclusively or one that measurably improves on a service that your competitor offers.
- Use celebrities. Let the press know how the connection works and why the celebrity was chosen.
- Throw a big party or event. If you can support the fact that your event is the largest or first, for example, you can use it as the central point in your news release.

Don't Forget Off-Line Promotion

Use traditional media as well as the Internet. As I mentioned in Chapter 8, my site was flooded with responses after a recommendation from something called the Marketing Report...which I still have not seen. Get your site mentioned in as many places as you can. Use the tricks and information in this chapter and utilize as many relevant media sources as possible.

Kinds of press releases

There are two kinds of press releases: (1) traditional (printed or broadcast) and (2) interactive media (anything that can be heard, seen, or read on the Web).

Both have their advantages and disadvantages, so you should be targeting each for your press campaigns. Traditional media have more specific deadlines. What's more, competition for space or airtime can be rough. Traditional media have more lag time. You may not know how your media strategy is performing until several months after your press release is sent out.

Interactive media tends to be frenetic with less consumer loyalty and credibility. It is comparatively easy to get placement because space is infinite.

The proper format

With either type of media, however, editors are sticklers for wanting a press release presented in a certain way. Here is the standard format:

Header
- For immediate release
- Contact info
- Headline
- Date

Body
- Lead
- Text—written in the third person
- Concluding paragraph
- Your URL
- Use Times Roman as your font, double-spaced, one side of sheet
- Include the word -*more*- at bottom of pages. It shows that your story will be completed on the next page or pages.
- Don't forget to put in your URL!
- 1–2 pages maximum (300–400 words)
- Place -30- or ### at end of the release. It is a universal notation that your story has ended.

> Editors are sticklers for wanting a press release presented in a certain way.

Creating the press release

Identify the strongest message. A good story must have the following four attributes:

1. Key message. This must be the most important part of the story.
2. Timeliness. Your chances for publication improve when your news release can say, "This is a hot topic and I am a great source." Years ago, I ran an ad in *Smithsonian* magazine for a company that was manufacturing copper wall plaques of sailing ships. Fortuitously, *Smithsonian* was running a cover

page story about the great tall ships. We sold a ton of plaques. Not all magazines will give you their editorial calendar (*Smithsonian* wouldn't—that's why I said it was fortuitous), but you should ask for it anyway and time your release to get to the editor at about the same time a related article is going to be published.

3. Uniqueness. Your message must be unique, newsworthy, or contrary to industry norms. Editors are busy. If you don't give them an immediate reason to keep reading, your audience is over.

4. Angle or spin. Get the info out quickly. It should be communicated in the headline and the lead. The five Ws and the H are important here. They stand for who, what, where, when, why, and how. This "all the news that fits in a sentence" lead should be the central part of your headline, lead, and first paragraph. When editors are in a space bind, they will often cut any material not in the first paragraph. Get all of your important info up front.

Some tricks for creating headlines and follow-up copy

- Use alliteration: "New Web site shows you how to add fashion flashes to flowers."
- Use colons to make your theme really stand out: "Wedding Flowers: A new look for an old custom."
- Offer business or consumer tips: "New Web site offers tips on making holiday decorations."

Here's an example of a good opening paragraph:

A new Web site, FloralFineries.com, debuting today, guarantees to turn even the most four-thumbed people into floral sculpture experts. The site promises to let consumers in on the techniques of floral arrangers that have been kept as trade secrets for many years.

> When editors are in a space bind, they will often cut any material not in the first paragraph.

Follow this opening paragraph with tips and how-tos that put the story in the right perspective. And follow that with details of your Web site.

Getting placed in interactive media

Although the format for e-releases is close to that of the traditional media, there are some key differences:

- Don't use more that 75 words in the first paragraph, and use no more than 300 words total. Though long (not too long!) paragraphs are okay for a release on a printed sheet of paper, they are much too long for reading on a computer screen.
- Use hyperlinks to photos and bios of your key people.
- Use hyperlinks to sources, articles, and resources that might be helpful to readers and employees.
- Attach FAQs about your Web site.
- Don't forget to add a hyperlink with your URL.

Write articles to create Web presence

Writing articles for various e-publications and print magazines is both cost effective and something you can do immediately. Ads and even press releases come and go, but articles can have a useful life of years and constantly generate new traffic. I've been getting responses to articles I wrote years ago on marketing that I didn't even know still existed. But writing is easy. The time-consuming part is contacting editors, but the final result is worth the trouble. Once you are published, you'll find that you've established a new level of credibility and trust. Strangely enough, people associate being published with expertise. This trust will result in more credibility for your Web site and draw in people who believe in what you're saying. There's a cyclical nature to being published. Once you get the first article published, you'll find that editors will be more amenable to publishing future releases and articles. Publications may even call you for further articles. Make sure you put the articles on your Web site.

> Articles can have a useful life of years and constantly generate new traffic.

Some tips on articles and getting published

- The article must be newsworthy and offer something of real value to the reader.
- Submit your article proposal (also called a query letter) to targeted publications. Although many editors say they're against cold calls, you can call editors directly and pitch your idea verbally. They won't always be responsive, so follow a verbal pitch with a letter.
- To pitch a story about your Web site, begin with your reason for writing or calling: "I am writing to suggest a story about . . ." or "I'd like to recommend an interview with . . ." Once you finally contact your esteemed editor, tell him or her why you're writing or calling. But make the main points in a sentence or less. That's usually all the time an editor needs to tell if a story is right for his or her publication. A rule of thumb is to write your idea—and your follow-up comment—on the back of your business card. If you can't get it all on a single card, then your story is unfocused or too complicated for an editor.
- Keep articles to about 800 words. That's the perfect size to fit on one typical magazine page. It makes it easier to get published.
- Make follow-up phone calls to the editor to further attract attention and expand on your information.
- Use every contact with an editor—even unsuccessful contacts—to build a mailing list.

Write articles for other Web sites or newsletters

Writing articles for your own newsletter or having them published in other newsletters is a very strong promotional tool. It helps establish you as an expert in your field and gets your name out in cyberspace. It can really drive traffic to your site, especially if you use hyperlinks in your column.

A rule of thumb is to write your idea—and your follow-up comment—on the back of your business card. If you can't get it all on a single card, then your story is unfocused or too complicated for an editor.

There are a great number of e-zines and newsletters out there with publishers who don't have the time or the inclination to write their own material. You write it, they get content, you get published, and everybody's happy. Every article you write should include your SIG. In doing research for this chapter, I found a Web site owner who had an article published in "Internet Day" one time, which had over 700 hits that day.

Most publications on the Internet are looking for material. Subscribe to as many of these e-magazines in your field that you can. Check out where and how to contribute articles. Yes, your e-mail box is going to get filled quickly, but one good story can get new visitors to your Web site fast. It's worth the inconvenience.

> Most publications on the Internet are looking for material.

What editors don't want

Now let's be fair and address issues that drive editors crazy. Violating any of these points can get you blackballed from an editor's publication for life.

- Don't promote your Web site until it is actually online and running perfectly. Partially open or unstable Web sites are the number-one complaint among editors I've contacted about Web site publicity.
- Do not use any sales pitch in your press release or contact. They will quickly refer you to the advertising sales department.
- Always speak in the third-person format. Remove "you," "I," "we," and "us," and replace them with "he," "she," and "they."
- Provide concrete, checkable references for any statistics, facts, and figures you use. (They usually won't check—but they might!)
- Do not use hype and flashy say-nothing adjectives. This is news, not a sales pitch. Write it the way you would want information presented to you if you were the reader.
- Proof your work. Then proof it again. And again. Editors make their living with words. Press releases with mechanical errors drive them to drink.

Whom to send your press release to

Now this seems important, but many people spend a week preparing a press release without giving much thought to whom it's going to be sent. You have a few choices here. You can pay a company to send it out to relevant media. This has some advantages because the people who send it out may have some knowledge and history with the people in the various media. But it may not be right for you because, money aside, the list may be outdated. PRWeb (*www.prweb.com*) is an excellent, free service that gets your releases out to the media the next day or any day you specify.

More important though, developing and following up on your lists gives you the opportunity to build your own relationships with the media. If you're really serious about making your Web site grow, you'll be sending out press releases and articles frequently–about once a month. And if you want a steady contact with media, you'll want to develop a friendly rapport. You'll be able to target your releases better if you create your own contacts. A site that offers many links to news media is *www.pressaccess.com*. Once you get there, click on Free Media Sources, then click on Publication Links.

> More important though, developing and following up on your lists gives you the opportunity to build your own relationships with the media.

Developing a list

Start by working in your own territory. Call the trade journals and the people who service your industry. Write down the contact name, phone number, e-mail and print addresses. The time and effort will be worth it.

Get used to talking with secretaries and being put on hold. An alternative to talking to secretaries is calling early in the morning or after five at night. Your editors will be grumpy, but more accessible.

Keep contacting media, and collect media names. Find authors who are currently writing for your target market. Keep adding names and updating your list. Update your list often. Constantly search for new magazines, newsletters, and e-magazines. And don't forget newsgroups.

Reaching people through Listserv

Listservs are another way of reaching many people with a single posting. A Listserv list is a collection of e-mail addresses. The idea is that people subscribe to a particular Listserv list, and then whenever a subscriber sends a message to the list, that message is automatically distributed to everyone who is subscribed to the list. Listserv lists work entirely via electronic mail.

There are more than 4,000 Listservs on the Internet, and membership may range from a few hundred to several thousand. Like newsgroups, Listservs are groupings of people who share a common interest. Unlike Usenet newsgroups, which require that you go to the group to give out information, Listservs deliver e-mails to the group members. In a Listserv, each member can get every message between every member e-mailed to them in real-time. Communications are maintained openly with the entire membership of the group. If you post to the group, your response will be delivered to *every* member of this limited interest group.

The site *www.list-universe.com* is the big honcho when it comes to Listservs, with listings of 30,000 newsgroups and a good search function. It's a good place to spend some time.

> Listservs are groupings of people who share a common interest.

Promoting offline

Though this book is mostly about the Web, you need to work all ends of the spectrum, both online and offline for maximum effectiveness.

- Newsletters offline. Locate newsletters or smaller print publications offline and submit articles. This can be a good way to increase your exposure and add to your press kit. Locate newsletters in your subject area by visiting the local university library reference section. Once you have been published in smaller magazines, it's easier to step up to the larger publications.
- Giving speeches in your area of expertise. Start locally at civic clubs and local educational programs. Then approach local talk radio shows and make your case to the producer.

Talk radio shows are actively looking for guests that have original material and thoughts.

- Publicity pitches: Put together several dynamic article ideas—just the ideas, not the actual article. Take those ideas and then pitch them to editors of targeted publications. Editors love ideas, especially ideas that are completely outlined and appropriate for their readership. Don't send sports article ideas to cooking magazines.

Quick tips

✓ Always have a reason to write a news release. Use content that meets the standard for print or broadcast media. Include facts that answer these questions: Who? What? When? Where? Why? How?

✓ Fame comes from planning and persistence. Make sure all of your press releases have an underlying theme

Summary

A strong press release should be sent as soon as your site is up and running. The media rely on an editorial calendar to dictate the release date of an article. You should find media outlets, especially popular and targeted ones, that have an opening or a scheduled article that relates to your product or service. This is an opportunity to discuss your site and product editorially and to build relationships with contacts in the media. The media has seen it all, so concentrate on the benefits that your audience will derive from your Web site and leave out the fluff.

The Power of Newsgroups

Here's an example of how powerful newsgroups can be. A New York Mets baseball fan posted a derogatory message about Mets manager Bobby Valentine on the Mets Web site. In the message, the member claimed that Valentine had made some disparaging remarks about the Mets organization and a few of his players at a university graduation ceremony. Although the claims were later proved to be unfounded, the story was picked up by the sports news media around the country. It was a lead story on ESPN. Valentine was vilified by his management and the press. He was almost fired, and the player that Valentine allegedly knocked was traded. All this because of a tiny (and incorrect) notice that someone posted to a discussion group. Newsgroups can be very powerful things.

For more information on this topic, visit our Web site at www.businesstown.com

Bringing in Mind-Boggling Traffic

Summary of Section III

- **How to bring in visitors (your #1 priority)**
- **Creating a synergy with similar sites**
- **Creating cross promotions with off-line companies**
- **How to build opt-in mail lists and eliminate spam**

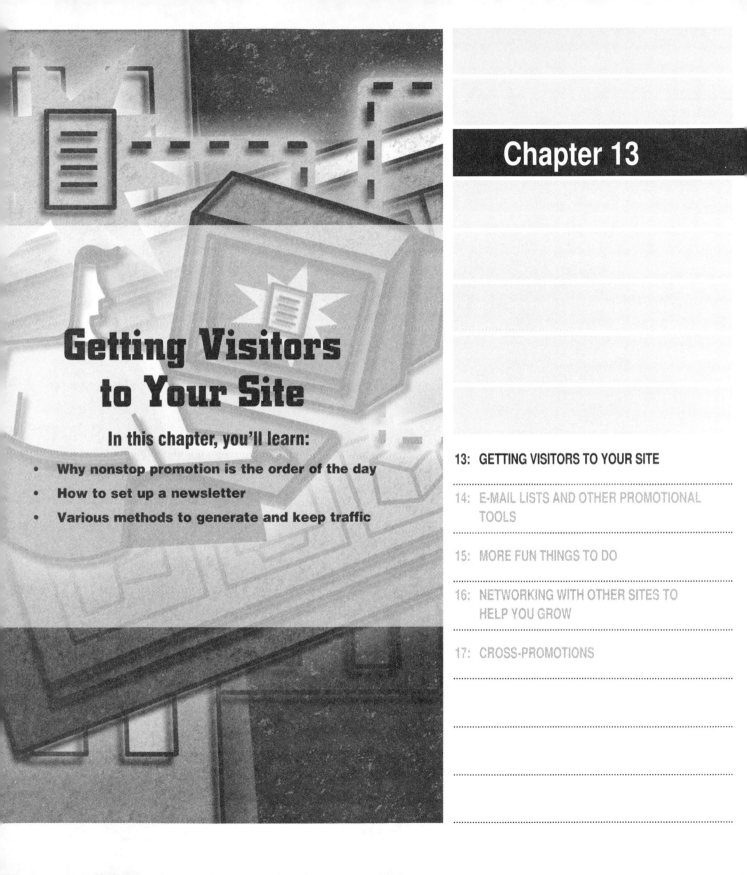

Chapter 13

Getting Visitors to Your Site

In this chapter, you'll learn:

- Why nonstop promotion is the order of the day
- How to set up a newsletter
- Various methods to generate and keep traffic

If you build it, they will come—not really

It may be true for brick-and-mortar stores, and it may be true for baseball fields in the middle of Iowa, but it's not necessarily true on the Internet.

In the real world, businesses rely on traffic, high visibility, and easy access. Ask a business that sits on a heavily trafficked street that is under construction how much business they lose when people can't get to them. When North Avenue, a major thoroughfare in Chicago, was under construction for six months, the businesses in the strip malls that lined that street nearly went belly up. They were either forced to shut down or cut their losses and relocate. Buyers just weren't willing to fight their way through the construction to get to them. Today, four years later, some of those strip malls are still dismal empty shells. Some are completely vacant, and some have precious few small shops that barely hang on. The interruption of business was just long enough. Customers and their travel patterns had been interrupted, and they found alternative places to go for their needs.

Consider how much planning goes into the positioning of a new business. When preparing to open a new shop, the owners spend a great deal of time and energy identifying the best possible location for their establishment. Burger King looks for positions close to McDonald's. Smaller clothing and housewares stores look for shopping centers where highly respected anchor stores create traffic. And savvy merchants seek out corner locations where they can get high visibility from all directions.

You can't do that in a virtual world where there are no corners and there is no clear roadway. So what do you do?

You begin by developing high visibility for your site. The next two chapters are about finding ways to turn your site into a people magnet.

> Begin by developing high visibility for your site.

A tangled Web

If you go to *www.companiesonline.com*, you'll find a database of an estimated 400,000 businesses online right now. The Thomas Register of American Manufacturers has a database of 150,000 manufacturers and many others in their databases for their Food Industry and Regional Business Directories. We haven't even scratched the surface or taken into account all the small entrepreneurial startups that inhabit the Internet. A comprehensive search would be mind-boggling. I don't believe anyone really knows how many businesses are on the Internet. But we do know these numbers will be magnified many times over by the time this book reaches your hands.

It's easy to get caught up in the enormousness of the Internet. It's easy to get lost in the crowd. When you get your site on the Web, it's just the beginning.

At first, you'll want to focus your online marketing efforts in the following six areas:

- Attract the right kind of traffic
- Place advertisements, classifieds
- Build your community using online lists, newsletters, e-mail lists, and additional services
- Capitalize on reciprocal linking
- Keep repeating your original marketing efforts

Attracting quality traffic

Attracting everyone in the Internet universe is difficult and pricey, especially if you're on a budget. The good news is you don't have to have hundreds of thousands of people coming to your site. It makes more sense to have 50 visitors a week who stay in touch, who visit and buy regularly, than to have 10,000 visitors who never look seriously at what you have to offer, surfers who keep right on truckin', never to return. The bulk of your efforts will be finding ways to let the people who do business with you know you're out there and how to get happily involved with you.

But be careful, just having people come to your site isn't all you're looking for. You want the kind of people who will come and see what you have to offer, and you want the kind of people who will come back time and again to do business with you. You want to

> It makes more sense to have 50 visitors a week who stay in touch, who visit and buy regularly, than to have 10,000 visitors who never look seriously at what you have to offer.

> Too many sites are trying to be everything to everyone. It doesn't work.

identify and capture the interest of those people who need you and what you have to offer. These people will keep coming back to your site over and over again, whenever they need the products or services you offer. People who simply surf on through and never come back are great if you're looking for venture capital and if you're looking only for hits. But I've never yet been able to pay my bills with hits. The phone company doesn't trade hits for service; nor does the gas company or my landlord. All the hits in the world will do nothing for your bottom line.

If you know whom you're trying to attract and do business with, then you can identify exactly what products or services you need to offer in order to get their attention. Too many sites are trying to be everything to everyone. It doesn't work. The more targeted you can be in terms of the people you want to come to your site and the products or services you are offering them, the easier your marketing efforts will be (and the more profitable).

This doesn't necessarily mean that you will make sales directly on your site. You may use the Internet as a piece of your business and a piece of your marketing. And this may work better for you than having an online storefront. Some businesses just aren't well suited to direct sales on the Internet. Some require direct face-to-face contact.

Use all the tools all the time

What is the biggest mistake that online businesses make? They set up an entity—a standalone, do-it-all business—with the expectation that they can go on vacation and let the business run itself. These are the businesses that bite the dust before they can even get a toehold in the cybermarket.

Here's another clue: If you're going to cram everything into your front page, you're going to scare off an awful lot of potential customers. Clutter and too much variety on a page confuse people. We all know that confused people do not buy, don't we? If you can be very clear up front about what you're offering and if you can clearly lead your visitors through your presentation, you stand a better chance of holding their attention. Giving them a department store or library-sized selection and expecting them to dig around until they find what interests them isn't going to cut it—at least until the general surfer is much more adept in getting around in cyberspace.

Use language that speaks to the surfer. Introduce yourself to the people who come to your site. Then convey the message that you really do understand them and that you care about them. The words that are recognized as the most effective selling words include "you" and "free," as well as words that speak about benefits more than features. Be sure you sprinkle them freely throughout your site. If you're not sure about these, go back and review the sidebars on pages 107 and 108.

> Use language that speaks to the surfer. Introduce yourself to the people who come to your site.

Cruise sites similar to yours

You need to do a lot of searching yourself to find where the people who would be interested in what you have to offer are going. At the same time, stay focused on other options for creating traffic. Start surfing. Go to all the places where your intended customers might be found. At every Web site you visit, look for any option it offers for adding your URL to theirs or adding an announcement or classified ad (free, of course). And add your URL to the list.

Surfing for links

Let's take an example. If you're a woman who offers custom purses to upscale businesswomen, you're going to look for sites where those women are likely to congregate. You'll look for sites that appeal to their interests and sites that encourage their participation. If you're marketing to women in business, you might check the women's sites like *www.fodreams.com* or *www.digital-gateways.com*. When you go to those sites, look for the option to "Submit your URL" or a directory for free announcements and offerings and advertisements. Look for invitations to join their mailing lists or to receive their newsletter. Be sure to get on those lists and participate in any discussion groups you find there. Check out other links you find. These are competitive and compatible sites that cater to your intended market. They are open doors to additional contacts.

Sign up through guestbooks

Some of these sites will have a guestbook. Sign it and take advantage of this opportunity to begin dialog with the owner(s) of the site. Also get familiar with others who have posted to those guestbooks. You'll find some interesting comments and feedback, and you may even find some potential clients there.

Likewise, if you're marketing to sports enthusiasts, go to sports sites and other merchants who cater to that market. Using your search engines and your personal list of bookmarks (which should include sites that you have a personal affinity with), go visiting and let everyone know that you're out there. Submit, submit, submit.

> If you're marketing to sports enthusiasts, go to sports sites and other merchants who cater to that market.

The initial approach

As you start getting acquainted with all these virtual communities, you will be taking the first step in building traffic to your site. You will be introducing yourself to others and inviting them to come to your site to see what you have to offer. Take an assertive approach to your marketing here. But you can't just go barging into cyberspace and announce, "Here I am; look how great I am." You're going to need to have a little more finesse than that.

The double opportunity with newsletters

A newsletter (or e-zine if you want to keep up with the buzzwords) can be a powerful promotional tool. A newsletter can be your number-one tool for bringing your visitors back to your site. If your aren't capturing them the first time with a free newsletter, then you have to keep going out and finding them. That's very expensive. Your newsletter is a permanent link to your clients and prospects. For a successful newsletter, you must offer useful content that informs, teaches, or enriches your audience. By doing so, your company's name, products, or services are brought to the subscriber's attention each time he or she receives your newsletter.

Composing your e-zine

Write newsworthy articles about subjects that you are knowledgeable about and that will target your marketing audience. Be subtle, and promote your products with one or two lines of text in each issue. You should use a SIG file at the end of each article, which consists of four to six lines of text that promote yourself, your business, your offer, and your Web site.

Newsletters are e-mail distributions to a specified list of recipients. The primary topic may be anything from apples to zebras. Whole Web businesses have been built strictly on newsletter promotions. It's a great way to stay in touch with your customers and keep them coming back. Newsletter promotions are one of the most powerful marketing techniques on the Web. When asked about receiving a personalized e-mail newsletter with only product information that matches their profile, half of the people asked in the survey said they'd appreciate receiving it. The real surprise for me was that about 25% of them said they want to receive an e-mail newsletter from a merchant once a week.

> Write newsworthy articles about subjects that you are knowledgeable about and that will target your marketing audience.

Four advantages of developing a newsletter

- They provide immediate traffic.
- You can tailor spending by audience size.
- You can tailor expenses by how many people you want to reach.
- They position you as an expert in your field.

Having people sign up for you newsletter is an example of opt-in marketing. Opt-in means that people are requesting that you send e-mail to them. It is not spam since they are requesting information from you.

In addition to being a communication vehicle between you and your market, your newsletters offer you a potential income stream—advertising. This works the same way as advertising in print media works: You pay your money, and you get your message in the newsletter. Only, you're the publisher and you're in the cat-bird seat. Sometimes you'll be able to insert an add for free or at substantial reductions in price in others' newsletters—or you can trade advertising opportunities in your newsletters with the newsletter publisher of other e-zines. Prices are all over the ballpark, often—but not always—determined by the number of recipients. You simply ask and see what can be negotiated.

How to get content for your newsletter

Creating a newsletter idea may seem a little daunting to the uninitiated at first, but there are only two priorities.

- You need to have words to fill up the newsletter.
- You need to recruit a critical mass of subscribers.

Getting content is not that difficult. There are many people who will actually find it an honor to write for you totally free. Well, not totally free. They're going to want a byline and a link to their Web site, just as you're going to want when you write for others. They may even want to use their SIG. There are a multitude of sites that offer free articles on all kinds of subjects, but first make sure you secure permission. I know of one company that posts articles and *then* asks for permission. I know it happened because she stole one of *my* articles. Contact other newsletter or e-zine owners who may have articles you can publish, or who may want to exchange ads with you. For example, Bizsuccess (*www.bizsuccess.com*) offers hundreds of free reports for business owners and small entrepreneurs, and

> Creating a newsletter idea may seem a little daunting to the uninitiated at first, but there are only two priorities.

intersuccess.com offers articles on a great many subjects. You'll find many sources if you run a search for your specific topic using any of the search engines.

How to get subscribers

The fastest way to gain subscribers, other than those surfers who happen on to your site, is to post information about your newsletter on various directories that exist for just this purpose. Visit them and register your newsletter. Sign up with as many of these sites as possible. One good one is *www.EzineArticles.com*, and there are more in the back of this book. Exchanging reciprocal links with sites that have complementary content (see Chapters 16 and 17) is another good way.

Here are some secrets to newsletter success, compiled by Mark Joyner of ROIbot:

1. Give the subscriber a reason to subscribe. Several psychological studies have demonstrated that giving people a reason to comply to your request will greatly increase their chances of compliance. And the reason doesn't even have to be good! Amazingly, just using the word *because* will increase your response.

2. Really "sell" the content of your newsletter. People don't know whether your newsletter contains pure junk or gold. You could have the greatest, most informative newsletter in the world, but if you don't tell them, they will never know. Now, here's the key. You don't want to tell them yourself "my newsletter is the best." No one will believe you. The best way to let people know how great you are is to have someone else tell them for you. You should get a testimonial or two about the content of your newsletter and use this to "sell" the content of your newsletter.

3. Provide an incentive to subscribe. How many people offer a free newsletter? No one can know for sure, but I'll tell you that the answer is "too many." What is unique about what you offer? If you tie your subscription into being able to

The fastest way to gain subscribers, other than those surfers who happen on to your site, is to post information about your newsletter on various directories that exist for just this purpose.

access something unique, I promise your subscriber rate will go through the roof. Can you offer a free service? Can you offer a free download? A free and unique report? Access to some exclusive information? Generate curiosity in your potential subscriber. People are inherently curious, and it is painful when curiosity is not satisfied. Set it up so subscribing to your newsletter is the only thing they can do to satisfy that curiosity.

Write for other newsletters

If you write for other newsletters, you can become an "expert of the day," and you get the traffic from people linking to your site from the articles. The best way to get an article (or articles) published is to create a "tip sheet." A tip sheet is a list of problem-solving steps to solve a particular problem, like getting people to come to your Web site.

Pick your topic, create an introduction, then list a series of problem-solving tips. This can be e-mailed to e-zines, magazines, newsletters, and even to newspapers.

Article submission

The reason to submit your articles to e-zines is to get additional subscribers, visitors to your Web site, and look for prospective buyers. E-mail for related e-zine publishers asking if they accept articles for submission. List some of your article titles, your contact information, or your Web site addresses where they can download or copy your articles. Build an e-mail mailing list where you can regularly submit your articles. Regularly submit to anyone who publishes you.

Keeping track of subscribers

Eudora Light is an easy-to-use e-mail program that you can be download at *www.eudora.com*. With this program, you can keep all of your subscribers' e-mail addresses in one or multiple address

> If you write for other newsletters, you can become an "expert of the day."

books, and you are able to send e-mail to all of your subscribers simultaneously.

How to use Eudora Light

Here's a simple way to write your e-zine in Eudora's e-mail program:

1. Put the e-mail address of you subscriber in the To: field.
2. The From: field is automatically filled in when your program is set up.
3. Put the title of the e-zine in the Subject: field. Take tips from the supermarket counter magazines to see how to write a catchy headline.
4. Place your cursor on the Bcc: field and click Address Book. Then, click your mouse cursor onto Folder, which holds your subscribers' addresses. Click Bcc. This e-mails all of your subscribers while hiding all the e-mail addresses from the readers.

Tips sheets

E-zines publish tip sheets for two reasons. Tip sheets are the easiest sells for a newsletter or e-zine because (1) they focus on solving their readers' problems; and (2) they're short, to-the-point, and valuable content separates the ads.

Here are four tip sheet ideas:

How-to articles include step-by-step instructions.

1. How-to articles. These include step-by-step instructions for solving a certain problem, for instance, insider tips on how to make soap.
2. Hot idea lists. These are a group of ideas listed in order.
3. Industry trade articles. These can include news about your industry or company information.
4. Interview articles. Includes interviews with customers, employees, or experts. Don't forget to link your articles back to your Web site.

Quick tips

✓ Create surveys. People love to tell you what you think. Develop a new survey each week, and be sure to share the responses with people for the previous surveys you've conducted. For best response, make your questions applicable to the interests of your potential customers.

✓ The text in the body of your e-mail, e-zine, or newsletter should consist of only 65 to 70 characters, including spaces per line. This will ensure that 95% of your readers will see exactly how you originally formatted your newsletter.

Create surveys. People love to tell you what you think. Develop a new survey each week, and be sure to share the responses with people for the previous surveys you've conducted.

Summary

Even five years ago, it wasn't too hard to get noticed. Cyberspace wasn't terribly heavily populated at that time, and people could find each other. It was like a small community where people pretty much knew each other, and their sites had the feel of the old-time general stores. People on the Web had the time and the interest to seek out each other and kept going back to the same sites to see what was new. They signed each other's guestbooks and followed up with each other by e-mail. But that's all changed. Now it takes constant use of all the tools at your disposal.

For more information on this topic, visit our Web site at www.businesstown.com

E-Mail Lists and Other Promotional Tools

In this chapter, you'll learn:

- **How to use e-mail lists to your best advantage**
- **What is and isn't considered spam**
- **How to use chat rooms to full advantage**
- **How to co-promote with other Web sites and companies**

Chapter 14

E-mail lists

There are two kinds of mailing lists: opt-ins and unethical lists. I'm sure that when you first got your computer, you were thrilled to get your first e-mails. I'm also sure that you got tired of them quickly. There are so many boundless groups of people who want to receive your e-mails, you don't need to waste your money on buying blind e-mail lists (spam). Many servers will actually rescind your e-mail privileges if you spam. Some of them may cancel your account entirely.

Opt-in mailing lists are typically e-mail groups where people with common interests share information and commiserate. People will be more receptive to your e-mail when they share similar goals. People participate in these groups the same way as they do in Usenet newsgroups. And the same protocol applies. Some of these groups are strictly controlled by a moderator who serves as gate-keeper and limits the content of messages that get distributed to the entire group. The primary difference is that the messages are sent to participants and arrive daily, or less frequently, along with participants' regular e-mail. They are rich resources for creating traffic. Some of these lists are highly active, generating 50 to 100 messages a day, whereas others are much less active. You won't know until you try them. Experiment. Join two or three at a time. You can submit and unsubmit to these lists at will, depending on how effective you find them to be for your needs.

These lists can be deceptive, however. Even a list that generates 100 e-mails a day may be distributed to thousands of others who are out there lurking. So, it's very important that anything you send to the group reflects yourself in the best light. Take care that your spelling is correct and that your messages are meaningful and positive.

As in newsgroups, you'll want to lurk for a little while, getting a feel for the participants and the topics at hand. When you are sure you understand the dynamics of the group, offer a very brief self-introduction that indicates your interest in the group and how you hope to contribute or gain from participation. You can either ask questions or give answers to questions when the discussion topic

> There are two kinds of mailing lists: opt-ins and unethical lists.

opens a door. Always make sure that your signature is attached to your posts.

Another reason for these groups is that they are highly reliable resources for locating people who are actively interested in the particular topics of discussion. These are people who want the information and resources you have to offer and will respond readily if you don't pressure them.

Direct-mail promotions

Like a newsletter promotion, for direct-mail promotions it's best to stick with one of the opt-in servers. They will ensure that you reach people who really want to receive your e-mail or information about your services or products. They will also make it easy for you to create and deliver a sales campaign that is specifically targeted to people who have a real interest in what you have to offer. There are lots of these services out there. In fact, you can start with that same list that you used to find groups to participate in. Many will charge you based on the number of deliveries you anticipate. Some of the best free options out there are eGroups, *www.egroups.yahoo.com*, or TargitMail, *www.targitmail.com/index_partners.html*.

Using these kinds of services you can conveniently connect with others, find other groups to join, and create your own. Make sure that the lists you create appeal to the kinds of people that you want to do business with and the kinds of people who need what you have to offer. Set up the list and announce it right on your Web site, giving surfers a way to sign up right then and there. Make it easy. And then go back and share the news with the newsgroups and lists that you're participating in.

Guestbooks

Guestbooks allow your visitors to post a public message right on your site. A guestbook will tell you who is at your site, and you can ask any questions you'd like—in any language! You can receive notification by e-mail when someone signs your guestbook. It's great way

Where to Find Lists and Newsletters

List Promotion Links

www.list-universe.com
http://egroups.yahoo.com
http://pages.ivillage.com/bc/ scifi_fan/promo.html
http://paml.net
http://tile.net/lists
www.listsnet.com
http://catalog.com/vivian/ interest-group-search.html
www.wcsu.ctstateu.edu/library/ rr_electronic_discussion_ groups.html
www.goodstuff.prodigy.com/ Lists/main.htm
http://alabanza.com/kabacoff/ Inter-Links/listserv.html
www.targitmail.com/index_ partners.html

Mailing Lists Devoted to Announcing Lists and Forums

Announce-lists@Onelist.com
listannouncements@listbot.com
bizrus@egroups.com
saf-t-mail@onelist.com
bizzopps@onelist.com
spam_free@egroups.com
safe-email2@egroups.com
announce@webpromote.com
emailsuccess@listbot.com
powermail@onelist.com
spamlegally@onelist.com
bizoppseeks@onelist.com

of seeing who is on your site at any given moment and a great research tool. Even more important, however, signing a guestbook will make a visitor feel more like a member of your Web site than just a visitor. A guestbook is a great, simple tool, especially when you copy the contact list into databases. Bravenet Web Services (*www.bravenet.com*) will set you up with free software to make your guestbook. Of course, you'll have to sign their guestbook. Put a guestbook on your site and give your visitors an opportunity to tell you what they think. This is a mighty good way to build a client list, by the way. Check that book regularly and make sure that you respond to any comments you find there.

Further information buttons and tabs

From the beginning of the book, we have talked about building promotional hooks into the content of your Web site. It doesn't get any easier than a button or tab that says "subscribe" or "for further information" on every important page of your Web site. The weary Web traveler clicks on the button and his or her e-mail address is sent right to you. Make sure your privacy preferences are posted right next to the tab or button assuring people that you will not sell their e-mail address. It makes a difference in the amount of clicks you will get. Do you have a sign-in option on your site? Do you offer a service that a person might apply for? Whenever a visitor fills out a form for any reason, be sure to include a radio button or check box that will allow him or her to be put on your mailing list for updated information.

Chat up your business in chat rooms

Real-time chats allow you not only to type in messages to others in the group but also to talk to them using a microphone. It's one of the most promising resources for qualified leads, according to Joan-Marie Moss, although, you need to be careful not to waste a lot of time in these groups. Only a few are devoted to serious discussions, but you can meet some interesting people. If you find a pocket of

> Make sure your privacy preferences are posted right next to the tab or button assuring people that you will not sell their e-mail address.

individuals who could potentially be converted into clients, your time will be well spent. Most of these discussion groups will have only a half dozen or so participants at a time, but if you're selective, you'll find groups where the participants will become strong sources of leads and inside industry information.

Because you don't have a signature attached to every comment you make in these real-time discussions, you're going to spend a bit more time building confidence and getting acquainted with others in these groups. Again, don't go barging in announcing that you are in business and need buyers. Take your time, get acquainted, participate in the group, get to know the people there, and gradually you'll find yourself developing alliances with other like spirits. Business and traffic will follow.

Start your own chat room

As you develop contacts and start becoming familiar with people through these various venues, and learn how each of these approaches work, you should stay alert to opportunities for starting your own chat groups. Firetalk is one of the software products that is head and shoulders above the rest. It's free, and that makes it highly desirable. Firetalk allows you to open your own specialized group discussion and to monitor it yourself. It also allows you to talk one-on-one or even to conduct seminars. Again, caution. This approach can be time consuming. But if you're running the show and you invite your potential clients and customers to join you in conversations that highly resemble focused phone conferences, you will find that you can get a lot accomplished in developing a network and a following that will lead to serious business. They're really quite easy to do. But they do require commitment on your part. Consistent delivery and focused discussions are critical to their success. But when you've started building a following of your own, people will be much more receptive and will think of you first when they're looking for the products and services you offer.

> Because you don't have a signature attached to every comment you make in these real-time discussions, you're going to spend a bit more time building confidence and getting acquainted with others in these groups.

More promotion ideas

You'll never be finished developing your Web site—not if you want people to keep coming back. Be on the lookout for ways to create interest in your site—reasons for people to keep coming back again and again. Here are just a couple of ideas that I like:

- Develop your site into an intranet or a gateway—or create a section of your Web site into an intranet specifically devoted to your regular contacts. You can see how this works by going to *www.creativeoptions.com* and selecting "Chicago Businesses" from the navigation bar. You can logon to an IntraNet there.
- Create a forum for discussion right on your Web site. The key is to develop topics of discussion that will captivate visitors—the ones you want to keep coming back. Announcements of this kind are well received on newsgroups and the lists we've discussed, particularly if they can be tied to a current discussion thread on those groups.

> You'll never be finished developing your Web site— not if you want people to keep coming back.

Quick tips

✓ Any time you set up a chat room or create a new topic of interest in your forum, tell everyone about it.

Summary

If you haven't figured it out yet, the Internet is a place that is open to promotion as never before. It's just a matter of you approaching it with an open mind and looking for opportunities to share what you have with others—as long as you're not pushy. Start thinking out of the box. When a door is open, walk through it. When a topic is opened for discussion, find ways you can contribute, and ease yourself and your business into that.

For more information on this topic, visit our Web site at www.businesstown.com

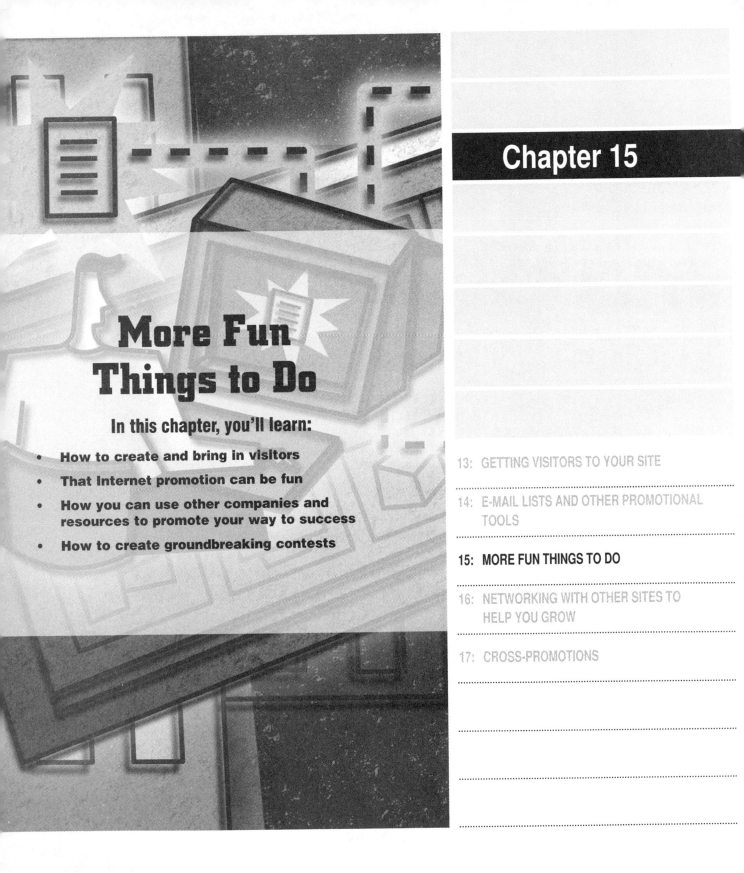

Chapter 15

More Fun Things to Do

In this chapter, you'll learn:

- How to create and bring in visitors
- That Internet promotion can be fun
- How you can use other companies and resources to promote your way to success
- How to create groundbreaking contests

Be a phone company

You can actually offer free phone service to bring in traffic. Another innovative approach to using the Internet for business that is free for the moment is PctoPhone, which allows you to place real phone calls through your computer. The cost savings alone make this worth looking into. It can really enhance your ability to stay in close touch with your prospects, clients, and customers. Right now you can use this software to place phone calls all across the United States for free while connected to the Internet. Develop your multitasking skills, and you can pick up the phone and call prospects while you're surfing their sites.

> You can actually offer free phone service to bring in traffic.

Chat with your visitors live

I mentioned this previously, but it's so much fun I wanted to mention it in this chapter. One of the cutest ideas we've found is called Humanclick, whose software is downloadable from *www.humanclick.com*. Using Humanclick you can monitor who is coming to your Web site and you can initiate a conversation with them, while they're there. It's not a voice-activated program, but it does give you the opportunity to send instant messages to people who are surfing your site.

Perhaps you can offer to help them find what they're looking for or ask them how they found your site so you'll know better how to promote it. This particular innovation is so new that you're going to need to be somewhat careful with it. A person surfing who gets a message popping up from a stranger (albeit the owner of the Web site) directed to him or her saying, essentially, "I know you're there and I'm watching you," can be intimidating. So, remember, easy does it. Be helpful, but not pushy—like the sales ladies in the finest clothing stores.

Frequent visitor programs

What's that, you say? Buyers are liars? They are fickle—especially on the Internet where they're dealing with thousands of faceless people. Take a look at some of the top merchants, and find ways to adapt the techniques they're applying right now. Some are so obvious that you'll miss them if you're not careful.

Arguably the best-known customer loyalty program in existence is the frequent traveler program. Pioneered by major airlines, frequent traveler or frequent buyer programs now abound. Hotels and rental car companies have them. Restaurants participate in them. Some credit card companies turn them into "Membership Miles" (American Express) or other kinds of frequent purchase rewards programs.

The recent trend toward Internet-based loyalty programs suggests that the same strategy applies online. This applies to business-to-business (B2B) as well as business-to-consumer (B2C) marketers. Loyalty or incentive programs reward prospects or customers for providing information, taking an action, or making a purchase. Incentive programs include sweepstakes and contests, volume deals, and price breaks, as well as online coupons, referral programs, and other forms of "instant payback" programs.

ClickRewards appropriated the frequent traveler miles concept and applied it to the Web. It offers ClickMiles for shopping at participating Web sites. MyPoints offers members "reward points" for taking an action or purchasing products. And there are completely customized, private-label loyalty rewards programs used by such companies as American Express, GTE, and ZDNet. MyPoints recently acquired CyberGold, another leader in the incentive program category. Flooz uses "online currency" to reward buyers and has recently entered the B2B marketplace. Some of these programs can be very expensive, so you'll want to be sure to check them out. Others are free.

> The recent trend toward Internet-based loyalty programs suggests that the same strategy applies online.

Affiliate programs

But you don't have to stop there. Consider something as basic as creating an affiliate program. Get others involved, and make it attractive for them to do business with you and to refer qualified leads to you. It's like building your own special sales force. And, of course, align yourself with other appropriate businesses that you can be an affiliate for. Bookstores are good for that. Powell's Books and Amazon.com enable you to promote their wares on your site and to target the selections you promote to the kinds of people who frequent your site. Many other businesses are incorporating this option into their Web site offerings.

Co-Promote

Give visitors ways that they can promote their own businesses and services at your site. Exchanging links is one of the easiest ways to generate interest. Simply find people you would like to do business with—people in compatible businesses, people who are experts in their fields and have Web sites of their own—and offer to put a link to their Web site in exchange for a link on theirs.

You'll be expanding your visibility and the likelihood of qualified people finding you. And as an added advantage of this approach (as opposed to banners and advertising), this kind of reciprocity lends an element of credibility since you're being referred by another site.

> Give visitors ways that they can promote their own businesses and services at your site.

Using auction sites to promote

Want to have some fun? Take a look at the potential for marketing your site and your online business using eBay and other auction sites. One young man I know has an online jewelry business. He generates leads for his site by offering a piece of jewelry from his inventory on eBay. Here's what he said when asked about his success:

> The hardest thing so far is to generate traffic. I have actually found that the best place is through eBay (*www.ebay.com*) so I have things listed there and people are then moving through there to my site.

Sweepstakes and contests

Develop sweepstakes and contests. Awards don't necessarily have to be extravagant. They can be your own products or services. Make it fun to come back to your site. People like to win. And whether it be a T-shirt that promotes your Web site (heck, let your efforts do double duty when you can), a product that you sell, a free consultation, or a trip to the Bahamas, you'll be amazed at how people will seek you out. Especially if you let them know that you are indeed awarding those prizes to real people.

Contests are a strong way to attract new traffic. You can advertise your contest in search engines, promotional material, word-of-mouth, link exchange, and programs—just about anywhere. If you're a computer service company, your prize could be a memory upgrade or a hard drive or anything that sounds as though it could be of real value to your visitors.

Ask contestants to complete a short form, which you will later use to help you understand your market audience. On the entry form, inquire about what products or services, content, or resources that they would like to see at your Web site. Ask them also if they would like to be informed of additional contests, related products, services, or to receive your newsletter.

Confirmation e-mail

Use an auto-responder with the entry form to confirm your contestant's entries. And use another that thanks them for entering your contest. You can also consider offering a discount for entering your contest and adding a mini-catalog to your auto-responder message. Always put a concluding date—for example, "Offer expires January 10." This will help your prospective customer to take action and make a purchase.

Your contest should last only a month or two at a time, but offer these contests regularly or monthly. It is very cheap to promote a contest while you gain loyal customers and repeat business. Keep in mind that you do not have to make a profit on your promotion. This will come back to you in repeat sales along with new customers.

Use Contests to Attract Viewers

OAK VIEW, CA - (INTERNET WIRE) - In their continuing effort to give small businesses a competitive edge on the Web, WHERE2GO.COM launched a free contest engine open to all businesses at *www.where2go. com/contests*. The free service allows anyone to host an online contest including the creation of rules and automatic picking of winners. Even if you already have a contest running (and do not need the contest engine), you can list it in the Where2go's contest database.

Customer follow-up

With the names and e-mail addresses you collect by having a contest, you can build a mailing list. You will want to regularly send everyone on your list information about product updates, sales, and discounts.

Another kind of message board

CoolBoard Express is a free hosted message board tailored to the specific needs of your site. Message boards can be customized to look just like your Web site, with your own graphics, backgrounds, fonts, and even navigation. Contact *www.coolboard.com*.

More freebies

And, of course, consider offering special promotions and free gimmes. We mentioned these before. These are pretty basic to all businesses. But they're so easy on the Internet. A "one-time special" offered through e-mail to your current mailing list (remember *no* spam) can generate some pretty good impulse purchases. Giving away online books that can be easily downloaded are nice. Free greeting cards, virtual bouquets, and such are better. Why? Because they are fun and people look for these regularly throughout the year. And, when they know they can get these from your site, they'll keep coming back.

Create a message board

A message board will help Web sites build relationships with its users. Message boards are a great way to make your Web site more active with new and interesting discussions posted every day. Strong discussions not only keep your current users coming back but also help attract new users. Message boards are also a lot of fun. You can get to know your users better and share information, ideas, and experiences.

Sample the Newest Technologies

If you scout around long enough, you'll find hundreds of new technological tips. Some of them are good. Some of them are not. But one thing is for sure. When you try a new service, you'll get tons of e-mail asking you to buy all sorts of things.

Move offline to promote online

Okay, you want do business on the Internet. And you can. But don't forget that people, potential customers, are everywhere. Promote offline as well as online. Use those business cards and letterheads. You *do* have your e-mail address and your Web site on them, don't you? Capitalize on your networking and your advertising and all the other activities you are involved in when you're away from your computer to make sure that everyone knows you're doing business online and that you're really serious about making it easy for them to do business with you.

Quick tips

✓ Let people get to know you, and sales will soar. Use chat rooms and offer a free, personal, one-hour chat with the renowned expert in your field (you).

✓ Message boards provide a safe way for everyone to feel important. It's an exchange of information that often builds the content of your site.

> Let people get to know you, and sales will soar.

Summary

Stay highly visible by speaking up and always staying helpful and positive and supportive of others. And, definitely be open to trying new ideas. Remember that rule that people generally need to see your name six or seven times before they start to think of doing business with you. This number, which has been touted among sales and marketing people for years, may be a bit higher on the Internet, especially when there's no face connected with the messages or the name. Repetition and following through on what you promise will ensure your success. Remember you want to reinforce that you're here for the long haul, not just fly-by-night and out for a quick killing.

For more information on this topic, visit our Web site at www.businesstown.com

Networking with Other Sites to Help You Grow

In this chapter, you'll learn:

- The value of networking
- How to acquire links
- How to grow by using other sites
- How to get your links placed on other sites
- The ins and outs of affiliate programs

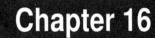

Chapter 16

It's time to start linking

Links, in banner or text forms, are probably the driving force behind the Web. Many people will find your site by following a link from another site, so cross-linking with other sites could represent your best method for increasing traffic. Your most effective strategy will span formal and informal linking, banner exchange networks, Web rings, and cybermalls. The right mix depends on your budget, target market, sales model, and current site traffic demographics. They can be either formal or informal in structure. It can be likened to a game of tag. Someone touches you, and you touch someone else.

Definitions

A link is a connection to another person's Web site. It's usually an all-text listing or a button that, when clicked, will take the person back to another site (ideally yours).

A banner is usually a paid link to another's Web site. But when we say "paid," it doesn't necessarily mean money. It can be a kind of barter arrangement. I'll show you mine if you'll show me yours.

A reciprocal link or banner means that in exchange for putting links on another person's Web site, you put their links on your site.

Let's look at informal links first. An informal link is one you have made with another Web site you have seen online. It might have come with a personal contact or with an e-mail you might have sent. You might surf for them over the Internet, or you might actually have a real-life friend who wants to help you out. The obvious advantage of having friends link to you is that you get free publicity.

Hosting links can also help you out. They can make your site more interesting and diverse. People, these days, expect links and the link you host can make your site more valuable to the surfer. If you host "prestige" sites, some of the prestige will rub off on you. Most informal links are text links that are simply lists that describe or refer your visitors to other sites. Text links can actually be more effective than banner links because they are perceived by surfers as additional help, coming from you, whereas banners are perceived of as advertising. Remember though, when you ask for a link to your site, the other host is going to want one back.

Here's how one site uses text links to other sites (the linked text is underlined):

TV Horror Hosts

<u>Chiller Cinerama</u>—Horror Host Doctor Gangrene (and Oogsley) create TV mayhem in Nashville, TN.

<u>Count Gore Devol</u>—Washington DC's long time running TV Horror Host (and "Internet Horror Host!")

<u>Count Zappula</u>—A favorite Michigan TV Horror Host from the 1970s and 80s.

<u>Dr. Creep</u>—On the air for over 30 years from Dayton, Ohio.

<u>Dr. San Guinary</u>—Tribute site to Omaha, Nebraska's longest running Horror Host (1971-1981.)

<u>E-gor's Chamber of TV Horror Hosts</u>—The Internet's prime source for TV Horror Host information. Names, cities, dates, whereabouts, etc. If you're looking for your home town TV Horror Host, this is the place to start.

<u>Jeepers Creepers Theatre</u>—Lots of info and images on one of LA's hometown favorites.

<u>Local Legends</u>—Covers many California TV Horror Hosts including Ghoulita, Jeepers Creepers, Vampira and more.

<u>Ravena and "Anok"</u>—Your Hosts for "Friday Fright" on cable TV's "B-Movie" channel.

<u>Sammy Terry</u>—Unofficial tribute site for this popular Indianapolis TV Horror Host.

<u>The Fearmonger</u>—Small tribute site to Louisville, Kentucky's TV Horror Host from 1971-1975.

<u>The Tomb of TV Horror Hosts</u>—Another TV Horror Host information site which has tons of information on Horror Host collectibles.

<u>Zacherley</u>—Zach has his very own site!

> Text links can actually be more effective than banner links because they are perceived by surfers as additional help.

Pros and Cons of Banners

Links and banners have their advantages and drawbacks. A heavy player on the Internet just eliminated all the links and banners on his site because they were leading people away from his site before he made the sale. Banners and links should be looked at carefully because they can lead surfers away from your site—no matter how creative and informational your site is.

How to get informal reciprocal links

- Surf for them over the Internet. Find a business that's complementary to your site, and ask the owner if he or she wants to link up with you. Any click on his or her site will be a new visitor. Let's say you have a site for selling dolls. You might link up to a site that makes clothing for dolls. Use the search engines to find your particular interest and follow up on the first 30 or so. Your best opportunity will be companies or sites that share the same target audience as you do. You should also check out the Web sites of your competitors and approach each of their links.
- Check out newsgroups. Look for companies with a complementary fit. In most newsgroups, the article has the person's e-mail address and SIG. Write the member a personal note listing the advantages of a reciprocal link. And, of course, don't forget to send him your URL or a hyperlink to your site in an e-mail. You can also post on newsgroups asking if anyone wants to link up with you.
- E-mail lists can be a great source of link leads. Find companies similar to yours and send bulk e-mails. Here is a nice, simple letter that does the job well:

Subject heading:
Reciprocal Link Request

Body of letter:
    I just visited your site at *http://www.smegly.com* and was wondering if you would be interested in setting up reciprocal links?
    Our company is Specialty Trade Group and we are producers and distributors of business forms. You can find our site at *http://www.specialtyforms.com*
    If this is of interest, please let me know and I can have a link up to your site some time today.
    Thank you!
    SIG file

Key notes about your letter

- In the subject heading, mention reciprocal links in one form or another. Tell them who you are.
- Make sure you tell them the site address you visited. They may own many sites.
- Tell the person the site you visited (include http:// and/or www as applicable in the address) since they may own multiple domains.
- Tell them who you are and your full site address.
- Offer to get their link up quickly so they feel you are serious.
- Include a clean-looking SIG file.
- Give a brief summary of your site. You want to come across as someone who is on the Internet for the long haul, not someone who may disappear tomorrow.

Don't overlook the obvious opportunities

Don't forget the usual business channels. Trade shows, phone contacts, networking opportunities all present an opportunity to exchange links. Your one common denominator is you both want to do more business on the Web. Add a line on your business cards that says you are looking for links.

- Find an industrywide Web site or trade Web sites that link to companies in your field. Negotiate reciprocal links to and from their Web pages. Trade associations are great places to start. For instance, the Seafood Association lists members from fishing boat owners to importers to shippers. Freelance writers can seek listings on Guru.com.
- Advertise on your Web site. One person mentions, "Cool links from around the Web. Reciprocal links always welcome" on his site.

> Trade shows, phone contacts, networking opportunities all present an opportunity to exchange links.

Banner ads

There is a great deal of controversy about the effectiveness of banners. Some people—often advertising agencies—swear by them. Others swear at them, saying few people really know if they work worth a darn. However, banners are still the "coin of the realm" as they relate to Web promotion and advertising. A banner is an ad that occupies a certain percentage of a computer screen, usually conforming to certain sizes. Although banners can advertise addresses and phone numbers, the real purpose of a banner is to get someone to click on it—and jump to the advertiser's site. Remember though, when a surfer jumps to another site, he is not interacting with yours. Banners can be static or animated, large or small, whimsical or deadly serious. One of the major advantages of banner advertising is that banners can be created fairly quickly. Many companies who sell banner space will even create one for you.

Banner advertising can be created with much shorter lead times than traditional print advertising or direct mail since they are essentially mini-ads that don't use up many creative resources. You can take advantage of this by timing your banners to run at exactly the same time as your other promotion extravaganzas kick off. Placing banner ads strategically on sites that reach the same prospects as your forthcoming print advertising or direct-mail campaign can provoke an action that traditional advertising simply can't provide. Your banner ad can act as a teaser, preparing it for the traditional media advertising messages to come.

Banners are a great way to focus on your target. Place your banners where you expect to get the greatest concentration of your key audience. Segmenting allows you to shoot your promotional arrow to focus on:

- Specific industries
- Geographical regions
- User interests
- User demographics

> A banner is an ad that occupies a certain percentage of a computer screen, usually conforming to certain sizes.

Although banners can be effective alone, they work best when they reinforce or communicate an integrated advertising message. Use banners for launching a new service or a media event. You can also use them to publicize an award or celebrity guest or as an invitation for a special Web promotion.

What banners cost

Banner ads are usually sold in two ways: cost per thousand impressions (CPM), or number of click-throughs (CTR). An impression is when someone looks at your banner ad. A click-through is when someone actually clicks on your banner. Though there is a huge variance in rates for either method, you can expect the typical cost of CPM to be between $50 and $70. It may be shown to a thousand different people, or it may be shown many times to a much smaller audience. You can save money by going to smaller, cheaper sites, but your effectiveness will be in direct ratio to the cost.

Buying on a CTR basis is usually more expensive (50% more) than a CPM basis, but can be more effective since people will be clicking to your site. Click-through hawkers promise that they will get people to your site, but a lot of these hits will be wasted and you can be responsible for paying as much as 15 cents per click. You will also get a great deal of poor traffic from people who are clicking to your site out of curiosity. Another drawback is that one person may click on your site many times and you will be charged for each click although some providers claim they have built in mechanisms to eliminate multiclick.

Whether you decide on CTR or CPM, the more targeted the visitors, the higher the rate charged. Many Web brokers set minimum charges. But as in most things in Internet-land, you can get by without paying anything if you're astute and committed enough.

Free ways to get banner placements

Many companies put together free programs where you can swap banners on a reciprocal arrangement. Your ad is placed on sites

Banners Are a Buyer's Market

As this is being written, advertising sales and banner exchanges are sliding down. Some people are selling spaces dirt cheap. Don't be afraid to negotiate, because many ad selling spaces are taking anything they can get. Be realistic and fair. Nah, don't be fair. Be ruthless. It's your money.

> Make sure you really want banners on your site. Sometimes they may be a distraction and detract from the professionalism of your Web site.

similar to yours in exchange for having a banner placed on your site. BCentral, once called Link Exchange, is a particularly good exchange firm. The exchange company keeps track of how many banners you have displayed on your site and gives you credit for the hits they receive. Some exchange companies may give you a fixed percentage of credits of the number of hits and sell the rest to advertisers. These hits are exchanged for banners on other sites. All the mechanics are handled by the exchange company. You can sit with your beer as your banner is magically placed on other sites and random banners show up on your site. You may have to put a small amount of HTML coding on your site, but it's no big deal.

You should choose your exchange company carefully. Here are some aspects of banner exchange programs that you should consider:

- Make sure you really want banners on your site. Sometimes they may be a distraction and detract from the professionalism of your Web site.
- Make sure that the banners on your pages are reasonable in byte size and that you can handle a number of banners without your site loading too slowly.
- Make sure that your banner company does not allow unlimited animation and that the banners that appear on your Web site are reasonably small. Complicated and large banners take precious loading time and can make your site look garish.
- If you let the exchange company design your banner, make sure it's on target. These companies use do-it-all banner-making programs that are usually untouched by human hands and not seen by human eyes or brains. Only you can tell if your banner looks as if it will be effective.
- Ask and insist that sites that your banner will appear on carry links that are complementary or appropriate for you audience. Choose exchange companies that allow you to specify what kinds of sites you will advertise. Alternatively, look for a specialty exchange company that targets your business or interest category.

Have your banners designed for free

Even if you are artistically challenged, you can create strong banners effectively. BannermakerPro is a shareware program that allows you to quickly create attractive banners and buttons for your Web site. Using a simple step-by-step interface, it walks you through creating your graphic. It's $25 to register but makes the process of creating banners easy—and almost fun.

If you don't want to take the creative approach and want someone to create it for you, you can have talented banner makers do it for you for free. Go to *www.bannertips.com/makers.shtml* and you'll find a list of people who do such things. Some of them might want their own banner placed on your Web site, but it's a small price to pay for a professional piece of work.

Using graphics and copy effectively

Although there is a controversy on how effective banners are on a return-on-investment (ROI) schema, there is some general agreement on the kind of art and copy that works to get better click-throughs:

> If you don't want to take the creative approach and want someone to create it for you, you can have talented banner makers do it for you for free.

- Say "Click here" on your banner. I know this sounds simplistic, but it can double your click-through rate.
- There's no room for subtlety in banners. Don't be subtle. Be brief and catchy. Grab your visitor like the old-time hook at vaudeville shows. It should scream your message.
- Use humor. It's the best way to get click-throughs.
- Pose questions. "Want to save 30% on your insurance in 10 minutes?" Questions work better than statements, particularly when they are used to "tease" your audience. Studies have shown they raise click-through rates by 16% over average.
- Use bright colors. Bright colors attract the user's eye. Research has shown that blue, green, and yellow are the most effective at eliciting click-throughs, whereas white, red, and black are less effective. Stay away from transparent colors either in the foreground or background. They tend to get

lost amid the colors of most Web sites. Always use a solid color for the background.

- Use simple animation. Moving images and blinking animations catch the eye. Strategic use of movement grabs attention more effectively than static banners. But don't make it so complicated that it takes your page too much time to load.
- Pique the curiosity of surfers. Cryptic ad banners involve the visitor. When the visitor gets to your site, he or she must be satisfied with the information on the other end.
- Offer a reward or something free when someone clicks on the banner. It's one of the biggest motivators for getting people to click. It can be a giveaway, a how-to tip, or a special offer. Tell how a click is going to change a person's life, if even for a few seconds. Of people who click banners, according to one source, 25% want to get something for free, 14% want information, and 10% want some fun.
- Change your banner often, or use multiple-cycling banners. One study concluded that, after the fourth impression, banner burnout was created. After the fourth look, click-through rates dropped drastically.
- Keep your copy short. If your text takes more than two seconds to read, you've got too many words. Have you ever noticed how few words are on billboards? The average time people spend looking at billboards is six seconds. You have only half that time on the Web.
- Use italics. They have been shown to raise click-through rates by about 1½% compared with standard typefaces.
- Grab the top position and grab it fast. Banners on the first fold are more likely to get clicked than banners in the middle or on the bottom of a page.
- Use wide banners. They're clicked on significantly more than smaller or skinnier ones.
- Make your banners load quickly. Slow-loading banners are a quick turnoff for surfers.

Offer a reward or something free when someone clicks on the banner. It's one of the biggest motivators for getting people to click.

Quick tips

✓ When you place a banner on your page, you are, in effect, giving your visitor a reason to leave your site.

✓ Your objective for using banners is to bring people to your site, not to sell. Don't give too much away.

✓ When constructing a banner, use the creative hints discussed in this chapter.

Summary

A banner is only a small part of the promotional chain. Just make your banners strong enough to get people to go to your site. The most important part of a linking strategy is to define the kinds of sites you wish to trade with. These sites should be in your Web site's category of interest. It is counterproductive to have your link on a totally unrelated site because you will have to furnish a link on your site also. If you want to have many visitors or subscribers, then you should have your link in as many places as possible.

> A banner is only a small part of the promotional chain. Just make your banners strong enough to get people to go to your site.

For more information on this topic, visit our Web site at www.businesstown.com

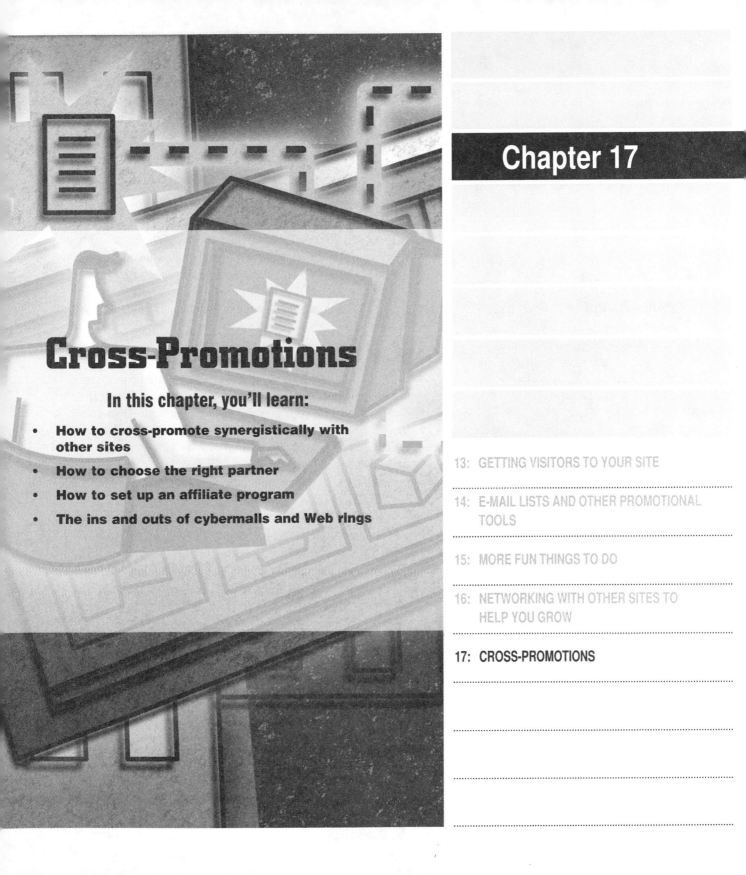

Cross-Promotions

In this chapter, you'll learn:

- **How to cross-promote synergistically with other sites**
- **How to choose the right partner**
- **How to set up an affiliate program**
- **The ins and outs of cybermalls and Web rings**

Chapter 17

The beauty of the Web is that you can get together with all sorts of businesses, both Web based and offline. Although using links and banners are ways to cross-promote to some degree, you can take the concept further and further. Cross-promoting, or partnering, as the phenomenon is called, has become a way to extend the value of your business and draw new traffic. Let's define a cross-promotion as two or more companies getting together to create traffic by linking up with each other on a formal or nonformal basis.

By dipping into each other's markets, both companies (or three or four, if your cross-promotion plans get really ambitious) can achieve higher visibility and efficiency than they might have achieved by going it alone.

There are many reasons to cross-promote.

- Cross-promoting works. By choosing the right partners, you can get your message across to greater numbers. Your traffic increases because your promotions are more unique and more people see them.
- Credibility—necessary for repeat traffic—is increased because when you partner with a respected company, their image can be transferred to your product. You get all the reflected glory of partnering with a well-known firm or site.
- Cross-promotions help you extend your reach. You can reach more potential buyers by partnering with companies that reach a similar demographic as you, or you can partner with a company that is targeting people you are missing. Frequency of impressions increases because your promotion appears in front of both customer bases.

How to choose the right partner

Some of the requisites you should be looking at when choosing a potential partner include:

- Partners must respect each other's businesses and goals.
- Partners must have equal commitment to the promotion or relationship.

> Cross-promoting, or partnering, as the phenomenon is called, has become a way to extend the value of your business and draw new traffic.

- Choose a company or a person that can enhance your product's value in the visitors' minds.
- Your prospective partner should offer added value—something extra, such as a unique demographic profile you lack or access to markets you can't reach.
- Choose a partner that has a natural fit with your Web site content.
- Look for similar market segmentation and buying demographics.
- The partnership should work synergistically. The cross-promotion should result in economical gains for both parties. At the very least it should offer the perception of added value for your partner.

Hot ideas for cross-promotions

But cross-promotion does not only mean you should partner with other Web sites. Think like the big boys and cross-promote with people and businesses that aren't even on the Web. Obviously, this list is not meant to be all-inclusive—there are thousands of different Web businesses out there. Use each one as a starting point and expand by using your own ideas.

- If you're a Web retailer, cross-promote with brick-and-mortar stores and manufacturers. Choose stores that cater to the same people demographically as you do. In return for getting your Web site in their flyers, place an ad or logo for them on your Web site. Run an online coupon for their products on your site.
- Sports are always a good outlet for your cross-promotions. Team up with local teams for reciprocal promotions. You furnish a small amount of space or publicity on your site and you get listed in their programs or yearbook. Bausch & Lomb Sports Optic created a "Fan of the Game" that appeared over the large-screen TVs in sports stadiums. Now, I know you can't afford anything that big, but you can create a fan of the game on your Web site.

> Think like the big boys and cross-promote with people and businesses that aren't even on the Web.

- Cross-promote with other manufacturers that serve a similar niche as your products.
- Cross-promote with new merchants and new businesses. Offer discounts or special deals at these and other retail stores when your URL is printed on their sales materials.
- Take a tip from the airlines, especially if your product is a parity product. In order to differentiate themselves from the competition, airlines are cross-promoting with everyone—and, they are being very creative about how and with whom they will cross-promote. United Airlines serves Starbucks Coffee and promotes it heavily. Most airlines continually cross-promote with rental car companies and hotels—and feature these promotions on their Web site.
- Piggyback on an exciting new technology. To reach people more effectively, American Online (which is really just one gigantic Web site) joined forces with Kodak to have photos available on AOL. The promotion shows off the new Kodak technology and also launched a new useful service for AOL.
- Partner with service groups to create goodwill and sales. Campbell's Soup Company has been partnering with schools for years, and they've taken the concept online. People save their labels to buy audiovisual hardware for schools. Yes, even you can partner with giant-sized Campbell's if you offer information about their programs.

Affiliate programs

Consider creating an affiliate program. Get others involved, and make it attractive for them to do business with you and to refer qualified leads to you. Affiliate programs are really just another form of partnering and networking. You pay an affiliate Web site—also called an associate or partner—a commission when their link leads to a sale or some other action on your site. This strategy is also known as performance-based marketing. Forrester Research, an Internet research firm, estimates that more than 20% of Internet revenues will be driven by affiliate marketing in 2003. The study also asserts that 54% of

> Cross-promote with new merchants and new businesses. Offer discounts or special deals at these and other retail stores when your URL is printed on their sales materials.

the online marketing dollars will derive from performance-based initiatives, affiliate marketing, and syndicated selling.

Performance-based marketing systems on the Internet go by different names: affiliate, associate, bounty, and referrals. I prefer the term *bounty* because it reminds me of the old Wild West days, which is the stage the Internet is still in. A bounty hunter grabs a suspect, 'er prospect, and you pay when the prospect buys from you. Basically, an affiliate program works as follows: A merchant, say, Barnes & Noble, pays a commission to a Web site owner for generating sales from either a banner or link from the Web site owner's site. The commissions are paid as either a flat fee, or a percentage of the transaction.

Sites that sell physical products typically have affiliate programs where they pay you when goods are purchased. Sites that have subscription models (ISPs, specialty services, and so on) have bounty programs where they pay you a flat fee when someone you referred joins their service.

The goal is to build a network of Web site owners who have a financial stake in promoting your site or product. You can advertise your products or services on thousands of Web sites while paying only for actual results. You supply the link or banner, so everything stays under your control. A special URL tracks where the visitor comes from and the purchases he or she makes.

An added benefit is that since you can supply multiple banners and keep track of what site is running which banner, you can test which ads or banners increase your traffic and which ads or banners fail dismally.

There are many companies that will help you start your affiliate program and recruit affiliates for you. The best way, though, is to do the recruiting yourself because you know exactly the kinds of people you want to publicize your Web site.

> I prefer the term *bounty* because it reminds me of the old Wild West days, which is the stage the Internet is still in.

Developing a successful affiliate program

1. Make sure you have excellent customer service or affiliate managers. Explicitly lay out the way your program works, provide marketing and sales tools, offer a variety of graphics,

and basically operate a model program. But one of the keys to success is to follow up with a telephone call to new affiliates to provide one-to-one help and guidance. It's easy to think of an affiliate program as a hands-off gold mine. But it takes people to run a gold mine, and it is often necessary to have a person dedicated to day-to-day operations. This person should be easily reached for customer service questions. If there is no name attached to the program, and little customer service, your program is doomed from the start.

2. Compile a list of frequently asked questions. Make sure your FAQs cover your site thoroughly. There are a wide variety of questions that are specific to your affiliate program: Does it cost anything to join? How does one sign up? How do the affiliates create a link to your site? What are the payment terms? As an experiment, walk some friends and neighbors through your program and ask them to each write down two or three questions. These are the beginnings of you FAQs. As your program grows, you will receive questions from your prospective affiliates. Whenever you answer a new question, be sure that the question and answer are added to the FAQs.

3. Get a privacy statement and contract. Will affiliates have access to your mailing list when they sign up for your program? Do you intend to sell or share your database of affiliates with other companies? Address everything. Your contract should spell out how often you will be paying your affiliates, how much you will be paying them, and under what circumstances they would forfeit their commissions. Although these documents may seem like unnecessary red tape, they are absolutely essential. Spell out your terms in a contract or operating agreement, and not only will you gain more credibility, but you will also avoid potential legal disputes. If you do not currently have a privacy policy, you can create one for free at *www.etrust.com/wizard*.

4. Invest in your affiliates. It's tough to figure out how low or high your commissions should be. There are many variables. Will you be paying a flat fee on each purchase, a percentage

> Compile a list of frequently asked questions. Make sure your FAQs cover your site thoroughly.

of the sale, or for each click? With low margins and high prices, it makes sense to pay out a low percentage. But in many segments, it is unacceptable to offer less than 5% of the gross sale. Flat fees and pay-per-click models are totally dependent on the product and cost. Research your competitors and outdo them. If you are offering a paltry commission, you will not have any affiliates. On the contrary, a small increase in commission will help to grow your program at a more rapid pace.

5. Publicize often, publicize well. There are many companies that operate affiliate programs, and they do not link to the program from their home page. People must be able to find your program if you want them to join you in marketing your product or service. Although the affiliate program directories, such as Refer-it and AssociatePrograms.com, will generate some traffic to your program, you cannot expect to operate a successful program if you don't use the tools in this book. It's also a good idea to incorporate a blurb in your e-mail signature. Everything you send out should plug your program.

6. Report statistics on a regular basis. Your affiliates are going to expect to track their statistics online. They are going to expect this feature, and if you do not provide it, your competitor probably does. If you use a third-party solution (there's one at *www.refer-it.com*), the online reporting should be a given. At a minimum, you should provide your affiliates with a breakdown of the pay periods, sales, returns, and total balance.

7. Don't forget the application. You should use a third-party affiliate application. If you choose to create your online application in-house, some potential affiliates will be sensitive about the transmission of their personal information. This is especially important if you do not have a secure server for transmission of their personal information. Your affiliate program has to reach a certain level of sophistication, and if it fails to do so, you are going to turn away a lot of prospective affiliates.

Publicize often, publicize well.

Affiliate programs are becoming more and more competitive in the growing e-commerce marketplace, so it is essential to research the competition. Affiliates will constantly measure you and your program against other affiliate programs.

According to a recent survey of 286 affiliates by Refer-it.com, the most valued aspect of an affiliate program is the commission. If your commission does not measure up to that of your competition, your program is going to be more of a struggle than an asset.

> Affiliate programs are becoming more and more competitive in the growing e-commerce marketplace, so it is essential to research the competition.

Driving traffic to your affiliate program

Most companies use banners to promote their affiliate programs. Though there's nothing wrong with this method, it can be tough for a Web site starting out. If you want to start your program immediately, you'll need money to establish a banner presence of any size. And since you're new to the banner game, you may get poor position among sites carrying your banner. Here are four other ways, suggested and offered by Declan Dunn, a noted expert in affiliate programs:

1. Targeted e-mail promotions to a qualified list. Throughout this book, I've mentioned that very few people buy during their first few visits to a Web sites. Direct sales work the same way. Sales are usually made only after repeat mailings or repeat e-mails asking people to visit your site. The real power of e-mail comes in the endorsed mailing. Once you have developed a newsletter or another service, you develop a certain trust between yourself and your readers. You can also gain trust by soliciting testimonials from respected leaders in your field or using the name of an important publication.
2. Text links and endorsements with banners. PCWorld.com does an excellent job of affiliate promoting with small banner ads on the side of the page. To the right of the small banner "button" is text that describes the benefits behind clicking on that banner ad. Both the banners and the text are links. It

is an extremely effective method of offering more than one product on a page, without overwhelming the visitor. Once again, words do the explaining that pictures can't, and a picture tells a thousand words. Together, they are a potent affiliate advertising tool.

3. Featured product. An excellent method to increase affiliate leads is to offer a page that acts as a featured product at the affiliate's Web site. This can be a standalone Web page or one that merges with Web page content at the affiliate's site. The key is to focus on the product being sold, a single-product offer that stands out from the rest of the page. This approach basically eliminates the grouping of affiliate programs and encourages people to click on this important product because it appears to be featured. The featured product enables you to gain exposure at the affiliate's site in a way that is perceived favorably by visitors.

4. Storefronts. The best affiliate responses can come from a storefront integrated into another Web site. This can be as simple as putting a logo graphic on top of the page with a return link to the affiliate's Web site so that the storefront appears to be an important part of the Web site as a whole. Storefronts increase credibility by offering a selection of products in a single setting. The storefront should not be one of many at an affiliate's Web site, but an integral part of their efforts. Although this requires more work on the part of the affiliate network, the returns can be much greater. Popular portal sites use this strategy often, but by extending it to highly trafficked sites, you can increase branding and the perceived value of what you offer.

A good idea is to mix the text and banner ad approach with a storefront, so you can offer multiple products. It's best not to offer more than three to five products at another Web site; too many choices confuse visitors.

> An excellent method to increase affiliate leads is to offer a page that acts as a featured product at the affiliate's Web site.

The most glaring problem, according to Dunn, in most affiliate networks is ad copy:

Without a good motivating headline, testimonial and ad copy, all your efforts will be wasted. Be sure that you look at the words you use in any of the four methods and find the ones that work best for you and for your affiliates. Adapt your words until you find the ones that pull the best.

> Without a good motivating headline, testimonial and ad copy, all your efforts will be wasted.

How to start your affiliate program

- Determine the commission you are willing to pay. It usually comes from advertising costs, so work out the details with your accountant. (Consider it your advertising cost.)
- Either set up the program yourself or hire a company that specializes in such programs; Be Free, Inc. (*www.befree.com*) and Comission Junction (*www.cj.com*) are a couple of good ones.
- For successful affiliate relationships, choose sites with a clear connection to your product or service. Marian Dieter, co-owner of Cleveland-based Princeton Watches (*www.princetonwatches.com*), hooked up with scuba-diving sites to sell her diving watches.
- Go to your favorite search engines and start plugging in some likely keywords. The sites that index well for your key-words are the sites you want to target. For instance, if you sell women's handbags, luggage shops are a good fit for you. Then think of sites luggage companies would want to be affiliated with. Leather goods and travel accessories may be promising.
- Once you find a site that you think would make a good affiliate, contact the Web site owner personally. (E-mails are considered personal contact.)
- E-mail them your proposition. If you can get a phone number, call them.
- Once you have your initial affiliates, look for their links. Sometimes they link to other great sites that would be a

perfect match for your program. In fact, affiliates that belong to Web rings and other link-trading programs can be tremendously helpful in uncovering more like-minded sites.

Web rings

A Web ring is a circular collection of Web sites joined by a common subject, product, or product line. The purpose of a Web ring is to allow visitors to reach member sites quickly and easily. Web rings are a fast, free way to build up links and traffic.

Visitors navigate to other sites in the same ring by using links, usually at the bottom of the page. Each site is connected to another site through a link. Visitors can traverse backwards and forwards by clicking on the links, and they will always be touching on links to a member of that specific Web ring.

Rings can have as few as 5 members to as many as 1,000. Every ring has a head honcho—usually a site owner—who sets up and maintains the ring. He or she controls all the member sites and their order in the sequence. Anyone with a Web site can join. All you need do is register and be reasonably compatible with the other participating sites. A list of Web rings can be found at *www.webring.org*. Choose the Web ring that's right for you and register. The person who runs the ring will review your site and send you the necessary code to join.

> The purpose of a Web ring is to allow visitors to reach member sites quickly and easily. Web rings are a fast, free way to build up links and traffic.

Cybermalls

Cybermalls are a collection of Internet stores and sites under one Web address. There is a store for virtually any category you can think of. Some cybermalls will set you up in your own Web site, or they may offer to maintain your Web site for you. Some cybermalls provide merchant accounts and handle the selling details for you. Cybermalls offer you excellent segmenting opportunities because they are organized by products lines, geographical regions, demographics, and psychographics.

Here is a standard barter agreement from *Inc.* magazine. It will ensure that you get placements on the sites of your tradees and they get promotion on your site. Many trade links work on an oral agreement, but it doesn't hurt to put things in writing.

> Many trade links work on an oral agreement, but it doesn't hurt to put things in writing.

BARER AGREEMENT (from *Inc.* magazine)

[Name]
[Company]
[Street Address]
[City, State ZIP]

Dear [Name],

To facilitate a barter agreement, we propose the following terms:

[Company name] will provide [partnering company name] with 1,000,000 advertising banner impressions (complete page views with your ad banner and link to your site) within [site URL]. This will commence on [date] and end on [date] (the "Advertising Period").

In return, [partnering company name] will provide [company name] with 1,000,000 advertising banner impressions (complete page views with a [company name] ad banner with a link to [company URL]) on [partnering site URL] commencing on [date] and ending on [date] ("Advertising Period").

Impressions will be provided by both parties on a space available basis. Any shortfall in performance by either party will be "made good" to the other party within the 60 days following the close of the Advertising Period.

Both parties will provide the other with their current advertising performance reports, weekly, or as requested, until completion of the Advertising Period. If either party must provide a "make good," additional advertising performance reports will be provided to the other party weekly, or as requested, until the agreed upon number of impressions has been delivered.

No money will change hands and no invoices will be created by either party. This is simply a barter of advertising by the parties.

Either party may terminate this agreement at any time upon 48 hours notice. Upon termination, each party must calculate the total impressions delivered, and the party that has delivered the fewest impressions must make up the difference to the other party within 60 days through providing advertising space for the number of impressions equal to the difference. Reporting will follow the terms specified above.

Ads are subject to approval by both parties and will be no larger than 468 pixels wide × 60 high (and not to exceed 10K in file size).

The terms of this agreement shall be kept confidential to both parties.

The advertising outlined above is non-transferable.

Both parties have the right to audit the books of the other party to verify number of impressions. The auditor must be reasonably acceptable to the party being audited. Audits must take place during ordinary business hours and only after 10 days written notice.

If this proposal is acceptable, please countersign this letter and return it to me at [fax number].

The proposal will be revoked if you have not returned a countersigned copy to me before [date].

SIGNED   SIGNED

_____ _____

DATE   DATE

Affiliate Success Story

Walt Frederick Associates sells architectural equipment and computers. For years they were dependent on their not-so-gigantic sales team—which consisted of three people. They decided to sell their wares on the Web. Bad move. Disastrous. Not a great many sales.

Walt Frederick's owner then persuaded other Web sites to display a link to Frederick's home page, *www.inkjetexpress.com*. Every time a customer linked to *inkjetexpress.com* from one of its affiliated Web sites that carried the banner—the site owner received a 5% commission, just like an in-the-flesh salesperson would. The referring site was thrilled. This was free money!

The result? In less than a month, Web affiliates helped bump Frederick's site traffic from five visitors per day to an average of 182. Today, affiliates drive more than half of the site's traffic. At the time of this writing, inkjet.com was growing at 25% per month. Those are serious numbers.

Quick tips

✓ Networking offline is a great way to approach businesses about linking to them. Keep a floppy disk, Zip disk, or CD with the coding for your banner.

✓ Although it is tempting, don't jump at the first place that accepts your banner. Make sure there is a synergistic relation between your banner and their site.

Summary

One of the most powerful ways to market online is through linking strategies. The goal is to get placed on high-traffic Web sites linking to you in a symbiotic relationship. Links will generate traffic to your site. However, trading links is not the only way to network. Affiliate programs, Web rings, and cybermalls can generate all kinds of traffic if approached with care and creativity.

Whatever path you decide to take (and you should try all these strategies), the sooner you get started, the better for you. Traffic that comes in from your links will increase as time goes on. If you link to a growing Web site, more traffic is going to flow from their site to yours.

> One of the most powerful ways to market online is through linking strategies.

For more information on this topic, visit our Web site at www.businesstown.com

SECTION IV

Search Engine Frenzy

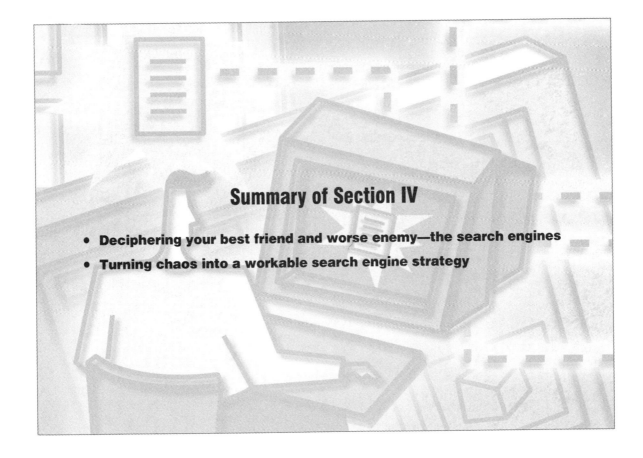

Summary of Section IV

- Deciphering your best friend and worse enemy—the search engines
- Turning chaos into a workable search engine strategy

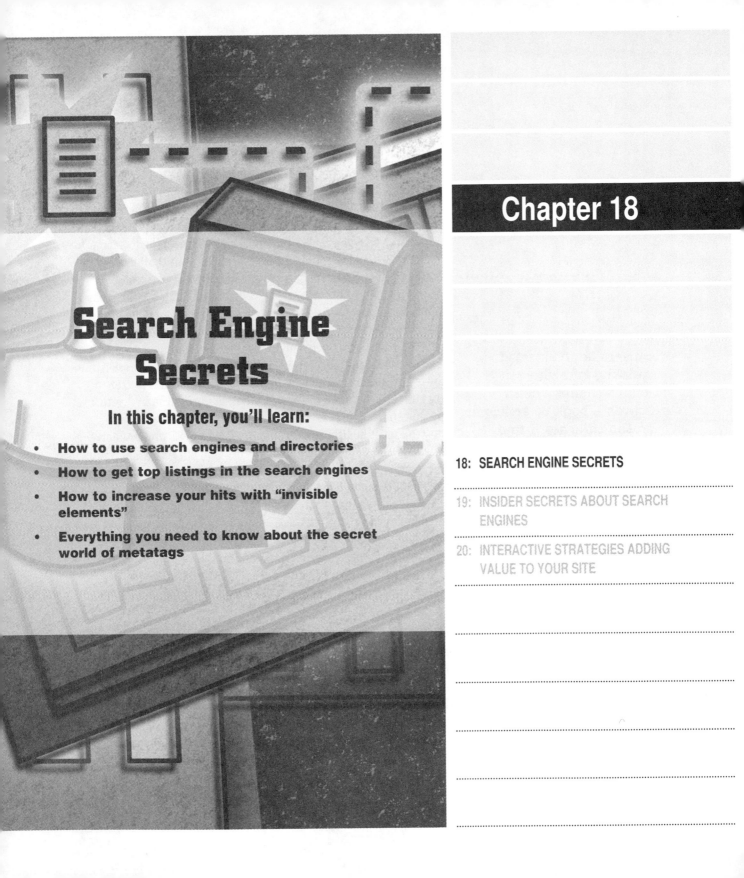

Search Engine Secrets

In this chapter, you'll learn:

- How to use search engines and directories
- How to get top listings in the search engines
- How to increase your hits with "invisible elements"
- Everything you need to know about the secret world of metatags

Chapter 18

When most people talk about promoting their Web sites, they immediately think of making nice with the search engines. We'll call them "engines" because that's what everyone else calls them. They're really giant computer programs that index sites. And you want to get indexed by them because 80% of all surfers start their hunt with the search engines. But the bad news is that a large number of people don't know how to search for what they're looking for. And possibly worse than that, most people don't go past the third page of "hits." Surfers get frustrated quickly, and who can blame them? When I research a book or article on the Internet, I find that only 1 hit in 15 hits is somewhat meaningful.

The trick is that you can do a shotgun submission to all the search engines and directories out there—and there are literally hundreds. But that is a lot of work for a very small return. Better to take the time to define the options that will bring the best return for your efforts.

You must be listed, and you must keep submitting regularly. Once just isn't enough. The goals of this chapter are to show you how to submit to search engines, how to get good positioning, and how to make sure your hits will result in a click-through to your site. I suggest you read through this whole chapter before doing anything—even submitting—because we're going to be covering a lot of ground here, and search engines are as finicky and set in their own ways as an old great uncle. Worse, you need them; they don't need you.

Generally, there are two types of search engines.

Those that are compiled by a computer spider— or robot

These are really just huge databases or indexes much like the index in the back of this book. They contain many of the Web sites that have been submitted to the engine. The word *many* is important here because if a search engine gets mad at you for violating its rules, it just might refuse to list you. And even the best search engines hit only about 27% of all Web sites.

> Surfers get frustrated quickly, and who can blame them? When I research a book or article on the Internet, I find that only 1 hit in 15 hits is somewhat meaningful.

A reasonable question you might ask is "What are these rules; I need to know so that I won't violate them." But search engines won't tell you. Most of them have their own proprietary methods. They're afraid that if you know how they go about doing their business, you might cheat, which is probably a reasonable assumption given how important they are.

Directories—those that are reviewed by real people

I guess they're the same kind of people who hide in your refrigerator and turn on the little light when you open the door. Real people manually review every Web site that is submitted to them. In some cases, the person who reviews your site may reject it because it is not the type or quality that is interesting to them. You might think of a directory as a shelf in the library. With these you'll be required to select which classification—which "shelf"—you want your site to be placed on. Not every directory is the same, so you'll want to take some time to find out just how the database is structured. With care you can select classifications that will give you top priority.

90% of the traffic is conducted by 10% of search engines. The ones that are most important to us are:

Yahoo!	HotBot	Northern Light
Lycos	Excite	Google
AltaVista	WebCrawler	DMOS
Go.com	AOL/Netfind	

There are also a few smaller engines, but they are usually powered by one of the big 11. The important thing to remember is that every major search engine has its own specific and quirky way of finding and indexing sites.

Preparing your site for submission

If you followed the sequence in this book, you'll find the preliminary work has been done. If you haven't, you might want to take a glance

The Best Search Engines

You have to be fast in cyber-world. Since this section was written, there have been major changes in search engine protocol, importance, and alliances. The following are now must haves:

AltaVista
AOL/Netfind
Direct Hit
Excite
Go.com
Google
GoTo
HotBot
iWon
LookSmart
Lycos
Magellan
MSN
NBCi
Netscape Netcenter
Northern Light
Open Directory Project
Raging
Yahoo!

backwards now, looking especially hard at the keywords section in Chapter 6. Even if you prepared correctly, you may want to fine-tune things a little further with some changes in your Web page title, metatags, and some of the first few, viewable, paragraphs on your site.

How search engines work

Search engines travel around the vast resources of the Web looking for sites. The important thing to know is that they are not working for you. Their reasons for being are for the people who are searching for things. The engines make money by being able to sell space based on the number of people who use their site, so it behooves them to be accurate and impartial. Actually, some search engines have toyed with the idea of selling their top listings, but for now it looks as if most are going to try to stay impartial.

When search engines find your pages, they give a certain weight to the elements on your site. Each engine uses a proprietary algorithm to rank Web pages according to a variety of factors. The search engine companies keep their algorithms secret for competitive reasons and to prevent people from making pages that spam them. It's essentially the same way your teacher graded your high school essays—giving a certain weight to your headers, some points for punctuation, and the majority of points for the content of your essay.

Most search engines scan everything on your page. They look through your text, your headlines, and some even look at the banners of your site. Here are some of the factors that search engines find meaningful when a specific query is made:

- Prominent keywords in the viewable text
- Frequency of the keywords in the viewable text
- Site popularity
- "Weight" of the keywords
- Proximity of keywords

Most search engines will also look at the hidden elements (the HTML code) of your page to see how they relate to the visible

> The important thing to know is that they are not working for you. Their reasons for being are for the people who are searching for things.

components. Some engines will scan your whole site, and some will just look at your first page. Some search engines, like Excite, limit the number of pages that can be submitted from each site. WebCrawler, on the other hand, crawls through your entire site focusing on the titles of your pages. Yet others (Infoseek, HotBot, Lycos, Northern Light, Searchking, AltaVista among them) allow you to submit each and every page in your site. Now that can be time consuming if you have a large site, but it certainly does increase your exposure.

The best way to work with the search engines is to make your entire site relevant. Since most of this book has been about the parts of your page that can actually be read by people, let's spend some time with the unseen elements.

Metatags—what they are

The term *metatags* is confusing because people use the word in different ways. Think of metatags as something in the coding of your site that search engines can see but people can't when typically viewing you site. Metatags are the first things that engines look for when indexing your site. Depending on the search engine and the mood it wakes up with in the day, metatags can carry a great deal of weight.

The important metatags are usually on the first part of your page and contain sections like "title," "description," "keywords," "author," and "content." You can look at almost anyone's metatags—including your own. Simply open up Netscape or Explorer and go to any site. Click on View and then on Source.

What search engines look for

Title

The title is the first thing the search engines look for. I'm not referring to the title of your pages that show on your site but that little rectangular box that comes up in whatever browser you're using.

> The best way to work with the search engines is to make your entire site relevant.

The title is the most important source of information for any search engine. Most engines place a high scoring weight on the title. If someone is searching for "open toed ballet shoes," and you have "open toed ballet shoes" spelled that same way in your title, there is a great chance it will show up in the first pages of the search engines' results. Every page should have its own unique title. If you look through the HTML coding of your site, it should look like this:

```
<title>open toed ballet shoes</title>
```

Don't use fewer than three words in your title or more than six. There's really no logical reason you should adhere to this word count, except that search engines like it that way. Most search engines will display your title page when it finds your site, so it should be brief and on target. I've seen cases where people have repeated the title many times in their coding like this:

```
<title>open toed ballet shoes</title>
<title>open toed ballet shoes</title>
<title>open toed ballet shoes</title>
<title>open toed ballet shoes</title>
```

Repetition, some people believe, will cause the search engine to give more weight to the title. Sometimes it works; sometimes it doesn't. I am not recommending this because the search engines may catch on and filter you out. But I have read about cases where it seemed to be effective.

> Don't use fewer than three words in your title or more than six.

Keywords

Although keywords are technically optional, they should be customized (1) for the various search engines and (2) for the vocabulary of the people you want to target.

Keywords announce all the details about your site to a search engine. They are hidden in the code of the Web site and can give different information to the search engines. It's really important to phrase your keywords carefully. Most search engines will look at the first 200 characters of your keywords (a character is a letter, space, or article of punctuation). Don't just use one-word keywords. Use a phrase that you think searchers might look for—"shoe repair" instead of "shoes" or "repairs." According to the latest research, 65% of all searches are conducted using phrases rather than individual words. Couple this with the fact that many of these people have no idea how to search for what they want.

A little intuition on your part comes into play here. Take the time to come up with a set of keywords that exactly fit into the content of your site and its goals and purpose. Put yourself in the shoes of the person looking for your site. What words or phrases would he or she use? Here's an example of good keyword usage for a company that makes steel buildings:

> metal buildings, buildings, metal systems, American Buildings, American Buildings Company, steel buildings, roofing materials, architectural products, heavy fabrication, self-storage, construction products, pre-engineered buildings, systems building, metal roofing, standing seam, metal buildings, metal panels, steel siding, American Steel buildings, metal walls, steel walls, mbma, pre-fabricated steel building.

You can use different keywords on each page of your site. Use plurals when possible instead of singulars because that's how people search—"parakeet breeds" rather than "parakeet breed." A good exercise is to "free associate" with your friends or colleagues. Have them come up with words that describe an aspect of your site.

Use these same keywords in the actual text on your site. However, you don't want to overuse them to the point that they take away from the readability of your document. Further, in an attempt to get the highest relevancy factor from search engines, some people use the keyword repeatedly. Some search engines will actually reject the keyword if it is repeated too often or spammed in your document.

It does no good to put the word *free* in your metatags on a page that includes a price list unless you are also offering something

Search Engine Fees

News alert. Because of heavy spamming, many search engines are now charging for a listing. While the amount is not great, some of them are charging a one-time fee, an annual submission charge, and in some cases monthly submission charges. Some are even charging for each page. Are they worth paying? Yes. Search engines are still the number one source that people turn to when they look for anything. Search engines are now saying "no more free rides." Make your search engine submissions as truthful and accurate as possible. Yahoo! is charging an optional fee. If you pay it they promise to index your site faster. Also, if you are registering several domain names on Yahoo! (or any directory) that are essentially the same site, submit each site on a separate day, so the same person doesn't review your listing.

for free. The mechanics of promotion on the Internet are designed to keep us honest. So you see, you need to put some real effort into designing your Web site, making it focused, and making sure that you deliver what you promise. The more often you use the keyword "free" on your Web page, the better your chances of getting the kind of traffic you want.

Description

The description is what the search engines will display when your Web site is found. It should contain some of your keywords and also sell your service, product, or Web site. It should be no more than a sentence, about 15 to 20 words long. It can be challenging to create a great description because you're trying to keep two masters happy. It has to be appealing enough to cause a surfer to click on it. On the other hand, it should contain good keywords and phrases to get a high ranking. Here's a description for a bridal gown company pulled up by Lycos:

> Discount bridal gowns, bridesmaid dresses, mother of the bride, veils, and accessories. Deep discounts off retail wedding designer retail prices. Free e-mail price quotes on any

It's an excellent description, but have you noticed one flaw? It was too long, so Lycos cut it after the word *any*.

> The description is what the search engines will display when your Web site is found.

Quick tips

✓ After submitting the first time, you may need to tweak your site. You may need to change the content to make sure the keywords are within the parameters for allowable repetition. Do not hesitate to modify your content.

✓ Software submission programs have their place but not for directories like Yahoo! Always take the time to submit properly to Yahoo!

Summary

You can learn the latest search engine strategies from articles available online. Try to subscribe to some newsletters with search engine news. You can use Web-based site promotion tools like Selfpromotion.com. This is a great tool that can help you a lot. You can also logon to *www.laisha.com* (Laisha Designs), a specialist in search engine strategy.

You can learn the latest search engine strategies from articles available online.

For more information on this topic, visit our Web site at www.businesstown.com

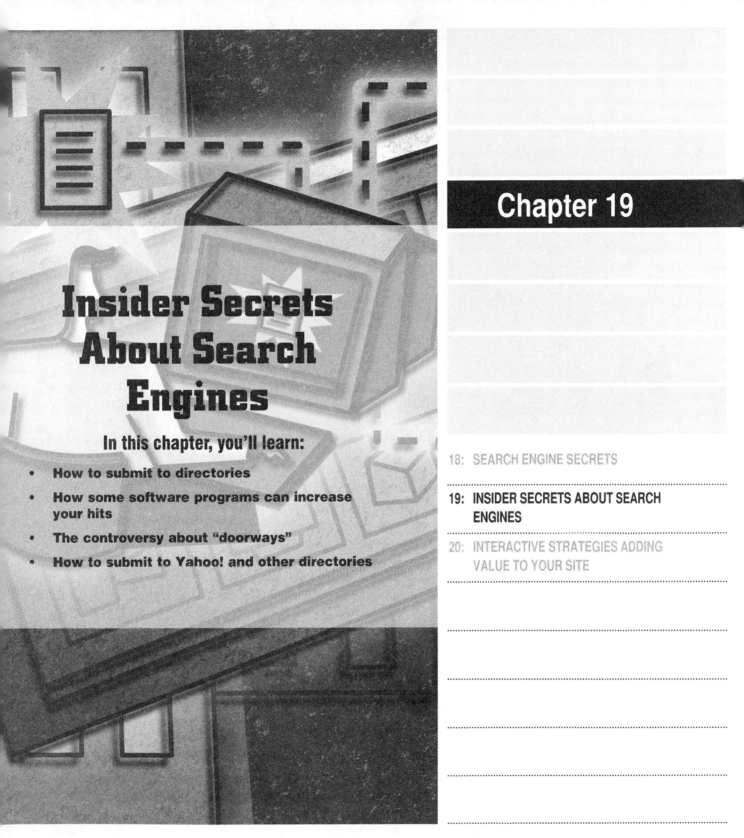

Insider Secrets About Search Engines

In this chapter, you'll learn:

- How to submit to directories
- How some software programs can increase your hits
- The controversy about "doorways"
- How to submit to Yahoo! and other directories

Chapter 19

Directory basics—again

After reading the last chapter, you may think you know everything about search engines. Wrong. To make things even a bit more complicated, some search engines are not search engines at all. They are directories. Yahoo! is representative of directory listings. Because real people man the process, Yahoo! and directories like it may take considerably longer to actually list your site. They tend to be highly selective about what they allow to be placed, and in which directory, so be sure that your site really fits where you want to place it. By the way, latest reports indicate that the easiest way to get into Yahoo! is to position yourself in the local classifications.

A word of caution: You really must read the directions for submission and each site's statement of agreement. They're put there for a reason. Some will give you some really valuable tips about how to get the most out of your listing. Others will define terms and conditions for being listed. Your site is submitted via an online form. Real humans read your submission and then logon to your site to make sure everything is as you say it is on the form. Yahoo! is the biggest of these directories; dmoz (*www.dmoz.org*) is another good one. I have found that their listings are thorough and accurate. Because Yahoo! is so big and so important, I've added a section about submitting to them properly at the end of this chapter.

Directories are great, but there are a few things you should know about them:

- Directories are looked at by humans. Spend time making sure that you're getting into the exact directory for your business or site. Take the time to look through all the listings and submit to the exact category you belong in. The people who edit these directories have their own specialties. If you don't submit to the proper specialist, they might turn down your submission.
- Because they are so backlogged, getting listed with them can take a few months or more. Be patient. Most directories usually don't confirm placement, so you'll have to keep checking back to see if you are indexed.

> Because real people man the process, Yahoo! and directories like it may take considerably longer to actually list your site. They tend to be highly selective about what they allow to be placed, and in which directory, so be sure that your site really fits where you want to place it.

- Once most directories accept your submission, there's no turning back. As a rule, they won't update their database to revise your listing, so take the time to do it right the first time.
- They take longer to process than search engines.

Search engine turnoffs

Just like working with newsgroups, you don't want search engines to think you're trying to trick them, so jettison the spam techniques. If engines think you're trying to get an unfair advantage—even though a mistake may be totally honest—they may ban you from getting listed for life. In Internet terms, life can be two weeks, a month, a year—or even forever. Here are some hard and fast rules to make sure search engines treat you like one of the good guys:

- Keep keywords relevant. If you use irrelevant words just to get traffic—I don't know why you would want to—their robots may spot it. Obviously, the relevancy of certain words is a judgment call, so my recommendation is just don't go too far overboard with your metatags.
- Hiding words in your copy. To get the search engines to look at keywords more than once, some sites hide them in their pages, say, by using black type on a black background. Although you and other surfers can't see them, the engines can. Search engines don't like being fooled. Their robots are getting more and more sophisticated, and it's not worth taking chances. The same goes with using almost microscopic type on your page.
- Don't use a keyword more than five times. Search engines filter for this and may decide to filter you out.
- Don't submit too often, more than once every two weeks or so is adequate.
- Don't submit virtually identical pages and give different file names. That will be interpreted as an attempt to flood the engine.

> Just like working with newsgroups, you don't want search engines to think you're trying to trick them, so jettison the spam techniques.

Optimizing your search engine program

If you really want to score high in the rankings, here's a method that works. Create a different page for each search engine.

1. Go to the search engine you are targeting. A quick way is to open your browser and type the engine name, for instance, HotBot with the suffix .com attached: *www.hotbot.com.*
2. Search for your potential keywords. You can also search through the keywords that your competitors are using.
3. Compare the documents and sites in the first 30 listings. If your enthusiasm wavers during this exercise, you can limit yourself to the first ten listings or even the top five.
4. Logon to each site in either Netscape or Explorer. Compare the source code and look at the sites' headers, especially the keywords. Now look at the actual text on the site. Compare the various sites to determine what they have in common.
5. Change your source code to make it similar to the pages you've just inspected.
6. Repeat these steps for each search engine.

Submitting your site

When it comes to submitting your site, you have many choices. The best rule to follow is "submit it right and submit it often."

- You can do it manually (free). This is the best way. Go to the home page of each search engine. You'll see rules and links for soliciting your site. Though each search engine has its own wording, you see phrases like "Add your site" or "Register URL." Click and follow the instructions. Directories can really boost your traffic and they should be done properly. You should always go to the directory sites like Yahoo! and dmoz, and do it yourself. Plan on about an hour a week doing nothing but submitting your sites to the various major and minor search engines.

Create a different page for each search engine.

- Go to a Web site that will do it for you (free). There are many sites that claim to register your site with a major search engine. In return, some require you to add your name to their mailing list. (And you will get mail—guaranteed.) These are called "auto-submit URL" sites. You will fill out a registration form that asks for keywords, description, Web site title, services offered, and so on. They will submit your information to the most important search engines and scads of smaller ones (over 1,000 at the time of this writing). Although there are no hidden charges—unless you buy their additional services—these sites don't tailor their registration process to the specific search engine, so they won't do the job as thoroughly as you would. There are also so many search engines cropping up and so many different criteria that something is always left out. Three auto-submit sites are *www.simplesubmit.com* (no registration required), *www.addme.com,* and *www.all4one.com.* You might want to try them, but don't rely on them to get you out there in front of your public. You really do need to go directly to the search engine submission pages and do the job right. Each and every search engine is different. Each has different requirements. Some will ask only for your e-mail address and site address, but others will want background information. Still others will want you to specify a classification and give descriptions of your site.
- Hire a company do the submitting for you. I must admit, I've been tempted by companies that charge a fee to submit my Web site. You've seen the ads—"we promise to get your URL in the top ten listings." As I see it, it can't be promised, with new sites coming and going every day. It takes time and skill. If you decide to invest in a service, monitor them closely and ask, "How do you do it?" If they claim they know the search engine secrets that no one else knows, be skeptical.
- Buy a software program to do it for you. Automated submission programs can save you valuable time. In the past,

The Top-rated Search Engines

Lycos
WebCrawler
Thunderstone
Direct Hit
NationalDirectory
Excite
AltaVista
Go.com
HotBot
Galaxy

The Top Rated Guides/Directories

Yahoo!
Open Directory
About.com
Surf Point
Snap
GoTo.com
Clearinghouse
Britannica.com
LookSmart
RealNames
Usenet
Deja.com
RemarQ

automated submitters fell into disfavor because there was (and still is) a cookie cutter reputation about them. Furthermore, many of the search engines are reported to place automated submissions into a lower priority. But things have been changing rapidly, and the software programs are much improved. Some of them keep up with the changing nature of the search engines by constantly updating their algorithm. All can be tried to sample their methodology before you have to pay money. All are available on ZDNet. Here's a rundown on a few of them and what ZDNet says about them:

- **AddWeb** collects and submits all the information required by search engines. You fill in a form, and the program uses your Internet connection to batch-process the submissions to more than 1,500 sites. When the job is done, you can check your ranking with a built-in utility that creates a log of how your site ranks with major directories. To see how well you've done, wait a few days and then run the ranking utility again for comparison.

- **SubmitWolf** provides a tabbed dialog for entering information about the pages you want to register and includes a list of more than 1,000 search engines and links lists to which you can submit your site. It lets you examine details for each engine and categorize engines into groups. After you submit your site, you can check out a submission report detailing the results of your efforts and maintain a history of submissions to avoid doubling up. SubmitWolf also claims to help you select the most appropriate category for each engine.

- **Submitta** is a free Web site promotional tool that automatically submits all of your Web pages to 60 search engines. You just fill in the blanks. It lets you pick from the list of search engines for submission based on size or importance, and then add a description and keywords. Alternatively, you can let Submitta automatically create them from URLs and page content.

Submitta is a free Web site promotional tool that automatically submits all of your Web pages to 60 search engines.

- **Engenius** is a collection of tools designed to help optimize your site—a keyword analyzer and generator, metatag generator, search engine position checker. You cut and paste the code from the Engenius generators into your own pages. Their tips are really helpful. Engenius avoids the most controversial techniques, such as overloading pages full of repeated keywords, and instead focuses on generally accepted techniques.
- **Web Position Gold** analyzes the design and keyword usage on any page in your site. It sees how and reports on how your rankings are doing, and analyzes the search engine performance of your pages over time. You can also use the scheduler to update the search engines regularly. Its real claim to fame is that it creates something called "doorway pages" or "gateway pages." These are pages that nobody sees, except, allegedly, search engines.

Doorway pages

A doorway page is a page designed specifically for a search engine. The search engine sees it, but your surfers do not. They're also known as entry or bridge pages. These pages act as info summaries about the real content of your site. The good thing about using them is you don't have to redesign or modify content in your current Web site's pages. An all-text page, designed for the search engines, make the search engines happy. This page links to your main site and invisibly whisks your visitors there. These pages can be especially useful for Web sites that have a lot of graphics. They also excel with those sites that are in highly competitive situations with everyone using the same keywords. The idea is to keep your current Web site as it is and create dozens of doorway pages, each optimized to rank well for a different keyword in a different engine.

But here's the controversy. Some search engines are now, either rightfully or wrongfully, seeing these pages as spam. As of this writing, however, they are not penalizing sites for using the technique.

> A doorway page is a page designed specifically for a search engine. The search engine sees it, but your surfers do not.

Prepare a set of doorway pages for each search word or search phrase that fits your site. For example, you might want to appear high on the search engines for the words *lobster, gourmet seafood,* and *lobster pot.* You can create a doorway page for each of these keywords—and for each search engine. The thinking is that you must write a page for each engine if you want optimum results.

You can prepare your own doorway site or use one of the programs designed for this purpose. Web Position Gold is one I use.

Here is a sample doorway page to my site. This was generated by Web Position Gold from my keyword input, and allegedly generated to be optimized for AltaVista. Surfers don't see the page, only the search engines do.

If you are searching for any of the following topics:

> new products, product positioning, brand positioning, Barry Feig, brand repositioning, new product marketing, new product development, product strategy, product strategies, product branding, line extensions, product names, new product concepts, concept boards, evaluate new product concepts, brainstorming

At barryfeig.com, you'll discover an easy to use, information packed Web site.

Look no further. You'll find it at barryfeig.com! At barryfeig.com, you'll discover an easy to use, information packed Web site.

Getting listed on top

Sometimes the best ideas are the most obvious. Some search engines alphabetize their lists. So if a site has similar keywords to yours, you can get on top by starting the title of your site with an "A." For example, if your title was "Wonderful Movies," you might want to change it to something like "Absolutely Wonderful Movies." Numbers are also good. In fact sometimes numbers are indexed ahead of the alphabet. It is best if the "A" is part of a word, not just the letter "A."

How long does it take to get listed?

Some search engines will search your site immediately, verifying that it exists, and add your site to their databases. Others will take two to four to six weeks. So if you are working under time constraints, say, for a launch or a special promotion, you'll want to plan accordingly. Submission to search engines will take anywhere from a couple of hours to a couple of months to complete. Now, it would be nice if you could just stop there. But you can't. The initial submission is just the beginning. You need to go back regularly and resubmit.

Search engines are backlogged. I've been hearing that some engines get 9,000 requests per hour! Directories take more time since they need human intervention. It is a good practice to resubmit the pages once every 30 or 40 days whether your site has been listed or not.

> Some search engines will search your site immediately, verifying that it exists, and add your site to their databases. Others will take two to four to six weeks.

Test your keywords

Once you've submitted you site, it's not the time to leave the Web promotion process and twiddle your thumbs. Now you must monitor your progress. To find out if you are listed in a particular search engine, query using your URL or domain name as the keyword.

If your site has been listed, you may want to know where you rank. To find your rank, you can use a position analysis tool. Many are available free on the Internet. You insert your keywords, and they will tell you how you rank in the major search engines. One good one is Position Agent at *www.bcentral.com*. You can also use one of the software submission programs mentioned earlier. If you can find your site in the first 20 positions, you have done a good job.

What people are looking for

Wouldn't it be great if you could read the minds of searchers and see what they're searching for right now and how they're searching?

The site *http://voyeur.mckinley.com/cgi-bin/voyeur.cgi* has a feature that allows you to see exactly what other people on the Internet are searching for. This will give you an idea of what the hot topics of the day are and what words people use to search with. If you can use some of that information on your own site, you will stand a better chance of getting traffic.

Though you'd like to hear that people are searching for *your* Web site, the answer may surprise you. At any given moment, 20 to 25% of all people searching on the Internet are searching for sex-related material. The good news is that about three-fourths of the people are *not* searching for porno. This site also shows common searches: *http://home.pon.net/kenw/keywords/index.htm*.

You can get a free list of the most popular keywords sent to you each week from *www.wordtracker.com*. They will filter out all the porno requests for you.

How individual search engines work

It is easier to get information on the molecular structure of the DNA double helix than to get information about the inner workings of search engines. The following information has been gleaned from the help sections of each engine, articles I have sifted through on the Internet, and research studies I have uncovered.

AltaVista

AltaVista indexes the description and keywords up to a limit of about 1,000 characters. They strongly dislike sites with numerous keywords or with keywords that have no relation to what browsers will see. They complain about sites that regularly submit large numbers of pages.

Excite

Excite claims they do not honor metatags at all, believing it protects users from unreliable information.

HotBot

HotBot uses a confidence or relevance factor that displays as a percentage of points. This relevance factor is determined by how many times the words used in a query are in a document and how close they are together. HotBot attaches a score to each document that matches the requirements of a search. In general, the more a certain word appears in a document, the higher the score. However, the uniqueness of the word also has an impact. Common words like "boat" contribute less to the score than rare and discriminating words like "dhow."

Pages that use search terms in the title are ranked significantly higher than documents that contain the search term in the text only. Pages that use your search terms in the keywords metatag will be weighted higher than text words. Document length is important, too. When the search words appear frequently in a short document, the page will be ranked higher than when the words appear in a long document.

On the negative side, HotBot looks unkindly at "spoofing," duplicating words thousands of times in comments or keywords, or including a large number of "invisible" words in a tiny font or in the same color as the background color of the page.

Infoseek

For Infoseek, the description should be no more than 200 characters. The keywords should be no more than 1,000 characters. Don't repeat words too often. If you do, they may remove your site from the index altogether. They rely on the contents of your page, as well as metatags to get the description and keywords.

WebCrawler

WebCrawler (which is owned by Excite) is on guard against irrelevant, unsolicited information. At the time of this writing, they have started reindexing their listed sites and are throwing off those that offend.

How Charlatans Can Cost You Money

I met a person the other day who was paying $2,000 a year for a person to watch and optimize Yahoo! It's a total waste of money because once Yahoo! (a directory) indexes something, they rarely update your listing. It's a great example of people spending money on the Internet and getting absolutely nothing in return. Monitor your spending closely, because even small expenses add up to a great deal of money and can diminish your profits.

Getting listed in Yahoo!

Yahoo! is the big kahuna in search engines with over 15 million hits every day. Since it is a must for both surfers and Web sites, I decided to devote a whole section to it.

Yahoo! looks for the keywords in the Web address, page title, and the description you enter when submitting on their form. They don't look at your metatags. The most important information is the description you enter on your form.

Do your homework. Search through Yahoo! for sites like your own and use similar descriptions to existing sites. Yahoo! lists sites alphabetically and sorts by the page title. Carefully eyeball the categories and try to find a category that starts with the beginning letters for the alphabet sorted by the page title. Always try to list in a category that starts with "A" or "B."

At the time of this writing, Yahoo! was using a new format that showed directories first and individual sites second, so with Yahoo! an alphabetical listing becomes more important. When you are deciding on the ideal directory, choose the most relevant "at the top of the selections."

Go to the category that best suits your site and enter your URL. The deeper and more specific the category, the better. Note, also, that Yahoo! gives preference to professionally designed graphics. Your site must be totally finished, or they will not list you.

Although Yahoo! asks for a 20-word description, I have heard they really only want about 10 words. Be honest and don't obscure the reason d'être of your site with too much hype. That kind of stuff is too hard for their indexers to read day in and day out. Indexers want to have fun, too.

Yahoo! may give extra points if you have a Yahoo! e-mail address. I was told this was true, and it sounded cute so I figured I would make the point. Sites with short domain names are listed faster that those with complicated names.

Fill out all fields on the form, even if the form says it is optional. Double check your work to make sure you fill out the form exactly as required. If this sounds like grade school stuff, that's because it is. Neatness counts with Yahoo!

> At the time of this writing, Yahoo! was using a new format that showed directories first and individual sites second.

The trick with Yahoo! is to be patient, follow the rules when submitting, and try to make it simple for them to list you. If you choose the wrong directory, they are unlikely to take the time to correct it. Yahoo! receives approximately 25,000 requests per week and can currently process about 10,000. So a backlog is created very quickly. They do not have the time to correct your mistakes.

If your site has not been listed after two weeks, you will have to resubmit since they have been known to lose information. You can resubmit every two weeks safely. Submit only by hand to Yahoo! since you need to be specific.

Getting and maintaining search engine positionings

This list was put together by Laisha Designs (*http://laisha.com*), the preeminent specialist in search engine positioning. Here they list the prerequisites for getting and staying on the top rungs of search engine listings:

- Optimization of Web site, including meta title, meta description, and meta keywords using terms that not only describe your site but are actually used by people utilizing the search engines.
- Manual submission to the major search engines and directories as well as any language-specific, geographic-specific, or industry-specific search engines you wish.
- Monthly search engine standings report that documents where you ranked for each search term and on each search engine and directory, and compares it to the last month's rankings. Monthly reassessment of search engine standings based on those reports.
- Monthly adjustment of metatags or descriptions and titles in order to bring your site higher in the search engines and directories, as appropriate

> Submit only by hand to Yahoo! since you need to be specific.

Keep good records

With all the search engines and their different specifications and rules, it's hard to keep track of what you sent to whom, especially if you're sending out multiple pages. This gets more problematical because some search engines will penalize you for submitting too often. Keep a record of the date you submitted, the page, the description (if you change it for each search engine), and the name of the search engine itself.

Some resources

Here are some links where you can find useful site promotion resources.

- *www.selfpromotion.com.* This is one of our favorite sites. A great and cool site, it contains a lot of information. It has a Web-based tool developed by the site's owner, Robert Woodhead, that will be really helpful. You can read his article on Yahoo! at our site. And you can make use of his secret tools like Rankulator if you pay a little.
- *www.freepromote.com.* There are lots of good articles and free promotional stuff at this site.
- *www.searchenginewatch.com.* This site offers great tips and news about each search engine's characteristics and secret tips for paid subscribers. It's a must for all Webmasters.
- *www.searchengineforums.com.* This is an archive of all the search engine message boards and some site promotion forums. You can post your questions on the board and exchange ideas with other users.
- *www.linkpopularity.com.* Link popularity is the total number of Web sites that link to your site. It's important because good link popularity can dramatically increase traffic to your Web site. Well-placed links are an excellent source of consistent and targeted traffic. And, because of recent developments, they can even generate additional search engine traffic to your site. You can check your link popularity here. We feel some search engines are giving weight to link popularity, too.

Exercise Diligence with Search Engines

This past year there was a big hullabaloo about one search engine that stated that all content submitted to it would become the property of that search engine. Of course, with public pressure, they rescinded that statement, but it caused a great deal of upheaval when people began to realize what was happening. Remember that we live in the information age and the most valuable commodity you have is your unique information and your work. If you give it away for lack of due diligence, you have no one to blame but yourself.

On the other hand, the vast majority of people and businesses on the Internet—like you and me—are honest and conscientious. There really is no reason to be paranoid—but *do* exercise caution.

On the other hand, the vast majority of people and businesses on the Internet—like you and me—are honest and conscientious. There really is no reason to be paranoid, but *do* exercise caution.

Quick tips

✓ Study the results of your strategic search engine program each month. If you don't land in the top 20 and your competitor's do, analyze their content and metatags.

✓ Don't forget the mantra: Submit often and submit well.

Summary

Although many people want to learn the ins and outs of registering with search engines and directories, it's hard to figure out because the rules are always changing. Directories are sorted by card-carrying humans who may be in a bad mood that one day you decide to submit, so it's best to be honest and forthcoming.

> Directories are sorted by card-carrying humans who may be in a bad mood that one day you decide to submit, so it's best to be honest and forthcoming.

For more information on this topic, visit our Web site at www.businesstown.com

Interactive Strategies Adding Value to Your Site

In this chapter, you'll learn:

- How to create interactive strategies that will earn you referrals from people who visit your site

- Interactive strategies to make your site a destination

- How to use cookies

Chapter 20

Back in the Stone Age days, before America Online became the powerhouse it is today, it was competing against Prodigy, which was then owned by the vast consortium of Sears and IBM. A no-brainer, most people thought. AOL would be relegated to the island of lost companies. There was no way tiny AOL would be able to stand against the financial might of two of the largest companies in America. Prodigy would step on and snuff out AOL like a half-smoked cigarette. Both companies prepared for a mighty war.

Both Prodigy and AOL tried to build their content up quickly and dramatically to capture visitors in the so-called Information Age. Both companies focused on education, creating huge lists of encyclopedias and reference material. Both had started e-mail services, but neither, then, knew how e-mail would change the face of the Internet.

Then Prodigy made a key mistake. They started charging for e-mails. It seemed like an innocent move at the time because the people who were using e-mails were few, and IBM noticed that just a few people were responsible for most of the e-mail. Heck, the U.S. Post Office charges money, and e-mails were going to cost only 10 cents each per address. Prodigy didn't plan on the media clamor that was soon to change everything. There was a ton of publicity. The publicity brought the term *e-mail* into the public realm. People quickly learned how this new form of communication would fit into their lives. Many people deserted Prodigy for AOL, which soon had the consumer e-mail business virtually to itself.

A little while later, AOL introduced a tiny little service called the Instant Message. People could talk with people online at their computer, by typing in text. Then came the Buddy List. People could see who was online and available to talk. Little by little, AOL kept adding value to its site.

> Although AOL was spending big bucks on content, people wanted community.

People flocked to AOL. Although AOL was spending big bucks on content, people wanted community. So AOL jettisoned most of its content and reinvented itself as a new medium of communication with more than 10 million subscribers. People feel a shared purpose between AOL and themselves—a sense of community. People feel that the interactivity that AOL offers is a real value.

In this chapter, we'll be exploring interactive ways to build and keep traffic by developing satisfied, long-term customers. We'll explore ways to add more value and ideas to make visitors to your Web site stick like glue.

Lots of traffic isn't enough anymore

To understand "sticky" sites (just try to use the phrase in a meeting without hearing at least one snicker), study the evolution of Yahoo! Ever since the Web gained mainstream popularity, Yahoo! has been one of the busiest sites around.

Three years ago, Yahoo! was much like a 7-Eleven store, which people popped in and out of rapidly to pick up the mere essentials. In fact, the average user was on Yahoo! less than two minutes per session and saw only three pages.

That makes it pretty tough to make money when the revenues come from exposing users to ads. So Yahoo! started the odd practice of adding unrelated functions to its search engine.

First came news headlines, then My Yahoo! with personalized pages, and later, stock portfolio tracking. In recent months, they've added online calendars, address books, and even airline flight tracking.

> Ever since the Web gained mainstream popularity, Yahoo! has been one of the busiest sites around.

How to keep people glued to your site

Simple, give people more of what they care about and keep adding the new services that give consumers what they want. Sure, your site needs to be visually appealing and easy to navigate, but most people aren't online to see cool, animated graphics or to test out the latest search engine. They are online to learn more about the subjects they care about. They are online because people like you develop content that shouts *"I'm there for you!"*

People go more frequently to their favorite sites and stay longer on those sites because they have discovered content that is meaningful. They stay on these sites—willingly and enthusiastically—because of the relationship they develop with the publishers of the site. They perceive a certain value.

When you give consumers what they want, they will come back for more. It's called a "value-added benefit." A true value should offer consumers something special. Value isn't what you put in your site; it's what your customer takes out of it. Though people probably aren't paying money to visit your site, they are investing time and want to spend their time wisely. The value of a Web site is its value to the visitor. The higher the value to the visitor, the higher the value will be to the advertiser. For a specialty site, stickiness is relatively easy. With a more general site, you need more interactive hooks.

Add new services

Service companies looking for greater stickiness can find it easily. The key is to think in terms of a wider scope of your overall customer's needs. You may have a niche market, but your visitor may want information beyond your narrow area. For example, a roofer looking for business can add insider information and tips that will show visitors how to do it themselves. The roofer may offer an evaluation of various types of shingles. It's really unimportant whether the visitors would actually shingle their own roofs; however, it is important to stickiness that the site owner gives the appearance of trying to help. Our roofer could start an advice column, answering questions about roofing or even home renovations. He could even start a traffic-building e-mail campaign from the addresses of the people asking questions.

One of the fun aspects of adding new services to your site is that it's often not a great deal of work. It involves partnering with other sites that provide complimentary services. Perhaps our roofer can branch out into vinyl and paint.

To get more traffic, focus on your core business and tend to as many of your visitors' needs as possible. Look for companies that are doing something better and cheaper than you can and make them an integral part of your site promotion.

> Service companies looking for greater stickiness can find it easily. The key is to think in terms of a wider scope of your overall customer's needs.

Using cookies to make your site more valuable

Most retail stores know that to be successful, they need to go out of their way to coddle good customers and create a file on their key preferences. The best salespeople address their customers by name and know their preferences. They bring specially selected merchandise to the front of the store and ask their customers to choose rather than having them go to the back of the store to the racks like the "riff-raff." Web visitors are no less important. Each Web visitor appreciates the extra attention that comes from being considered special. It's a natural part of having a relationship with a customer. It pays to recognize steady Web visitors and to treat them differently from people who stop by once or twice a year. According to recent studies on online shopping, shoppers feel strong about personalizing their Web experience. They show a high level of acceptance and appreciation of the use of profiles and personalization to improve their online experience.

A strategy for personalizing a Web site is to use cookies. Cookies are tiny pieces of information that are placed on your visitors' computer. It's a small file that stores personal information. You can retrieve this information any time a visitor logs on. Using this information, you can create a custom page for the visitor.

A cookie helps you track who is on your Web site and where they go in your Web site. With cookies, you can customize your site so that it best appeals to each individual Web traveler. When a visitor logs on, a cookie will tell you when his previous visits were, what he bought, which pages he stopped on . . . and even his name so you can custom tailor his Web experience with you. It happens automatically. When a purchase is made in the site ordering system, the cookie is retrieved and a record is made of the source of the sale. You can use cookies to your best advantage by creating custom pages for each visitor.

For example, let's say you have a business that issues tickets for sporting and entertainment events. When a visitor enters your site, you can display the best tickets according to the person's interest, schedule, and habits. By using cookies, you can even determine if the person would rather see offerings from Santana (a classic rock group) or the Boston Philharmonic.

It should be noted that cookies are getting a bad rap from consumer privacy organizations. They say that they invade privacy. They're not entirely wrong. I have had many requests from people who wanted me to rid their computers of cookies so others could not track where they went. If you are going to use cookies, make it clear on your site and tell consumers how to shut the cookie option off. (By the way, even though people can turn off their cookies, 80% of people don't.)

> Cookies are tiny pieces of information that are placed on your visitors' computer.

Five ways to use cookies

- Obtain information about your customers' visits and make the experience better for you and for them with specially designed navigation tools.
- Customize your site for each visitor.
- Generate banners that only some people will see.
  - Modify the information you present to each of your Web visitors to fit that particular visitor's interests and habits.
  - Save visitors time by identifying them from their cookie instead of forcing them to use passwords. It's a great deal friendlier.

Figures 20.1, 20.2, and 20.3 show screen shots of cookies. Notice how each page is personalized with my name and preferences.

The technological aspects and the ins and outs of using cookies are beyond the scope of this book. If you're interested in fine-tuning your Web marketing effort in this way, ask your ISP, Web-hosting provider, or a consultant to help.

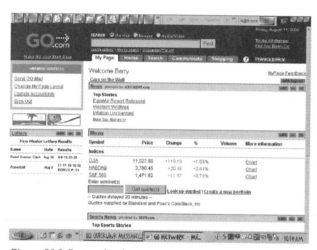

Figure 20.1: Personalized *www.go.com*

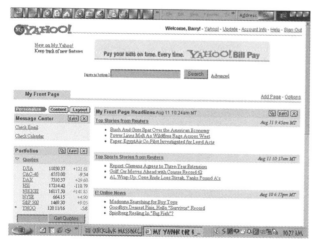

Figure 20.2: Personalized *www.yahoo.com*

Figure 20.3: Personalized *www.espn.com*

Create an advice or a review column

The Web is a place where you can convince clients that you are an expert in your field and that you understand their needs. Your know-how is marketable on the Web. It's part of what keeps people coming back. Creating an opinion center helps to establish your site as a "no-holds-barred" authority in your field.

Although many sites like to put professional opinions (taken from magazines, newspapers, and such) of products they sell on a site, it's a fact of life that people frequently attach more credence to the opinions of their friends and peers.

Some years ago when Amazon.com was just a bookstore, it started the trend of soliciting and presenting the opinions of its visitors. In addition to including excerpts from the standard publishers, Amazon allowed readers to rate books based on a five-star scale and to post comments of their own. It was an immediate hit.

Don't underestimate the power of helping people make decisions about buying something or helping them choose a supplier. Siskel and Ebert built a franchise by helping people decide what movies to see or not to see. In my other life as a marketing columnist, I make my living by reviewing new products and telling retailers what products to stock and what products to stay away from. Advice on consumer purchasing decisions has been the staple of magazines like *Consumer Reports, PC Magazine, Car and Driver,* and others.

Bond with surfers and create strong word-of-mouth referrals by recommending which products and services to buy and warning what products to stay away from. Many Internet retailers and some publishers have already capitalized on this by allowing users to post opinions about products the companies sell or review. It keeps users coming to the site to get information that is available "nowhere else."

Epinions (*www.epinions.com*) is a site that has grown by leaps and bounds—even relative to the freneticism of the Internet. The site's sole purpose is to furnish advice on products. Prospective shoppers browse through categories of reviews and select the reviews that they're most interested in. I just came across

> It's a fact of life that people frequently attach more credence to the opinions of their friends and peers.

that site, and it is causing me a lot of delays because I am now addicted. I've been looking at the reviews to see how my feelings about a particular product stack up against the raters. Since I'm looking at some new pieces of office equipment, I'm finding out which are a good buy and which sound as if they would quickly become useless trash. Because of several reviews I read on the site, I have narrowed the list of laptops I was considering. Thank you, Epinions.

It's easy to get opinions from people. Just ask your visitors. Put a button on your site that says, "Give an opinion on (whatever)." To get reviews, Epinions offers royalties of $1 to $5 for every 10 times a person's review is read by an Epinions member. Sometimes Epinions features the reviewer's bio and even a photo. Because of the impartiality of the reviews, the site has built up a spirit of trust, which brings surfers back time and again. It works like a word-of-mouth advertising campaign.

> To set up a review column, you can either write your own opinion or have visitors write them, but you must give an appearance of impartiality.

To set up a review column, you can either write your own opinion or have visitors write them, but you must give an appearance of impartiality. Opinions should be free and unbiased, and be based on the real-life experiences of you and your visitors. Surprisingly, you don't have to worry about hurting the feelings of companies and products that you review negatively. My experience has shown that most take the criticism good-naturedly and welcome (maybe "welcome" isn't the right word) the feedback.

Opinion columns can be tailored for a great many sites. If you're selling beauty products on the Web, you can run a poll on which wrinkle cream works best. If you're selling sporting goods, you can offer your valued knowledge on which tennis racquets are best, even which racquet strings perform best.

Cater to an informed surfer

In keeping with this concept of valuing your visitors' opinions and input, keep in mind that there are a lot of offshoot benefits that come from soliciting the input of others (your customers).

Informed clientele can work to the advantage of an enterprise. Lee Noga, of Z Master Productions, a company that publishes sex-oriented CD-ROMs, agrees that online consumers are more critical than street buyers but says that their suggestions are more useful. She claims she's developed entire productions from e-mail input. And Karen Fritsche, of the Stockroom (which sells sex aids and toys), says that customers have voluntarily posted the company's catalog on bulletin boards and have distributed links to its catalog archives.

Give expert advice

It's said that free advice is worth what you pay for it. But based on the e-mail from my site, it's something everyone wants. It's probably one of the simplest ways to get and keep traffic—and there are many ways to implement advice sections. Newspapers know that Q&A (question and answer) columns are the most widely read sections of the newspaper.

For this reason, you should position yourself as an expert and set aside time each week to update your site and answer visitors' questions. Include a department where you can regularly solicit questions—called something like "ask the experts." Readers will come back to see if you have responded to their personal questions, but more will avidly read your column to see how you answered others' questions. At the beginning, seed your advice sections with your own questions to get the ball rolling.

EXP.com offers real opinions and answers to site visitors' questions at their Web site. It covers a wide range of subject areas and enables consumers to buy advice and services on topics ranging from career planning and tax shelters to what types of roses to plant.

EXP.com currently serves millions of unique visitors each week. Individual advice seekers can find an expert who suits their needs by scanning all experts' profiles in a topic area.

You can create a how-to and advice column for your site, or you can generate name and Web site recognition by signing on as

> It's said that free advice is worth what you pay for it. But based on the e-mail from my site, it's something everyone wants.

> Offering free classified ads brings both sellers and buyers to your site. The seller needs to place an ad and come back time and again to see how the ad is doing.

an expert at EXP.com. Whichever way you decide to do it, free advice can be golden to attracting and keeping traffic.

Go classified

Before the Internet became popular in the days when people got their hands ink-stained and slippery by turning pages in a newspaper, there was a big newspaper strike. A poll asked readers what they missed most by not having a daily paper to thumb through. By a landslide, people missed the classified advertising most. Consider developing a classified section for your site.

Developing a classified ad section works on several different levels. Offering free classified ads brings both sellers and buyers to your site. The seller needs to place an ad and come back time and again to see how the ad is doing. The buyer who is looking for a particular product has to keep coming back to see what's being offered.

To see two classified ad sections fully optimized, look at *www.recycler.com* and *www.iwant.com.* Recycler.com allows business ads to run two weeks for $5 and will add a link to your Web site for another $5 for two weeks. It is also possible to have links published in the local print editions.

iWant.com focuses on the "wanted to buy" side of the classified advertising equation. The site also offers sellers the opportunity to look for shoppers they want to sell their products to.

Quick tips

✓ If you don't want to create an opinion column but want to establish your expertise as an expert reviewer, go to one of the opinion sites and offer to review products in return for a link to your page.

✓ Personalize your site well, and you will offer more value to your customers.

Summary

You can create your own sense of community and dramatically increase traffic by adding more services to your site. One of the keys to making people stay on your site longer and visit more often is for you to build relations with them. People stay on sites they know and trust, and on sites that provide a perceived value. In Internet-speak, this is called stickiness.

> You can create your own sense of community and dramatically increase traffic by adding more services to your site.

For more information on this topic, visit our Web site at www.businesstown.com

Tools You Can Use Right Now

Summary of Section V

- **Building community, not just a site**
- **Adapting strategies from the seedier side of the Net**
- **Learning about banners, ads, and how to measure your success**
- **Business to business strategies**

Create a Portal to the World and More Strategies for Building Community

In this chapter, you'll learn:

- How to further foster community
- How to build your own portal to the world
- How to create and use Web logs and Blogs
- How to create a push strategy
- Further ideas to keep people coming back to your site and staying there longer

Chapter 21

Sometimes people want information on more than your products and services. Sometimes they want to expand their range beyond your products and into the rest of the Web. Promote as the big guys do by putting a mini-portal on your Web site. Yes, this is the same type of portal that made Yahoo! and Netscape famous.

A mini-portal is both a starting point and a gateway to many other sites on the net. Though they work the same way as links, they are much larger in scale. There are more links, and there is a larger variety. Your portal revolves around your industry and your target market.

You don't have to be one of the big guys to design your own portal. You can create an "affinity mini-portal." This is a gateway aimed at a small segment of the Internet population, usually a small interest group. Some segmented mini-portals that exist deal only with hobbies, jobs, political parties, or religions. Although at one time, designing a portal program would have been insanely expensive, there is a new idea emerging that has brought renewed spirit to them.

Rather than spend large amounts of money to attract groups to come to a particular portal—it's the promotional money that eats the bucks—you can work with associations that already cater to specialized groups to build portals aimed at their own memberships. It ensures a loyal user base and even a free flow of revenue from advertising and commercial transactions.

At least two companies specialize in designing mini-portals—Verilytics (the biggest) and Everyone.net. Both companies build and maintain the portal.

The portal, which becomes the startup page for subscribers, includes smaller versions of features that users would find on the big portals, including e-mail, shopping, chat areas, and news and financial information. The difference is that the content for each organization is tailored to that group's interests.

For instance, if you were a financial services company, you might offer news on financial matters and courtroom disputes. The Teamsters site (*http://teamsters.workingfamilies.com*) includes information on sports labor disputes. In the shopping area, users find

---

Promote as the big guys do by putting a mini-portal on your Web site.

Web Sites Need Constant Updates

Portals, advice columns, and especially chat rooms and forums can help keep traffic on your Web site. But they take daily care and activity. Before you choose an interactive feature, make sure you have the time to keep it current and newsy. For most of these interactive programs, you'll have to update your site once or even twice daily.

items sold by manufacturers with unionized workforces. For example, union-friendly shoppers can purchase Callaway golf clubs, which are made by members of the United Steelworkers of America, or Easter candy from See's, whose workers also are unionized.

The portal makers say they pay the marketing costs to raise awareness of each group's site among its membership. In return, the groups sign a five-year contract. Verilytics gets 75% of the revenue generated from shopping and advertising. Your group agrees to help Verilytics market the site within their organizations. Promotion is typically through newsletters, e-mail, and publicity at trade shows. The physical layout of the portal is headlined with your logo or the group's logo. Members get standard Internet portal features like news, weather, stock quotes, and specific content; links to group Web sites and activities; and community-building tools and activities. Groups control the content of their custom portal; members use the portal to combine their group affiliations and interests with personal ones. A smaller version, Travelhost, has an excellent mini-portal.

To create community, create Web logs

You may not have heard of them, but Web logs have been around a while. As a "community builder," they are a hybrid of a bulletin board and a link list. Web logs let people post commentary and Web sites in a sort of shared portal-building/media-creating frenzy. Web logs consist of shared posts and responses from thousands of people on a diverse variety of subjects. They bring news, community, and Web surfing together into an incredible collage of content.

One company to look at for examples and software is Blog. As the originator of Blog (also called Web logs) says on her Web site:

> It was (originally) a place to put bookmarks. I was constantly quoting articles that I could never find the links for again. A journal was born at the same time. I needed to vent my frustrations about how miserable I was at my job. (All the good bits have since been removed.) Those ventings that actually had a topic, other than my job, landed in the rants section.

> You may not have heard of them, but Web logs have been around a while. As a "community builder," they are a hybrid of a bulletin board and a link list.

Blogs represent several opportunities. They are a great way to do informal market research, and they are a great place to find out what your customers are thinking and doing. You can learn what's troubling customers, what they do on the Web, and where they cruise.

You can organize Blogs around your industry. Blogs can be a great way to build community and create word-of-mouth about your site. As the supersites know, combining information with community can be lightning in a bottle—a powerful mix. Creating your own Web log for your product lets you combine customer support with customer input and vertical market news in one compelling package.

A simple way to develop your own Web Blog is to use a program called Blogger (what else?). It lets you post your own Web logs without installing any software on your site. It's simple. You get e-mails from your customers, decide which should be posted, and then you post it. The logs blend into your server. You can get the software and some more samples of Blogs at *www.blogger.com*.

> A simple way to develop your own Web Blog is to use a program called Blogger (what else?).

Let's talk about chat rooms

Create even more community with chat rooms Give people an easier way to find and talk to like-minded people. They will form ad-hoc special-interest groups and extend into other community activities. As I mentioned earlier, when AOL created Instant Messaging and chat rooms, I'm not sure they knew how powerful these devices would be in creating community and traffic. There are really only two kinds of chat rooms that you have to be aware of:

- The chat "event," where a celebrity or alleged expert answers questions from users (I say "alleged" because I have hosted several of these). These can help generate traffic and allow you to become the voice of authority. For examples, go to AOL's business forum—use the keyword BusinessKnowHow. It's run by Janet Attard, and she is the best on conducting professional forums with real meat.

- The open forum, where a community chats in a moderated free-form session. Open chat forums, on the other hand, can build a loyal community, but can also wreak havoc on a company's image if a user chooses to criticize or "flame" the site during a chat. Garden.com hosts open chat rooms while peddling goods mentioned in the chats. When folks go to a chat site, they tend to linger awhile (an average of 26 minutes) and return regularly.

Chats can be loud and boisterous, informative and inane, but they're a great way to attract people to your site and make them stay there. Out of 10 million subscribers on AOL, 300,000 of them are in chat rooms at any given moment.

The push concept

Push, the granddaddy of Internet marketing paradigms, is a simple concept—deliver an extremely important message (in your eyes, anyway) to an Internet consumer instead of making him or her go get it. It's unlike TV where you need to change channels to find what you want. It's also the opposite of surfing where people have to jump from Web site to Web site in hopes of finding what they want. Push marketing is an interactive method for responding to your customers' needs—even before he or she asks. With push technology, in theory, people get what they want automatically. Let's say you like wine from a certain vintner and you want your favorite e-store to tell you whenever that vintner introduces a new product. The store will send you an e-mail telling you a new product is now in stock. Push technology has become more and more popular to Web marketers who want to go after business rather than waiting for it to come to them

Sending e-mails offering information to a list of subscribers is the simplest form of push. You can actually send your whole Web site to subscribers with HTML coding.

A common mistake is to push too hard. When you allow a consumer to subscribe to a flow of content, keep it simple. Send small

> Chats can be loud and boisterous, informative and inane, but they're a great way to attract people to your site and make them stay there.

amounts of highly targeted information. The trick is to offer to deliver small bits of valuable content. Make it sharp, and make it pertinent. Specificity makes the customer appreciate it without relegating it to the junk mail quick delete e-mail box:

- Create a triggered push. Travelocity.com offers a great bit of push technology. When an airfare rises or falls to a certain point, they send me an e-mail (hoping obviously) that I will buy the ticket from them.
- If you're a stockbroker, you might want to notify specific customers when a price falls.
- If you're a wine broker, you can let your customer know when a new case of his favorites has arrived.

> The average person has six e-mail accounts from a variety of sites.

Offer e-mail and datebooks

The average person has six e-mail accounts from a variety of sites. The beauty of an e-mail account is that people have to come to your site to check it. Going a bit further, companies are offering third-party online calendars, datebooks, reminder services, and task minders through their sites. This means that people feel welcome; they feel that you care about what happens to them and that some aspect of your Web site will help them solve their problem.

Homesteading creates a base for surfers

Give people a free plot of land in cyberspace (a free home page), and then let them gather into neighborhoods of interest. GeoCities is the best known of these sites. Other favorites include Tripod and WhoWhere? (both now owned by Lycos) and theglobe.com. Users can create a place within the site where they can post personal pages and photo albums, set up group calendars and group address books, participate in private chat rooms, and create newsgroups.

Quick tips

✓ Build value into your Web site to make visitors stick around longer.

✓ Keep offering freebies and small gimmicks. Then sell visitors on your other services.

Summary

Don't think that the options we've explored here to keep visitors at your site for longer periods of time is a strategy just for the big boys of the Internet. A sticky strategy of this kind makes even more sense for companies that don't have ambitions of making their sites a portal. Strategic partnerships make it possible to provide lots of resources so as to maintain the involvement of visitors for relatively little cost.

A demanding customer base can easily eat up the savings gained on the marketing side of the ledger.

Traffic is a marketable commodity. With substantial traffic and repeat visitors, a Web site becomes a valuable commodity, one that is sought out by power marketers who are willing to pay to expand their exposure.

> Build value into your Web site to make visitors stick around longer.

For more information on this topic, visit our Web site at www.businesstown.com

Follow the Lead of the Seedier Side of the Net and Even More Strategies

In this chapter, you'll learn:

- **How the sex industry brought about many changes to the Internet**
- **How to use viral marketing**
- **How to enter and win Web award competitions**

Chapter 22

The seedier side of the Internet

Whether you approve of porn sites and such or not, they do provide insights into strong marketing methods that work on the Internet. Pornography sites have pioneered technical and marketing developments that are at the heart of the business plans of many enterprises that would not be caught dead on the same server.

An informal survey of developers of sex sites shows that nearly all of them are planning to add new categories of business rather than target narrower niches. Some of those sites function like small Internets, branching off more and more services. New World Erotica runs classified advertising and operates online movie theaters, chat rooms, videoconferences, and a "mall" that sells videos, CDs, and other physical goods. We can learn from the sex industry. One lesson is that selling information, products, and services in a high-competition arena means keeping up with the demand for ever-friendlier sites and the use of new multimedia toys.

The sex category was the first to commercialize videoconferencing over ordinary phone lines, a service that brings the industry the largest share of its revenues. Before this, videoconferencing over the slow connections used by home computers was difficult, requiring special software and direct connections for videoconferencing.

Sex sites were probably also the first to make marketable products out of online animation delivery, downloadable video clips, interactive videos, real-time video feeds, and streaming video (video that runs while it's being downloaded).

Viral marketing

Wouldn't it be great if you could have your site visitors serve as missionaries for your Web site and carry your site promotion to others? You can. It's called viral marketing—named after the way viruses multiply rapidly—and it's an increasingly important process. It is an advertising method that, once released, is quickly spread

> An informal survey of developers of sex sites shows that nearly all of them are planning to add new categories of business rather than target narrower niches.

by others with little or no control from the originator. But it is still yours. You create an e-mail about your product, service, or site, and you encourage others to send the e-mail to still others, using their own network or relationships.

Perhaps the most famous and successful example of viral marketing is Hotmail. Their message ("get your private, free e-mail from Hotmail") was tagged to the bottom of every e-mail sent by customers using their Hotmail account. It spread like wildfire. This resulted in explosive growth for Hotmail—within a few short years, the company had over 30 million accounts.

Hotmail's viral marketing strategy was quite accidental; the concept of the signature line was an afterthought and almost never implemented!

So, Hotmail proved without doubt how effective viral marketing could be. The concept has now been online for a few years, and it is still successful. Another example is the ubiquitous chain mails or "jokes of the day." Each carries a message encouraging the recipient to send the note to a friend—carrying the site owner's marketing message. If you can write quality articles, or offer unique services, you can offer them to others to use on their Web sites or in their newsletters. Each article should carry a link to your Web site and a notice suggesting that readers send it along to their friends.

The best thing about viral marketing is that it's free. Viral marketing methods have evolved over the years. The viral approach can be one of the most cost-effective and explosive marketing strategies found online—if used right.

> Hotmail's viral marketing strategy was quite accidental; the concept of the signature line was an afterthought and almost never implemented!

How to construct your own campaign

First, you must consider and understand the basic principles of how a real virus thrives. To thrive, a virus must be able to survive and reproduce. At its center, or nucleus, is something useful or interesting—something that users are motivated to pass on. Therefore, we need something that people are going to be interested in. What products, then, can be transformed into an effective marketing virus?

Here are some tips from Internet Day:

- Signature lines. Although they are now more mainstream than viral, signature lines can work much like Hotmail if you supply free e-mail addresses. Make your message as intriguing as possible so people click through to your site.
- Free e-books. These can be short books on a subject related to everything related to your business. Perhaps it can be a book of hints and tips, or a compilation of articles branded with your company details, and an encouragement to pass it on.
- Free software. You could approach the author of an application you consider useful (a useful freeware utility, perhaps) and brand it with your name. Then give it away from your site, and submit it to download sites such as *www.tucows.com* and *www.download.com.*
- Screensaver. This doesn't have to be directly related to your product line, as long as it is interesting enough and contains advertising for your company or Web site.
- Humorous images. Imprint them with your company Web address and slogan in a corner.
- Little desktop games. I've lost count of the funny games friends and colleagues have sent me—branding them with your company details would be a great opportunity.
- Free content for other Web sites. Pass on to others any original content you have devised, and be sure your credits are retained.
- E-postcards. If you can tailor them to be industry specific, and humorous, so much the better.

> You could approach the author of an application you consider useful (a useful freeware utility, perhaps) and brand it with your name.

Awards and award sites

If your business won any awards or received official recognition, it's always helpful to have a small blurb that says something like, "MyBusiness.com is a nationally recognized Web site and winner of the Cool.net award for superior customer service." It makes you sound like an expert, and makes your business appear cutting edge.

Awards are a way to gain recognition for you and your Web site. They bring prestige and more traffic to your site, and they enhance your credibility. Besides, it's good for the soul. We all want to know that our peers like our work. Tangentially, it can increase the number of hits to your site. Though winning awards won't do much to build traffic for business sites, trophies always feel good.

Remember, the true spirit of award seeking is the desire to receive outside opinion about one's site. It is far too easy to fall in love with the design we've worked so hard on and ask for criticism from people whom we care about. But, unfortunately, those are the people we should not ask. Usually they'll say something like, "It's nice," or they may say, "It's awful." But those opinions shouldn't count. Awards are, without exception, the best way to seek objective opinion. If we ask our friends and family what they think, we are asking them to make us feel good, and they will. They will applaud our efforts and often go out of their way to make us feel as though we were the final word in Web design. They do this because they love us and want us to feel good. Hey, remember how your mom loved your finger paintings so much, she hung them on the refrigerator for everyone to see? Mother put mine on the refrigerator in an attempt to build my self-esteem. This is hardly objective.

Here's how to prepare your site for awards. These suggestions are based on the experiences of a veteran of the awards, Don Chisholm, who has applied for hundreds of awards. He has studied the criteria at the award sites, and has had many discussions with reviewers at some of the best award sites in the world. Follow these proven guidelines, refine your Web site, and it will be a winner!

Before you start to apply for awards, it's a good idea to make sure your Web site is ready for the test. It has to be perfect and meet the criteria of the award you're shooting for. To meet their criteria, you must know what is required, and you must prepare your site.

> Awards are a way to gain recognition for you and your Web site. They bring prestige and more traffic to your site, and they enhance your credibility.

Purpose

You must have a clear purpose for your Web site. Every element in your site must contribute to that purpose. Extraneous material will lead to points being subtracted.

Content

Most award groups want to see comprehensive, useful material. The Internet was created to share information and comprehensive, useful content. The content should be original, concise, accurate, well written, and up to date. It should be meaningful and useful to your target audience.

Web sites that present a new idea or concept and sites that offer a unique or useful service have the best chance of winning awards. Try to be original or creative. Some of the best ideas are simply a new twist on an old idea.

> Graphics should be used solely to improve the presentation of content. They should enhance and be enhanced by the Web site theme.

Graphics

Graphics should be used solely to improve the presentation of content. They should enhance and be enhanced by the Web site theme. Properly used, they can greatly enhance a Web site and its content. Clip art should be held to an absolute minimum. Most awards give extra points for using original graphics, and they should be relevant to your theme. The page should load fast. Use animation only when it is relevant to the content of the page.

Design

The design of your Web site, how you combine the content and graphics, can transform good content into a great site. A great site will have a layout that is pleasing to the eye, and all the pages will have a consistent look and feel. It will be well organized, logical, and easy to navigate. A color scheme for your site should be established, and the number of colors should be held to a minimum. Colors should complement your Web site.

The color scheme will help to create a consistent look and feel, and the pages will flow more smoothly from one to another.

Here are some more rules from Mr. Chisholm:

- Don't try to cram your entire site into the first page, keep it short.
- Your pages should look clean and crisp, not crowded and cluttered.
- Break large areas of text into smaller paragraphs with subheadings; it's easier to read.
- Don't use backgrounds that make it difficult to read the text.
- If possible, use the same background throughout your entire Web site.
- Keep advertising banners to an absolute minimum.
- Don't use blinking text; it's very distracting.
- If you use music anywhere in your site, there should be a way to turn it off.
- If you use frames, make sure that you use the <noframes> tag as well.
- Your Web pages should display properly in all the major browsers.
- Don't use "Under Construction" signs; good Web sites are always under construction.
- Don't post more than one or two awards on your home page. They increase the loading time and almost always conflict with the color scheme you selected for your Web site. Create a section called "My Awards," or something similar, and post them there. Longer loading times and a myriad of colors are expected, and acceptable, in the awards section of your site.

> A Web site should be easy to navigate, and visitors should know where they are in the site at all times.

Navigation

A Web site should be easy to navigate, and visitors should know where they are in the site at all times. If you use an image map, or a menu consisting of graphical links, you should have a text version as well.

The following suggestions will help you meet the criteria that most award sites use for judging the navigation of your Web site:

- Navigation should be easy and intuitive.
- On longer pages, you should use more than one menu unless you're using frames.
- Use a "Back to Top" link at the bottom of longer pages.
- Supply a "Back button for navigation." Visitors should not have to use the Back button on their browsers to navigate.
- Make sure everything works. Check your links. Then check them again. Then check them again. Missing graphics and broken links, especially internal links, are a great way to ensure that you don't win awards.

> Proofread all of your work; then proofread it again. Check for grammatical errors and spelling mistakes.

Check, test, and retest

Proofread all of your work; then proofread it again. Check for grammatical errors and spelling mistakes. If possible, get a friend or relative to proofread it as well. It's very easy to miss errors and mistakes while checking your own work. Use a text-to-speech program like Monolog or Talk to Me (both are shareware programs available on ZDNet).

Try your Web site with different screen resolutions and different modem speed connections. Make sure your site works on platforms other than Windows, Explorer, or Netscape. Free services from Web Site Garage, ANYBrowser.com, and the Web Page Backward Compatibility Viewer will check compatibility.

Real awards programs are objective. The judge or judges will have no reason to tell you anything but the truth about your design. Feel free to write to the judges in a given contest to ask how they can improve your site.

Quick tips

✓ Use awards to obtain credibility. Display them in a conspicuous area on your site.

✓ Suggest people pass around to others copies of your freebies and articles from your Web site.

Summary

Since you are, by now, living and breathing your Web site, you are going to find it hard to believe that there is a world of people out there who are not totally interested in your product or site. But these people are interested in your category. Get people in the habit of starting their Internet experience at your site. Then make it easy for them to navigate into a community.

> Get people in the habit of starting their Internet experience at your site.

For more information on this topic, visit our Web site at www.businesstown.com

Business-to-Business Sites

In this chapter, you'll learn:

- **What businesses really want**
- **Why you should sell relationships rather than just products**
- **How to find your target market**

Chapter 23

What businesses really want

I had a conversation last night with a very successful salesperson from Office Max (a huge office supply company), a firm that has gone from bricks and mortar to clicks and mortar. That means it markets on the Web as well as with storefronts (that's the mortar part). He mentioned that sales for OfficeMax on the Web has sky-rocketed to huge numbers. I asked him if he was losing sales:

> Not at all. The Web actually helps me keep the OfficeMax name in front of the public. I service large and medium-sized businesses in our stores; while the smaller companies prefer to buy on our Web site. Selling personally and getting traffic to the Web are two different animals. Both have a place. I even keep my customers loyal to me by telling them how to get a good deal on the Internet. I'm probably their best selling tool because I get commissions from my accounts on Web sales, too.

OfficeMax has obviously got it all together

Business-to-business Web site owners—called "B2B" by marketers who like to use the latest buzzwords—have at least three goals:

1. To generate sales.
2. To facilitate communications.
3. To generate traffic so that the prior two get done.

> A B2B site should function as a virtual office or virtual storefront—depending on whether you're offering a product or a service.

A B2B site should function as a virtual office or virtual store-front—depending on whether you're offering a product or a service. When surfers hit your site, they should feel as though they are coming to a real office or store. So, don't forget that most stores rely on repeat traffic and building relationships with their customers.

The relationship starts when a person first logs on to your site. Shoppers surfing the Web want to know what you can do for them. They want to know what makes you special. Give them solid information. Set a mood from the very first fold. Let people know that you know your stuff. Let people know you care about their businesses and their problems. Recognize the fact that a B2B Web site is a working office for transacting business. That's the way to attract people and keep them coming back.

Your Web site should tell a potential client that you are well versed in a given area of law and that the potential client could well use your services, just as you would be sure to let him or her know if he or she were in your office. Your Web site should give straight answers to what you offer and why the client should buy from you.

Here's where you need to be very careful. Because shoppers who purchase online are very savvy—they generally know exactly what they want and how much they want to pay for it. If they've taken the time to come to your Web site, they typically don't need fluff and feathers, and they don't want in-your-face sales tactics.

What they're looking for is whether you can deliver what they want, at the price they want and when they want. And whether they can trust you to be everything you say your are (and then some).

With that in mind, your goal should be to create the most professional Web site you can and to make sure that every possible objection your potential client might have is handled.

Some tools that are magical, and often overlooked, include:

- FAQs. A page that includes a list of all the questions you can anticipate a visitor wanting clarified about your business, your products, your services, and how they can safely do business with you.
- Testimonials. Quotes from satisfied customers (preferably the most highly recognized ones you've worked with and ones that are among your target market.)
- A bio, and even sometimes a picture. I know, I don't like my picture broadcast either. But a personal touch does wonders for a business-to-business Web site. Remember when all is said and done, business to business is really person to person. You need to satisfy the needs of the individual who represents the business in the transaction.
- Information. Is your firm retained because of the solid advice you give? Make sure that your testimonials and examples point to ways that you have satisfied customers with the

> Your Web site should tell a potential client that you are well versed in a given area of law and that the potential client could well use your services, just as you would be sure to let him or her know if he or she were in your office.

advice you've given them. Include a subsection in your Web site that offers articles and newsletters that demonstrate your expertise. In short, the content of the site is dictated by the target client and his or her methods for making a decision.

The ultimate goal

The goal is to develop a sense of community and a relationship so as to presell your potential customers and make them *want* to do business with you, even before you get to your sales pitch. Surfers want you to inform them and to convince them, that's true. But they also want you to woo them. They want a relationship with you, and they want to feel you really care.

Keep your Web site lively

There's nothing wrong with entertaining as well as informing. Businesses of all kinds are exciting. Even business-to-business law firms can be exciting when you hear about the successes their clients have had. The Web is a place where you must convince clients that you are exciting—and even fun to work with.

Of course, you want to be somewhat selective. Bells and whistles are great *if* your typical client expects them, if their system can handle them, and if they do not mislead the customer. If you're an attorney, you probably don't want to include a lottery on your site although lotteries do generate repeat business. And if you sell caskets, you probably would be well advised to avoid the latest online games.

If you were courting, you'd look for fun things to do with that special someone. You want to do the same thing with surfers on the Internet. But you would want to do things that are supportive of your end goal, which is to establish a mutually profitable relationship with another—and that's true whether the other is an individual or a business.

In B2B, Relationships Mean Sales

The key to selling on a business-to-business site is to build relationships Every person who signs your guestbook is interested in what you have to say. Follow up all leads with telephone calls, and of course, respond to all e-mails. In your guestbook (a crucial tool for building a database) request your visitor's name, e-mail address, phone and fax numbers. Because the e-mail address usually has the domain name, you can log onto their Web sites to see what their business is and how you can help.

Keep your site targeted

One key difference between a B2B site and a general site is that surfers to a business site are more narrow-minded in their surfing outlook. They want you to answer their questions quickly and thoroughly, and they want no variances or digressions to sidetrack them from their mission, whatever it happens to be. Keep your site relevant. Make sure your artwork, banners, and discussion groups, if you have any, stay highly focused.

Targeting can be just as efficient as direct mail in reaching particular audiences. There are as many specialized Web sites as there are specialized trade publications—primarily because virtually every specialized publication has established a sister Web site.

Look at the trade journals that you use to stay abreast of the latest developments in your industry every day. Use them to target and categorize your site. Concentrate your efforts on marketing to the people who need your services or products. Audit your marketing and sales data to find out who is actually buying your product or service and why a sale is made.

Eliminate or change Web site strategies and extraneous features that don't serve the needs of your customers.

Integrate everything, and plaster your name on all of your promotional material.

Let's not forget that traditional media will play an important part in your announcements. Use all traditional marketing tools that you would in your business offline to announce the opening of your Web office. Send out paper announcements as well as Web announcements. Put your site address on everything, including brochures, ads, letters, business cards, published articles, and even briefs filed with courts.

Encourage your employees to participate in newsgroups and to use your URL in their signatures when they post. This applies to newsgroups concerning your hobbies as well as business-focused newsgroups. After all, people who play also need to work and earn money.

> Integrate everything, and plaster your name on all of your promotional material.

Sell your site through the phone

With the use of voice mail, e-mail, and the Internet in our day-to-day business activities, we sometimes forget that one of our most powerful tools for promotion is the telephone. I've found that in calling my clients, they often have an Internet connection at all times. I've briefly mentioned my Web site to them, and they'd often say, "I'll check it right now." This is exactly what you want. Immediacy. And, it's sitting right in front of us . . . the telephone. You can network, sell, close, research, and advertise your site all right now through your telephone.

As often as not, we're all influenced—sold—by the warmth of another's voice even more than we are by looking over something in print. Use the phone and use it wisely.

No matter how tempting it may be, do not call yourself a consultant. To a great many people "consultant" means "out of work."

A quick note for consultants

No matter how tempting it may be, do not call yourself a consultant. To a great many people "consultant" means "out of work." Remember, perception is everything. When most people see the word *consultant* in a search engine description, they typically will ignore the listing. Rather, use terms like "specialist" or "strategist."

Besides, when you use the word *consultant*, a lot of people will request free advice and drive you crazy.

The Internet is great for services as well as products, but you need to be a little bit more discriminating when you target your potential customer.

Target, target, target

To determine what information is needed and how to target your promotion, you must first know your target customer. Is he or she a top-rank decision maker or the purchasing agent for office supplies? Are you targeting small businesses where the owner of the company surfs the Web as well as sweeps the floor? Are you a niche provider targeting small, segmented businesses, or is your market bigger and less amorphous? Are you selling advice or a service?

One of the keys to creating a great traffic-building strategy is knowing how to find the customers who will be genuinely interested in what your Web site has to say. Especially in B2B sites, your business won't survive by relying on "walk-ins" or by accidental happenstance. The first thing you have to determine is where they "walk that walk." Many B2B site owners forget to put themselves into the heads of their target market and post their messages accordingly. Prospects are all over the Web:

- They congregate in chatrooms.
- They get involved in discussion groups and newsgroups.
- They read specialized media and newsletters.
- They join online clubs and organizations.
- They network online and participate in online seminars.
- They frequent specialized portals.
- They trade links with suppliers.
- They use specialized search engines.

The key is to market proactively and reach out to your prospects. And don't forget the other strategies we discussed in this book. To reach prospects, you could:

- Write a specialized newsletter and make it available through your Web site or through an opt-in server like Topica or eGroups.com.
- Publish articles. Include them on your own Web site and offer them to other Web sites, especially those that offer content, like FreeContent.com or Contentious, as well as compatible newsletters that target your selected market.
- Send highly targeted e-mails. Just be careful that you get permission. Use those opt-in providers like YesMail, egroups.compuserve.com (still a recognized leader in information and networking for businesses), and your own personal in-house mailing list.

> The key is to market proactively and reach out to your prospects.

More than one target?

Many businesses target more than one segment of the market. Yours may be one of those. If so, don't despair. Your Web site can handle that if you plan carefully. Simply set off various parts of the Web site to deal with the specific issues of each individual segment. For example, you might use the approach that Microsoft and Lotus use on their Web sites. If you go to those sites, and the sites of many others like them, you'll see that they have menu selections that guide specific visitors in different directions depending on what their individual interests are. Creative Options is a much smaller example. You'll see that part of the site caters to the SOHO market, part to the Chicago market, and part to writers and other creative people. In each of these examples, you'll note that there may be some overlap, but the companies each recognize and appeal to the interests of each individual special interest group.

> Build relations, and that will build sales.

Quick tips

✓ Build relations, and that will build sales.

✓ Business-to-business marketing works best when coupled with offline promotion.

Summary

People come to a B2B site for solid information. A primary reason that many B2B sites fail to meet goals is they don't give the information that prospects seek when they arrive at their sites.

For more information on this topic, visit our Web site at www.businesstown.com

Here's How to Get Your B2B Site Up and Running

In this chapter, you'll learn:

- **How to get your B2B site up and running**
- **Tips for generating leads and proposals**
- **How to network your way to success**

Chapter 24

Although there are many theories and ideas about building a client base through the Web, this six-step formula can act as a blueprint for success:

1. Identify your niche and your market. Focus. Focus. Focus. For instance, you may be focusing on small publishers. Work that group with everything you have.
2. Surf on over to Lizst.com and find discussion groups that you think your prospects read. And get happily involved as both a recipient and a contributor.
3. Make your pitch by contributing whenever you can. Use a strong SIG that tells what you can do for clients and how you can be reached.
4. Answer every note with an auto-responder and follow up with a personal letter.
5. Build your in-house mailing list, and develop a newsletter that you can send out to that list and to an opt-in list on a regular basis.
6. Constantly ask for referrals and testimonials.

A Great Lead Generator

Bloombergs (*www.bloomberg.com*) is an excellent place to find business leads and information on what is happening in your business areas. Use it to research your prospects and categories.

How to get on bid lists

Web sites *www.mondus.com, www.guru.com*, and *www.iwant.com* have services that allow both business buyers and venders to get together. These are sorts of clearinghouses where businesses put their purchasing needs out for bid, and venders have the opportunity to submit detailed proposals.

Specifically, mondus.com, for example, targets small and medium-sized companies. It's a buyer-driven site that allows venders to submit a bid to buyers tailored to their business needs, rather than competing solely on price.

Using their online templates, buyers complete and submit a purchase order form (POF), detailing their purchasing criteria. Mondus.com then sends the POF to venders in their database that are qualified to bid on the project. You then get to review the POF and submit a bid. Even if you don't get that particular order, you can get traffic just because the company gets to know you.

At the time of this writing, mondus.com has 116,000 members in its database and is adding new categories all the time.

Network your way to online traffic

The Internet business is all about partnerships and connections and your network; for the salesperson or deal maker, this is a key benefit of an industry event. Ask yourself what your goals are in participating in the various networking events that we've discussed in this book so that you will pick groups that will help you get what you are looking for. Some activities are based more on learning, making contacts, or volunteering rather than on strictly making business connections.

Visit as many groups as possible that spark your interest. Notice the tone and attitude of the group. Do the people sound supportive of one another? Does the leadership appear competent? Determine whether the group is one where you'll find a ready source of potential clients, or if it is a group of peers who share techniques and inside industry information. Or maybe it's just a place where you can make some friends, have some fun with any business that might come your way as an added bonus—one that you're not expecting.

As in any networking situation, volunteering, and thus maintaining high visibility, is essential. Groups need lots of work done, especially when they're online. There are Web sites to maintain, newsletters to coordinate and write for, opportunities for moderating discussions, and most easily overlooked, a need for people to share their expertise. Don't just lurk, get involved. Give freely and let your strengths shine.

Ask open-ended questions in all networking conversations. It's surprising how many overlook this simple technique in online discussions. If you make it a practice to spout off your, admittedly, outstanding knowledge and don't encourage feedback from others on the list, you'll never build relationships. And though you may impress others, you will not encourage them to interact with you. What we're talking about are the questions that ask who, what, where, when, how, and what do you think as opposed to those that can be answered with a simple yes or no. This form of questioning opens up the discussion and shows others that you are interested in them.

> The Internet business is all about partnerships and connections and your network; for the salesperson or deal maker, this is a key benefit of an industry event.

By consistently participating and offering to help, you will become known as a powerful resource for others. When you are known as a strong resource, they will remember to turn to you for suggestions, ideas, names of other people, and so on. This keeps you visible to them.

Have a clear understanding of what you do and why, for whom, and what makes your doing it special or different from others doing the same thing. In order to get referrals, you must first have a clear understanding of what you do that you can easily articulate to others.

Take care to articulate specifically what you are looking for and how others may help you. Too often people in conversations ask, "How may I help you?" and no immediate answer comes to mind. But if you ask, "May I show you how this product will save you three hours a day so you can enjoy more family time?" you may be surprised by the responses you receive.

Follow through quickly and efficiently on referrals you are given. When people give you referrals, your actions are a reflection on them. Respect and honor that, and your referrals will grow. When sifting through your e-mail—particularly if you're one of those who are swamped with more mail than you can handle—learn to skim the senders and subjects to be sure that pressing mail is handled first. And respond immediately. If you put off an answer "until later" even if you flag the item, it's likely to get lost. Time management is even more critical online than offline.

Call those you meet who may benefit from what you do, and encourage others to call you. Express that you enjoyed meeting them, and ask if you could get together and share ideas.

There is no single networking activity that will ensure your success in building traffic. But learning to look for opportunities like those mentioned here, you'll soon see that traffic to your Web site is pretty much taking care of itself.

Generate traffic and learn at the same time

Although you want to lurk for a while, you don't want to let too much time go by before introducing yourself to the group. You don't need to give your entire life history. A brief two- to three-paragraph bio works

> By consistently participating and offering to help, you will become known as a powerful resource for others.

well for the first time. You can expose yourself gradually as you begin contributing to various topics of interest. Don't worry about pitching your business, just get acquainted and let your SIG do the work.

During the course of your participation, you'll identify people who will be particularly good to network with for any of a number of reasons. You may want to add their names, e-mail addresses, and a little bit about them to your address book, and you might also want to send a private self-introduction or acknowledgment of their contribution to the group. That's certainly acceptable.

You'll continue to network in the real world at the same time. Remember to exchange cards with everyone you meet. They came to tell you about your business and pitch theirs, so you're on the same page.

Always feel free to ask questions of the speaker, panelists, and other contributors. Don't do it with the purpose of delivering your sales pitch, but do prepare a one-liner about your company for when you introduce yourself at the start of your question. Smart, relevant questions can say a lot about the person asking, and may well have prospective customers seeking you out in the halls later.

Attend as many group discussions as you possibly can fit into your time. Keep in mind that your mission here is to meet, to connect, and to sell—in that order.

> ### Use How-To Articles to Increase Traffic
>
> One of the features of my business site is the number of helpful articles on it. Add articles to your site whether they were written by you or not and advertise them on your very first page as a teaser. If you use articles written by others, make sure you get permission. Make sure you also include bios of your key people. On business-to-business sites, content is incredibly important, as is image.

Six common sense tactics to keep business and traffic rolling in

1. Respond to e-mail quickly, in less than 24 hours or less; immediately is best online. By responding quickly, you send the message that your customers are important and you are genuinely interested in meeting their needs.
2. Follow up on orders. Make sure your customers are thoroughly satisfied with their purchase and offer additional services related to their purchase. Remember, it's much easier to sell to current customers than it is to find new ones, especially if you deliver products and services as well as first-rate customer service.

3. Give refunds promptly and unconditionally. Customers are often happier with a mistake that is corrected without a hassle than they are when it is right the first time.

4. Ask your customers to fill out a survey so you can better understand their needs. Offer a valuable freebie or a discounted service for participating. This strategy establishes a dialogue between you and the customer, and helps determine the direction of your business.

5. Be sure to include tips and information on your site that your customers can't get anywhere else, and don't forget to offer subscriber-only discounts and freebies.

6. Make your site easy to navigate. Customers value their time and appreciate finding what they want quickly and effortlessly.

More networking strategies

Effective business networking is the linking of individuals who, through trust and relationship building, become walking, talking advertisements for one another. Keep an eye out for opportunities to put buyers and sellers together—even if they aren't in your own organization. Those you help are more likely to reciprocate in kind.

But remember that you can't tack on good-quality networking to the outside and expect it to work. Keep in mind that networking is about being genuine and authentic, building trust and relationships, and finding ways to help others.

So, here you are, at Jupiter's Consumer Online Forum, or Thunder Lizard's Web Marketing Monterey Event, the Variety Summit, or any of the hundreds of other Internet advertising or e-commerce events. Are you ready to work the event to your best sales advantage? If you are not sure, here are some tips to help.

Ask for action

Whether your pages are trying to generate an online sale, incite press interest, answer customer questions, or capture market

> Keep in mind that networking is about being genuine and authentic, building trust and relationships, and finding ways to help others.

research information, it's the action that you ask your visitors to perform that yields beneficial results.

But for actions to occur, you have to tell visitors exactly what you want them to do. Some may figure it out on their own, but without a stated "call to action," you run the risk of becoming just another browse-and-run victim on the information superhighway.

Calls to action can be bold or subtle. For example, if you're interested in generating sales, don't use a static subhead on your page such as "More than 150,000 products listed." Instead, drop an action hint by telling the visitor to "Save 25% off your first order. With more than 150,000 products to choose from, we guarantee you'll find the right product for your needs." Both subheads boast the 150,000 products, but the second—the upfront announcement of a 25% discount—let's visitors know that this is a sales catalog that they can order from. And there's an incentive to do it.

Once you've defined your site's message, which should take only a sentence or two at most, the next step is to dedicate every word, graphic, and effect to the domination of every page of your Web site.

> Calls to action can be bold or subtle.

Quick tips

✓ Business-to-business Web sites should be clearly focused on your clients' needs and problems.

✓ People rarely buy on one visit. Constant follow-up by e-mail or personal contact will make the ultimate sale.

Summary

What rules a successful business site is offering something concrete and building a relationship. Don't waste the readers' time with a bottomless bandwidth of self-gratifying drivel that leaves people unfulfilled. State your story clearly and quickly.

For more information on this topic, visit our Web site at www.businesstown.com

Advertising That Costs Money

In this chapter, you'll learn:

- **The different benefits of paid and free media**
- **How to tie in traditional marketing with Internet marketing**
- **The correlation between velocity and budget**
- **How to use free and paid advertising**

The Internet is a true advertising medium. If you watch TV, drive past billboards, listen to the radio, or open a newspaper, you'll find that dotcom companies are flooding traditional media with advertising. You've probably seen a ton of look-alike dotcom commercials on TV and are wondering how they are working. For some, they are; for others, they aren't. It depends on the goals of the companies. For many, just being on TV is enough because many are chasing venture capital and they want to *look* established, and TV is the fastest way to do so.

The beauty of advertising on the Internet is that people are sharing the same workspace with you. With most of your online advertising, your prospect is only one click from finding you.

Since we're dealing primarily with the Internet, it's easy to forget that traditional media can be effective in promoting your Web site. Most people still get the majority of their marketing messages through traditional channels. Most people spend more time going through life than sitting at their keyboards. It can be helpful to place small ads in magazines that are similar in spirit to your Web site. A very effective way to promote your site is to place a small display ad in a targeted trade publication, offering some teaser copy, perhaps a free report or discount, and pointing readers to your URL.

Integrated marketing

Integrated marketing is the practice of promoting by using several forms of media simultaneously. Because it's a tried-and-true business strategy, it's been used by offline merchants and advertisers forever. Integrated marketing has undergone a transformation with the explosion of the Internet. The successful Web marketer uses each medium to feed the others, generating power by combining different media in just the right way. To make it work, you use each medium to its best advantage.

> Integrated marketing is the practice of promoting by using several forms of media simultaneously.

- Traditional media. Using traditional media—television, radio, and print—is a great way to build awareness of your Web site.

Collateral material, like brochures, flyers, and advertising gimmicks, can introduce your site or remind people of your site's usefulness. Yes, the offline world can peacefully co-exist with the online world.

- "Multimedia-tasking." Fifty-seven percent of U.S Internet users have the capability to use their PC and television simultaneously. Of those who have this ability, 86% actually go online and watch TV at the same time. This means that almost half of U.S. home users are multimedia-taskers.
  - Offline branding and online surfing. Among multimedia-taskers, 91% report they became aware of a URL through an offline source and then visited that site. With a mouse in one hand and a remote in the other, a whopping 62% of multimedia-taskers say they visited the site of a URL advertised on television, equivalent to 30% of home users. And forget about visiting the bathroom during TV breaks. Almost three-fourths of multimedia-taskers report they sometimes, usually, or always are occupied online during TV commercials. Yet, unlike advertised URLs, only one-fifth of users said they visited a site related to the program they were actually watching.
- Content and click-through. Users are much more likely to notice and click on ads promoting entertainment, technology, or financial-related products and services. Online advertising can get people to your site with a single mouse click.

The advantages of electronic or online promotional methods are:

- Lower cost
- Wider exposure
- Much easier to make changes
- Much easier to test ads
- Only a mouse click away (can't stress that too much)

Add Your Web Site to Your Personal Sales Pitch

When you have a prospect on the phone, they are often on the Web at the same time. Suggest they logon to the Web during your call and get their reactions. Suggest they send your URL to other key people. If you're a service company, the Web can be used to support and reinforce your business image.

Valuing visibility

Visibility is paramount in building traffic with both offline and online choices. With enough money, you can create an instant presence and expose your site to the multitudes. However, since most sites don't have Amazon.com-type marketing budgets or Amazon.com word-of-mouth capabilities, where to advertise becomes very "strategic."

Budget dictates what percentage of the world will see your advertising online just as it does offline. The good news is that even if you don't have an enormous advertising budget, you can still make waves on the Internet. It's up to you to decide how fast you want to go with your Web site. Here is an immutable formula:

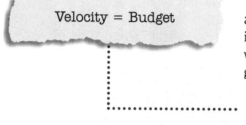

Velocity = Budget

The more money you have, the faster you can gain mass-market visibility (as opposed to selectively targeting your market). However, if you don't have a huge advertising budget, you can take solace in the words of a retail store tycoon, who looked at his massive advertising expenditures and said, "Half of my advertising dollars are wasted, but I can't figure out which half." Yes, as you've noticed throughout this book, you can create visibility with free promotion, but you don't have the control you do with paid advertising. Here are some tradeoffs when comparing free promotion and trade promotion:

- Free Web publicity works just as hard as advertising, but it takes longer.
- Link exchange programs work just as hard as paid advertising, but link exchange programs take longer to get rolling, and you usually can't specify where or when your ads will appear.
- Paid advertising enables you to be somewhat assured of positioning in printed media or on Web pages. Free Internet advertising might, too, but getting the positioning is more challenging.
- Paid advertising allows you to target your market specifically. Free advertising can, too, but you may not be able to

tap into the sites that generate the greatest traffic, and you'll work harder to locate the most effective free advertising opportunities.

The more money you have, the faster you will get attention. Lots of dotcoms enjoyed their 30 seconds of fame during Super Bowl XXXIV. Many of the commercials were quite entertaining. The advertisers got a big bang for the buck, and many got a big boost in traffic because of it. Of course, what they did with that traffic and whether it ever came back again is another story—so the accountants still have to decide if they got a real return on that huge investment.

- 80% increase in Web traffic to Monster.com after ad ran during Super Bowl XXXIV
- 541% increase in Web traffic to Brittanica.com after ad ran during the game
- 2,350% increase in Web traffic to MicroStrategy after ad ran during the game
- 2,502% increase in Web traffic to Computer4SURE.com after ad ran during the game
- 300,000 people per minute visited a Web site during the game

Even if you want to go the pay-as-you-go route, you don't need to spend thousands of dollars on advertising. You don't need to advertise in the *Tribune* or whatever the major daily newspaper in your neck of the woods might be. Take a serious look at the small specialty newspapers—the free ones you'll find at the entrances of Barnes & Noble and other major bookstores. They may target 10,000 or so readers, all of who fall into a highly targeted niche. They offer wonderful bargains for entrepreneurs: much less expensive ads, a predisposed readership that wants the information enough to pick up the paper, and more often than not, a place in which you can tell your story, not just buy an ad.

But no matter how you slice and dice it, online advertising is the most important component of your marketing mix because the consumer is just one mouse click away from entering your store.

Don't Forget Your Sales Staff

Don't cut you salespeople out of the loop. Create a commission structure for Web recommendations. It will give people greater incentive to sell the site.

Targeting your spending

Targeting your market is of utmost importance. It's always better to show consumers ads for products of interest than those for products or services they'll never buy. But knowing what a Web user is interested in seeing—and, you hope, purchasing—is the tricky part. If you followed my discussion about newsgroups, you should have a strong feeling about whom to target.

Free and classified ads

There are many free or cheap ad sites listed in back of this book. Free ad sites run the gamut of categories and should be one aspect of your marketing plan. Others that you should also consider are direct e-mail (not spamming) and targeted ads in online e-zines or newsletters. You can also run classifieds on supersites like America Online, Microsoft Network, and CompuServe.

Here are some places to explore when looking for free or cheap ad placement:

- Newsgroups. Find a newsgroup that is highly targeted to your particular product or service. Look through the ads and the content of the newsgroups to make sure that it is focused and that it accepts ads.
- Bulletin boards. Some bulletin boards also offer classified ads.
- Mailing lists and newsletters. Many mailing lists and newsletters are really collections of ads broken up in bits and pieces of words. A good place to start is *www.factsheet5.com*. They have a very eclectic and thorough list of current e-zines. Another good one is *www.etext.org/zines*.

When placing ads at free locations, you should do several things:

- You should have your ad and several variations ready when you go online to place them. The number of words allowed at each site can vary from 25 to 50.

> Targeting your market is of utmost importance. It's always better to show consumers ads for products of interest than those for products or services they'll never buy.

- When you go to a site, check out the ads in the category you are thinking about placing your ad in. See how they are laid out and whether they have active e-mail or URL links.
- Review the site's policies and procedures to see what they allow and don't allow.
- Determine how long your ad will stay up on the site. Some are for a week, a month, several months, or a year, and some just stay on until newer ads push them off.
- Keep a record, on index cards or in a three-ring binder, so you know when to go back and resubmit your ad.
- Have your ad and its variations already typed up on your word processor or text editor. This way when you are ready to fill in the ad text at the site, you can just call the ad up from your editor, copy and paste it in, rather than typing each one individually.

Search engine placement

You can purchase advertising for your Web site on many of the popular search engines and in many of the portals we discussed earlier. Your advertising can be national, regional, or even local in nature. In addition, many special-interest sites sell advertising banners and other types of related advertising. These costs can range from several hundred dollars to tens of thousands of dollars each month. They all give you the opportunity to reach specific demographics at a cost that cannot be reached by conventional media. What you can do with this information is unlimited. For instance, it is possible to have your advertisement or link appear whenever a particular search word is used in a specific search engine. Here is what came up when I ran a search for "sporting goods" on AltaVista:

> You can purchase advertising for your Web site on many of the popular search engines and in many of the portals we discussed earlier.

Comparison shop for "sporting goods" Get answers on "sporting goods" from an expert at EXP.com Let the merchants come to you! Shop by request for "sporting goods" at Respond.com Find Yellow Page information on "sporting goods" at WorldPages.com Click here for more on "sporting goods" at

Britannica.com Refine your search on "sporting goods" with LookSmart Categories and here's more:

- Dicks Sporting Goods—sporting goods stores
- Big 5 Sporting Goods—Wilson sporting goods
- Discount Sporting goods

For the height of target marketing, you can purchase advertising packages that show your ad when a specific company is running the search. There are usually minimum-dollar figures that you need to spend when doing this kind of targeted advertising. WebConnect, a large Web media broker, for example, requires a monthly expenditure of at least $750 (which can be spread over several Web sites).

Here are some other costs:

- Yahoo! charges $1,000 per month when you purchase a word on their search engine. Let's say a banner ad for your boat company pops up anytime someone searches for the word *sloop* or *sailboat*. For the $1,000 per word per month, Yahoo! will guarantee you 10,000 impressions (a CPM—cost per 1,000 impressions—of $100, or 10 cents per impression).
- Lycos charges $500 minimum per month per word, at 5 cents per impression over 10,000 impressions (CPM of $50).

As we saw in Chapter 16 (on banner advertising), people may see your banner ad, but that doesn't necessarily mean that they will click on it to go to your site. If you put an ad on the first page of Yahoo!, for example, millions of people will see it, but you can expect a low rate of interest because your click-through rate is intensely correlated with your target audience.

Here are some typical click-through rates from various search engines taken from CyberAtlas reports for a general-purpose site:

Go.com, 1.1 percent   HotWired, 2.8 percent
WebCrawler, 0.7 percent   Mr. ShowBiz, 1.5 percent

More closely targeted sites might bring click rates of 8%, 13%, or even higher.

> For the height of target marketing, you can purchase advertising packages that show your ad when a specific company is running the search.

HotWired advertising effectiveness study

Since advertising on the World Wide Web began in 1994, marketers have asked the same question they ask of all media: Does it work? More specifically, do banner ads—those small, hyperlinked pixel displays popping up on public Web sites everywhere these days—actually provide a vehicle for effective commercial communication? As marketers are projected to spend billions of dollars on Web advertising in the next few years, this question has become increasingly urgent.

Until now, the only available answer has been partial at best: Yes, ad banners do work as direct marketing vehicles. But only when their viewers click on them for transport to the advertiser's own Web site, where a wide range of customized marketing processes can then begin.

The problem, of course, is that only a small fraction of all viewers click on the banners they see. As a consequence, a few marketers have elected to pay only for proven click-throughs, while the rest of the marketing community, which pays for ad placements according to CPM, is left to wonder whether the millions of impressions its banner ads generate without click-through are simply wasted.

Well, are they? To answer this question, the HotWired advertising effectiveness study was designed to examine whether banner ads also work in the traditional sense. In other words, can banners build brands on their own without the benefit of click-through? Can they stimulate brand awareness, affinity, and purchase interest in the same way traditional broadcast advertisements can? Or do they fail to work in these ways, perhaps because their communication space is simply too small (as some have alleged) or because their environment—the computer screen—is fundamentally unfriendly to advertising?

To construct this study, two research teams collaborated. The Research Department of HotWired, Inc., the Internet publisher that innovated the ad banner format that is now a Web standard, partnered with Millward Brown International, a recognized leader in advertising effectiveness research. Together, these teams designed a rigorous study that applied to the Web the same proven metrics used

> Only a small fraction of all viewers click on the banners they see.

by Millward Brown to assess the effectiveness of print and television advertising.

Using these metrics, their study was able to accurately test the communication impact of a single advertising impression generated by an ad banner, regardless of its ability to garner click-through.

This, in sum, is what they found:

Banner ads on the HotWired Network make a significant impact on their viewers. An impact that demonstrably builds the advertised brand, even upon first impression. To this extent, every ad impression is important.

When we add the ability to build brands in a classical sense to the Web's established advantages in selective targeting and direct marketing, we arrive at the first complete picture of the World Wide Web (or at least of the HotWired Network) as a medium with truly superior potential for conducting marketing.

Successful banner design

Although we did discuss banner making previously, it is worth taking a moment to review. The purpose of a banner is to stop—interrupt really—your chain of thought. Clicking on a banner is similar to the impulse decision you make to buy a piece of candy at the supermarket. When a person makes an impulse decision, the logical thought processes are derailed. A banner ad on a site like Yahoo! is the only chance you have to make a first impression and grab the attention of the surfer. Your goal is to compel the surfer to leave that site and go to your own site to find out more. Here are some tips for making your banners achieve click-through:

- Use a call to action. Just as all offline advertising should end with a request to do something, so should your banner. A call to action increases click-through rates dramatically. Creating a call to action can be done by simply adding the words "Click Here."

> The purpose of a banner is to stop—interrupt really—your chain of thought.

- Add a button. You can just add the words "click here" or "click on me," but placing an actual or obvious button on your banner improves response. An important part of a banner is a call to action.
- Give surfers a reason to do your bidding. For example, "Save $199 on your car insurance" or "10% off your next purchase when you click here now!" (by the way, exclamation points have been shown to increase click-through rates).
- Keep your "clickable words" short and sweet, and compelling. They've got to interrupt the person's thought processes and compel them to find out more. Don't forget, the surfer is not looking for your banner. He or she is looking for information, and your banner is usually an unwanted intrusion.

Your ability to write compelling headlines is the key to more effective banners. Use words that motivate. Use active words rather than passive words. Keep the wording simple and short. Incorporate a major benefit into the headline. How is clicking on your banners going to make the surfer's life faster, more productive, more positive—for a few seconds anyway? You only have a few words on a banner. Make them short, punchy, and dramatic.

Your first step in developing a banner is to make sure someone sees it. But remember, though a clean design is helpful, it does not grab the wandering eye like animation. A little animation will go a long way in grabbing your target's attention. Animated banners have been proved to be much more effective than static banners. But don't go too wild. If you get carried away, the animation may overwhelm the message you are trying to convey with your banner. Besides, too much animation will increase the file size of your banner, which will cause the banner to download too slowly. If this happens, surfers may be gone before they even see the banner. Remember, surfers get impatient and bored quickly. More often, they're on a mission and looking for something else, so you've got to be there before they move on.

Another important factor is the actual banner ad itself. "The banner is like the outer envelope of a direct-mail piece," says Roy Schwedelson, CEO of WebConnect. "The Web site content compares

> Your ability to write compelling headlines is the key to more effective banners.

to what is in the envelope. Like direct mail, on the banner ad, you might offer a free premium, special value, or question."

Quick tips

✓ The key to a successful and fully integrated campaign is creating one message that reinforces itself throughout your promotion activities.

✓ The most important part of a banner is the wording. Always include a call for action.

✓ Once you have made some sales, you're ready to put some money toward advertising, display ads, and direct mail (opt-in mailings). Put aside a budget of at least 5% of sales.

Summary

Advertising on and off the Web can create awareness, create impressions, and supply your customers with the key information they need to make a purchase decision.

Advertising on the Web offers greater flexibility and can be more cost effective than traditional media because people are only a mouse click away from entering your site. You can create an advertising program with no money at all or with a budget of $10 million. In either case, review all media closely, and allocate a percentage of sales for paid adverting.

> The key to a successful and fully integrated campaign is creating one message that reinforces itself throughout your promotion activities.

For more information on this topic, visit our Web site at www.businesstown.com

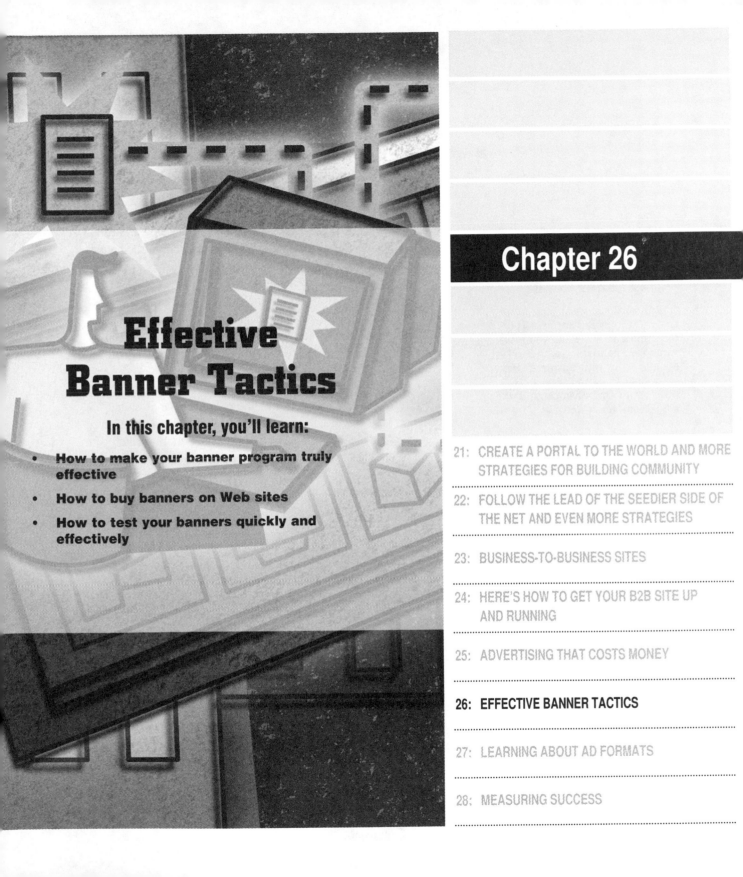

Effective Banner Tactics

In this chapter, you'll learn:

- **How to make your banner program truly effective**
- **How to buy banners on Web sites**
- **How to test your banners quickly and effectively**

Chapter 26

Breakthrough banner tactics

Here are some banner tactics that you can use to achieve high visibility and click-throughs. All a click-through means is that it is an opportunity to see (OTS) your page.

- Make a game. I saw a cute banner that had monkeys running back and forth. The object was to click on the banner to receive a small prize. Games for many surfers are like a cat chasing catnip. They have to give in.
- Run a series of banners. It may take more than one message to tell your story or to go after a particular market. Run sequential banners, and vary your message. Keep your message consistent to make your visitors want to read further.
- Make your banners—and your Web site—interactive. The Internet is an interactive medium. Let people do something on your site or achieve a goal. Get as many senses involved as possible. Look at the interactive banners that catch your attention for examples of how you can involve your audience. Go to the Web and find ones that make you sit up and take notice, the ones that make you want to get involved. What is it about those banners that grabs you? Those are the elements you want to apply to your own advertising, banners, and Web site.
- Create curiosity. A large number of those who click on ads do so because they're curious. Studies show that curious clickers vary widely by demographics and other characteristics, so targeting based on curiosity can be effective. The curiosity value works best when you have a general-interest product or service.
- Offer a coupon. When someone clicks on a banner, he or she goes to your site and sees a coupon for merchandise from your store or from one of your affiliates. Product discounts and coupons are attractive to users. Keep in mind that users are more interested in definite discounts than they are in that one-in-a-million chance of winning a contest.

Believability and trust play a major part here, as does the ability to satisfy an immediate need.

- Create product interest. One of the major conclusions of a study quoted by Jeff Moore on clickz.com is that by far the most powerful driver of click-throughs is product interest. Eighty-nine percent of users who click on ads do so because they are interested in the product being advertised.
- Combine interest and targeting. Look at your target market carefully. When you understand the demographics and motivations of your customers, you can come up with the exact banner placement and cost.
- Know thy user. So how do you plan your ad strategy to maximize its effectiveness? Understand who is likely to buy your product. What does you target audience do online? Where do they go? What kinds of approaches appeal to them?

How to implement you banner campaign

Here's a roadmap to develop your online advertising and banner campaign:

1. Determine where to purchase advertising space. Find a Web site that complements yours. Run searches on all the search engines, directories, and industry-specific sites to see which sites cater to your target audience. Subscribe to all related Web rings. On major portals, enter keywords that match or complement your banner ad campaign. Follow the links from the search results to see whether and where these sites are showing banner ads.
2. Determine the right keywords and categories. Make a list of keywords, categories, and sites where you would like your banner ads to appear.
3. Choose between general or specific target sites. You need to determine if a large portal site suits your needs or if a site specific to your industry is a more cost-effective choice.

> Determine where to purchase advertising space. Find a Web site that complements yours.

STREETWISE LOW-COST WEB SITE PROMOTION

Portal sites have more visitors, but industry-specific sites are usually cheaper and may be better for reaching your target audience in a concentrated fashion.

4. Contact the representative or the site. Most sites that carry advertising have an e-mail link or telephone number to request information. Ask for a rate card and placement options. Remember that ad positions on the top right of a Web page work better than others, so it might be worthwhile to pay a little extra for the space.

5. Learn the submission guidelines. Most Web sites have guidelines and policies for banner submissions. Here's what you need to know:

- Maximum file size
- File formats used
- Banner dimensions
- Deadlines for submission
- How many banners you can submit (if you are rotating messages)
- Where your banner ad will be featured on the page
- How often they rotate banners

6. Check for special rates. Here are some questions you should ask:

- Do they sell based on click-throughs or impressions?
- Do they have special rates to be positioned near their search engine?
- Can you do it cheaper by buying in bulk?

7. Retrieve banner ad statistics. Most sites that advertise should be able to tell you how well your ads are doing (or not doing). Make sure that the sites will send you details on impressions and click-through rates. These should be broken down by daily, weekly, monthly, and hourly rates.

Contact the representative or the site. Most sites that carry advertising have an e-mail link or telephone number to request information.

Banner Info Site

There are many tips for creating banners. For a comparison on what works and what doesn't, go to *www.bannertips.com*. You'll find more than you ever wanted to know about banners and their pulling power (or lack of it). Spend a great deal of time there and really soak up the information. A bad banner is worse than none at all.

Which banner pulled best?

Now that you know the basics for creating hard-hitting banners, let's see if you can tell which banner in Figure 26.1 achieved the greatest click-through rate and which achieved the lowest.

Figure 26.1: Banner Comparisons

Answer:
B. CTR = 0.60% (167:1)
A. CTR = 0.45% (223:1)
C. CTR = 0.12% (862:1)
D. CTR = 0.08% (1,250:1)

A note on testing to improve your results

To be successful and to improve your banner, testing and measuring are important. First, define what results you are looking at. For example, is it the number of sales made from your site or the number of people who subscribe to your newsletter that will determine your success ratio? You will also need to keep track of your banner click-throughs. Most banner exchanges and ad agencies you advertise with will keep track of this for you.

Change the variables in your banner to test each component individually over a finite amount of time. For example, change the background color of the banner, or change the wording slightly, such as from "take 10% off each purchase" to "$10 off each purchase."

Keep track of the click-throughs and your desired results. Compare the two. You are aiming for an increase in both. When you find the best results, keep that banner for a while.

Quick tips

✓ People will get bored with your banner after a certain amount of time. Replace your banners regularly with new ones after the banner starts to lose its effectiveness.

✓ Match your message to your targeting and to the self-interests of the people you want to come to your site; make sure your banner is targeted.

Summary

Banners are the coin of the realm when it comes to advertising. Banners can be large or small, animated or static. Each kind of banner you use says a great deal about your Web site. Keep testing and retesting your banners until you have a banner that calls out to the surfer.

> Keep testing and retesting your banners until you have a banner that calls out to the surfer.

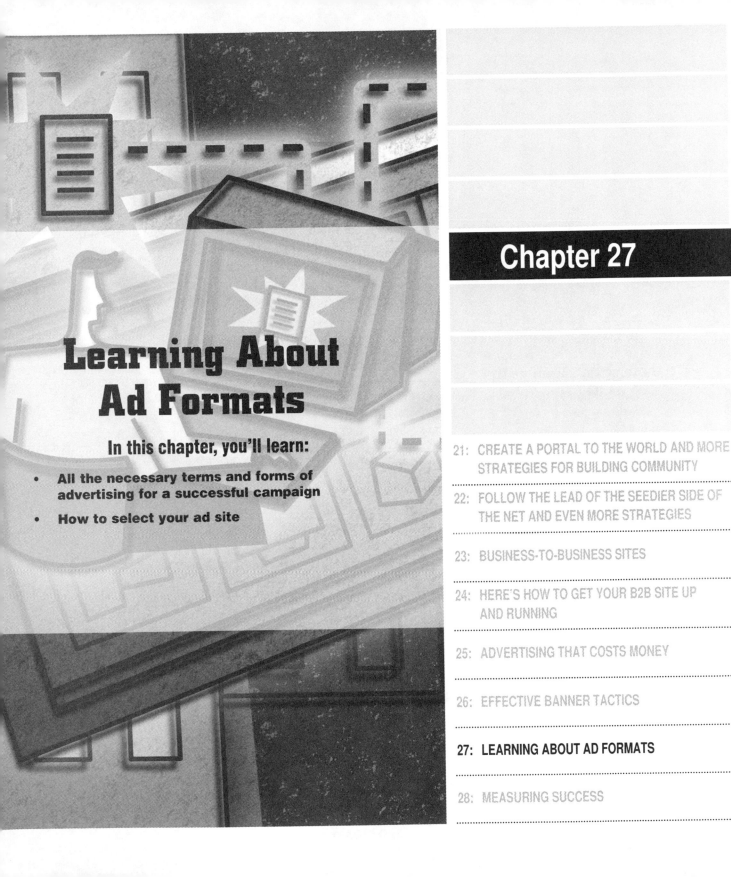

Learning About Ad Formats

In this chapter, you'll learn:

- All the necessary terms and forms of advertising for a successful campaign
- How to select your ad site

Chapter 27

Forms of advertising and how they apply to you

Run of site (ROS)

You can choose where on a specific page or section of the site your ad will run, or you can settle for where the site wants to put you. Advertisements can be focused on a specific page or section of a site. A run of site campaign simply means that the advertisement is rotated across all the pages of a site. ROS should always be less expensive than a targeted ad campaign.

Text ads

Text ads are growing in popularity because they sometimes disguise the fact that they are ads at all. A text ad consists of a few lines of copy together with a link or an e-mail address for action. Text ads are usually priced like banner ads on a cost per impression or click-through basis. Text ads in newsletters are usually specified as a number of lines, with a maximum number of characters per line.

Pop-up ads

Pop-up ads are little boxes that "pop up" over the main browser window when you enter a site, leave it, or leap to a certain page (I use one to set up a presentation). It can contain just about anything you would put on a particular Web page.

Hybrid ads

Hybrid ads combine aspects of other advertising types, such as text and banners, to make a more effective pitch to visitors.

Sponsorships and partnerships

A sponsorship is a paid effort from an advertiser to tie its name to a company, an event, or a venue that reinforces its brand in a positive, yet not overtly commercial, manner.

> You can choose where on a specific page or section of the site your ad will run, or you can settle for where the site wants to put you.

Sponsorships are a different way of promoting your business. You don't usually run a banner for your sponsorship program (although you can), but you connect yourself in more subtle ways. You can use a text notation or just a link. Many times it's hard to see the connection between the company and the event that is being sponsored. And that's OK since, in their classic form, sponsorships are about branding, not about immediate sales. A sponsorship is but one piece of a larger plan to create warm fuzzies in the heart of consumers whenever they see the brand.

A common form of sponsorship is the advertorial. These are usually free, targeted messages that are part hype and part real information. Crayola sponsors numerous arts and crafts sites, and is very happy to transfer the good feeling of sponsorships into day-to-day sales. Banner or text ads offer an integrated appeal when used with the branding of your site. Sponsorships, when done well, can be both discreet and effective. Many sponsorships take the form "Site brought to you by [Sponsor]" or "[Sponsor's] guide by Site."

Interstitials

The Web is very effective for coming up with names that nobody really cares about. Now that I've said that, interstitials are ads that are shown in the transition between two pages of a site. So you click on a link on one page, but instead of going to a page you expected, you arrive at an intermediate page containing the sales pitch. Interstitials are gaining in popularity with advertisers since they offer an almost unlimited amount of space to pitch a product.

Opt-in mailing

Although we have suggested that you refrain from spamming, e-mail advertising has proved fast and effective. Opt-in mailings consist of sending an e-mail message to a "prequalified" list of people, that is, an audience that has expressed an interest in receiving information on a given topic. You can buy lists of newsletter recipients from advertisers, but most advertisers prefer to keep their e-mail addresses secret. If you want to advertise using opt-in mailing, approach mailing lists with caution, and check to be sure that they are being offered by a

Research What Works

You may, as I do, feel a bias against certain kinds of ads, like pop ups or interstitials. That doesn't mean you shouldn't use them. Research companies that use them and find out how well they work. Call or e-mail a principal in a company or even a Webmaster.

reputable firm. Some unscrupulous companies think nothing of "padding" their lists with the names of people who have no real interest, but who have been virtually press-ganged into joining.

Barter instead of paying

The mighty dollar is not always the prime focus of every business transaction. There are ways to get something that's for sale, without ever exchanging any money. Likewise, you can get your advertising into the strongest promotional sites without exchanging money. The Internet has made bartering, or trading, products and services easier than ever before.

I'm sure, in doing your own surfing, that you've found sites where you'd like to place your banner or ad. The problem is they're too expensive. Don't give up. Anybody and everybody who markets a product or service online is always looking for good deals. Just because the Webmaster of that great site is asking for a great deal of money to use some of his or her Web real estate does not mean that he or she won't take less, or even something other than money.

I've been asked many times to swap space for a banner or copies of my books. The point is goods or services in exchange for space can be a great deal for you. Since I'm always short on time, I can't always promote my Web site personally. I just bartered with a search engine expert to promote my site in exchange for copies of this book. It was profitable for us both. We both saved some money and received something we wanted.

Web space is like airline seats. They are both transient. If a plane leaves with an empty seat, the airline loses revenue. If a Web site doesn't have a banner sold it is useless.

Six rules for successful bartering

1. Be realistic. Think about the inventory you have. What value would it have for the prospect? You may have 2,000 salad rinsers on hand. Why would anyone want them? Hint: It may make a good promotion for the site you're trying to sell to.

> The mighty dollar is not always the prime focus of every business transaction.

2. Use the suggested retail price as your benchmark. It allows you to get paid for the cost of making or buying the salad rinsers and to make a profit. Leave room for negotiations.
3. Target properly. What site will want your product? Any site that sells cooking products or gifts might be perfect for you.
4. Be creative. Think about whom your products sell to. If they sell cooking items, you have a wonderful product that they can add to their selection. When you approach Macy's, you have a sought-after gift that will last newlyweds their entire marriage.
5. Make sure you are getting what you are worth. If you are negotiating with another site, they typically have a rate card posted on their site. These rates, just like your salad rinsers, are negotiable.
6. Look at traditional media. Most media outlets have done barter deals at some point in their history. There are no rules that say you have to exchange a banner ad for a banner ad. Determine what's right for you.

> The Web is wide-open territory that you can liken to the old Gold Rush days in Alaska.

How to select your ad site

The Web is wide-open territory that you can liken to the old Gold Rush days in Alaska. No one knew what they would find, but people went there anyway. If this book has shown you anything, it should be that planning should be your buzzword. If you decide to advertise on the Internet, treat it as you would any media and research project. First, you want to check out the advertising on the site. Navigation should be easy; the site should be well thought out and professional. Look closely at the ads offered on the site. Are they similar to yours? You might even e-mail the advertisers to see what kind of service they are getting and what you might expect. The trick is to apply some of the same criteria you would in placing an ad in traditional media.

As in the traditional media target, your decision-making criteria should be based on circulation and your target market. Whatever your figures, the actual target circulation should be part of your decision. Select the publications you use based on the circulation they go to. You'll see things like "Put your ad or page in front of 10 million customers who want your product." Obviously, you are not going to believe that. Stay away from any site that makes outlandish claims. If the offer is to good to be true, it probably is.

When you place an ad on the Internet, you will usually get the URL and that's it! If you hope for placement when you place an ad on the Internet, let's say a page, you get an address where it is located. But the goal is to look for targeted placement. You also need to ask how the site promotes itself. If it's not promoted well, you will probably get the sound of one hand clapping.

If you just say, "fine" and leave it at that, you may get some visitors to look at the ad, but you probably won't get many. If it is on a highly promoted site, you should get some exposure from visitors going to the site itself. If this is not the case, you will probably hear the sound of one hand clapping, too.

Nevertheless, when you do decide where to promote and get that URL, put it on all of your mailing material, business cards, advertising, signature files, and so on. I admit that I've been lax about checking my advertising. If you just put the ad out there and forget about it, it will be like taking your 8 1/2-by-11-inch ad and leaving it on the restaurant table (with your tip) when you order a cup of coffee and forgetting about it. It may pull in some leads—and then, again . . . .

Quick tips

✓ Test all the free ways to use banners before you spend a great deal of money.

✓ Check your ads regularly to make sure you're getting what you're paying for.

Summary

The vast majority of Web sites are exploring and experimenting with different kinds of ad designs. Although many tests have been run, there is no set formula for what kind of ad works best because there are so many variables. Place more emphasis on targeted media and banners rather than using just a shotgun approach. Keep modifying and improving your ad program. If you don't, you will find that your ad budget will be depleted quickly.

Although many tests have been run, there is no set formula for what kind of ad works best because there are so many variables.

For more information on this topic, visit our Web site at www.businesstown.com

Measuring Success

In this chapter, you'll learn:

- **How to make sense of statistics**
- **Key numbers your host should provide**
- **How to track where your visitors are coming or going**
- **Lot's more about measuring the success of your Web site**

Chapter 28

Overview

When we started this book, we spent a few pages going over your goals. What is the true measure of how your Internet site is doing? It depends.

If you're running a business, your goal might be to add to your bottom line or, at least, to know you eventually will be adding to your bottom line. It may be that your goal is just to have a presence on the Web or to free your tech support personnel from the same old questions day after day. If you're running a fun site, getting a few hits per week might seem like fun.

But no matter what your goals are, to check on your Web site, to keep your promotion plan running on optimal capacity, you're going to need steady analysis—someone or something that will give you all the information you need to achieve your goals. Something that is going to analyze your traffic patterns and point you in the right direction. The good news is that it's there on hidden pages of your Web site.

Measuring Web site success is different from measuring stats in traditional business areas. With tried-and-true business statistics, you can measure effectiveness through sales, inquiries, and benchmarks of some kind. The effectiveness of your Web site is measured differently and, in many respects, better than any other form of advertising or marketing.

It is necessary to know if your Internet marketing scheme is successful. But as in all forms of communication that use statistics, the Internet is still so new that it is being redefined every day. As the following paragraphs will show you, even measurements that were once considered finite and definitive are being challenged and changed.

Statistics can be interpreted in any number of ways. It's sort of like the two-horse race between an American and a Russian horse. The American horse won, but the Russian newspapers bragged that the Russian horse came in second against international competition.

All these numbers start from the log file on your server that tracks the myriad of people who come to your Web site. The log file

> When we started this book, we spent a few pages going over your goals. What is the true measure of how your Internet site is doing? It depends.

is then translated by software that interprets the numbers and makes them accessible to you.

Some of the numbers that usually show up in your Web site statistics are:

- Hits
- Files
- Page views
- Sessions
- Data sent (in KB) and the amount of data requested, transferred, and saved by cache (in KB)
- The number of unique URL sites and sessions per month
- The number of all response codes other than 200 (OK)—that is, error codes like the infamous 404, "Page not found" or "The page can not be displayed"
- The average hits per weekday and for last week
- The maximum/average hits per day and per hour
- The number of hits, files, 304s
- Data sent by day, the top 5 days, 24 hours, 5 minutes, and 5 seconds of the summary period
- The top 30 most commonly accessed pages (hits, 304s, data sent)
- The 10 least frequently accessed pages
- The top 30 client domains accessing your server most often
- The top 30 browser types that access your site
- The 30 referrer hosts

About hits

Marketers used to wax enthusiastic discussing the use of hits. Hits seemed to be the only concrete measure of site effectiveness. And the fun thing about hits is that most stats show a lot of them. It's easy to get caught up in hits because every Web statistical program shows them up front and at the top of the charts because they are the biggest numbers. However, as with most things on the Web, counting

> Marketers used to wax enthusiastic discussing the use of hits. Hits seemed to be the only concrete measure of site effectiveness.

> When someone spouts off that their site gets such-and-such number of hits, he or she is spewing out meaningless drivel.

is very self-serving. It's the most inaccurate measurement of anything pertaining to efficacy.

The word first came on the scene as a way to determine Web site traffic because there was nothing else by which to judge online activity. So it was determined that hits should be a defining measurement.

What a hit actually consists of is a file request from a server. And here's the rub. One page may have 20 graphic and image files. Thus the records show that the site received 20 hits each time someone accesses it. Now want to have some fun? Set up a page for yourself with a bunch of graphics. And then go back to your site a dozen times a day. Just watch your stats jump!

When someone spouts off that their site gets such-and-such number of hits, he or she is spewing out meaningless drivel. The number of hits a site gets depends more on how the site was designed than on how many people visit it. Up to this point, it is unclear what hits can tell you and how you want to measure them. A hit is any response from the server on behalf of a request sent from a browser. This includes any response from the server, not only text files or documents. If, for example, an HTML page has two images embedded, the server usually generates three hits if this page is requested: one hit for the HTML page itself and two hits for the two inline images.

The hits question can even undermine the profitability of your site. Suppose you hire an Internet advertising company and base their payments on the number of hits you get. If you have five images on your page and someone accesses your page, your server gets hit six times. And you have to pay for those six hits. That makes your pay-by-hit advertising agency very happy. However, your page really only got one hit and the fact that you have to pay for six of them makes your accountant very sad. The problem with paying for hit performance is that this scheme really does very little to ensure that your objective is met. It ensures only that your page will be seen, not understood, or enjoyed or even appreciated.

An alternative to measuring hits to determine your Web site's effectiveness is to judge which hits are important. Try setting up pages so that the hits to certain pages express different levels of interest. For example, you can measure hits to your splash page, home page, a middle page, your back page, or an order form.

One of the most misleading hits to consider are those to your front page. The result you get is basically how many people have been kicking tires out of mere curiosity. Although this can give you decent analysis of how many people are stopping by and window shopping, it is hard to tell from this method if people are actually shopping or if they are just breezing through on aimless, mindless surfing expeditions. On the other hand, if you count the hits mainly on the back page, you won't know how many people are taking an interest in your whole site.

In other words, a person should not put all the emphasis on one page. Commercial Web users need to be conscious of the structure and layout of their pages. A well-organized set of pages will not only be an oasis to the user, but will also yield very pertinent statistics that will indicate the effectiveness of the individual pages.

Working with statistics accurately

In Chapter 4, we talked about the 5 Ws and the H. In doing your Web site review, you need to use them a different way. If you're trying to please your Web audience, you need to know who, what, when, why, where, and how your visitors are responding to your entire Web site. You should track statistics based on these bits of information if you want to give your products more exposure or keep your audience at your site long enough to see your products or services.

When someone—anyone—visits your Web site, your hosting company tracks *all* the visitor's movements. They know in real time where each visitor came from (the search engine), where they've been, and how many times they clicked when at your site. When someone visits your Web pages, your hosting company can track that visitor's activities, then record them in a log file. Here is some useful information you can access from the files your server should be providing you to track your traffic.

Statistics Can Be Misleading

While this section will give you a lot of tips about using statistics, it doesn't always jive with the number of sales you make. One site gets 25,000 hits per month but hardly sells any goods. Use statistics as an informational tool—and then you can turn it into a marketing tool.

Sessions

If you go to my home page, besides earning my undying gratitude, it counts as one page view—or session but, as we've seen, it can count as many, many hits. You might have looked at only the first fold, or you might have gotten there totally accidentally. All I actually know is that my page sent your computer some files. You have paid me a visit or engaged in a session. But I really want to know what you do when you are on my site. I want to track your moves so I can measure the effectiveness of my layout, information, navigation, and graphics. And I want to check out the pages you've been to

> If you go to my home page, besides earning my undying gratitude, it counts as one page view—or session but, as we've seen, it can count as many, many hits.

Total number of page impressions

The number of page impressions tells you exactly how many people have visited your Web site. You can use this information to prove to potential advertisers the number of visitors your Web site receives. You can also use a page view history to see how you are growing. Your number of page views should grow geometrically as your promotional programs are launched. All files that either have a text file suffix (.html or .text) or are directory index files are included in your page views statistics. By keeping track of page views, you can estimate the number of real documents that your visitor has looked at. If defined correctly, the analyzer rates text files (documents) as page views. Those page views do not include images, CGI scripts, Java applets, or any other HTML objects other than those files that end with one of the predefined page view suffixes, such as .html or .text.

Statistics—the short and the long of it

In short statistics mode, your server provides your history from the first day of the current month until the previous day. In full statistics mode, your site's history log contains summaries for a full year broken down by months so you can see how well your site has grown, or not grown as the case may be. You can rotate the log file at the first day of a new month to keep a constant flow of traffic.

Which advertising campaign works best

One of the best things about tracking statistics on the Internet: you can track how well your advertising is working. Unlike traditional advertising where you're almost always speculating about what's working, you can easily track the results of your banner advertising campaigns and the various links that you've exchanged with others. For example, if you have placed your banner, or your link, on someone else's Web site, you can set it up to link to a specific Web page. You can also use the ?keyword after each of your banner's URL links to track your banner results. Doing this will allow you to see exactly where those visitors are coming from when they come to your site. Just keep in mind, in order for this technique to be effective, you need to set up unique banner links for every banner and link you want to track.

> One of the best things about tracking statistics on the Internet: you can track how well your advertising is working.

Average viewing time

The average time a visitor spends at your site is a particularly important statistic to watch. It tells you:

- Whether your site is keeping the attention of your visitors. If your visitors leave after a couple of minutes, you can pretty much figure out your site is not what they are looking for. If they leave after 30 seconds, you can probably figure that your site is loading too slowly. Statistics show that after 30 seconds, many people get bored and give up.
- How effective your site navigation plan works. You can determine how long it takes to read a page and gauge how long it takes for a visitor to figure out how to navigate through your site to other pages that interest him or her.

Once you understand the movement of surfers and, most specifically, those who come to your site, you can tweak your site to maximize your exposure.

Which pages were most visited and when

What really interests your visitors? By watching the stats that show which pages were most visited and on which day, you can understand what interests your visitors. This information will be especially helpful if you change your site often. Knowing this, you may want to expand or change your site's content to cater to your desired audience. You may have to change just the elements, or you may want to catalog the front page more fully and do more introductory, headline, or graphics work on the first page. Kid Trainers (Chapter 3) had many hits on the first page, but the offers were just not appealing or focused enough to tempt people to read further. And that's why you have to take a cold, hard look at statistics.

> By watching the stats that show which pages were most visited and on which day, you can understand what interests your visitors.

Which pages were visited least often

Consider changing your content on the least popular pages in your site. But don't stop there, you might not be getting the responses you want from the search engines. You may need to optimize those pages and resubmit them to get better search engine rankings. Perhaps you should change the page title to get the engine to reindex the page. There's no written law that says page three *has* to be page three. Changing the page order may add greater flow and ensure more consistent follow-through on you site.

Which pages of your site are the top entry pages

The top entry page is the most visited page on your site. Knowing where people enter your site and where they go next will enable you to promote sales, discounts, special offers, and so on, and to place them where they would be seen the most.

Which pages are the top exit pages

I know, it's difficult to believe and hard to take without getting moist eyes, but everyone leaves even the most interesting site sometime. The top exit page is the last page your visitors see before they leave your Web site. Maybe your visitors are leaving your site too soon because you have too many tempting links that take them out of your site. Perhaps the links to other parts of your Web site aren't easy enough to use.

Here's one way to keep visitors at your site when using outside links. It takes a bit of HTML code. Use the **target="new"** HTML code. When visitors click on links that take them to another site, this code makes a new browser window open leaving your own page right there for the visitor to return to by simply closing the new window. This is a quick and easy way to keep your visitors and have your links, too. Your html code must have **target="new"** inside it. Here's how:

```
<a href=http://www.outsidelinks.com target="new"></a>
```

> It's difficult to believe and hard to take without getting moist eyes, but everyone leaves even the most interesting site sometime.

Where your traffic is coming from

I can't emphasize too strongly how critical it is to know which search engines and which keywords are motivating visitors to come to your site. Without knowing this information, you may change or delete a keyword that brings in the bulk of your traffic. Understanding this information, you will also be able to focus on the search engines you receive the least amount of traffic from by making a specific copy of a Web page that is optimized for those specific search engines.

And don't forget to monitor your reciprocal links to find out who is linking to your site and how many hits you are getting from them.

Table 28.1 shows some more key definitions you might use to monitor your site. I'll use my own server, Superior Hosts, as an example. It's a bit technical but will give you a feeling for the language that is probably used for statistics on you own server.

Table 28.1   DEFINITIONS OF KEY TRAFFIC STATISTICS

KBytes saved by cache

The amount of data saved by various caching mechanisms such as in proxy servers or in browsers. This value is computed by multiplying the number of *Code 304 (Not Modified)* requests per file with the size of the corresponding file. Note: Because http-analyze can determine the size of a file only if the file has been requested at least once in the same summary period, the values for *KBytes saved by cache* and *KBytes requested* are just approximations of the real values.

Unique URLs

Unique URLs are the number of all different, valid URLs requested in a given summary period. This shows you the number of all different files requested at least once in the corresponding summary period.

Unique sites

This is the sum of all unique hosts accessing the server during a given time-window. The time-window is hardwired to the length of the current month. This means that if a host accesses your server very often, it gets counted only once during the whole month. Only the sum of the unique hosts per month is listed in the statistics report.

Sessions

Similar to *unique sites*, this is the number of unique hosts accessing the server during a given time-window. This time-window is one day by default for backward compatibility, but it can be changed with the option -u or the directive in the configuration file. For example, if the time-window is two hours, all accesses from a certain host in less than two hours after the first access from this host are lumped together into one session. All following accesses more than two hours apart from the first access will be counted as new sessions. This way you may get an estimated number of how many sessions are started on different sites to access your server.

Check out another highly rated statistical program

A highly rated statistics program is FlashStats. It generates the following reports:

- Summary report—number of hits, bytes transferred
- Top URLs requested—which pages are the most popular?
- Top referrers to your site—who is linking to your site?
- Search phrases—what are users searching for to find your site?
- Most common browsers—what browsers are being used?
- Bad URLs—what requests are generating errors?
- Bad referrers—who has bad links to your site?
- User domain analysis—which domains accessed your site?
- Types of domains—where are your users coming from?
- Daily totals—how many hits in total did you receive on each day?
- Hits per day of week—which day of the week is busiest?
- Hits per hour—what hour of the day is busiest?

You can try a live online demo or download a 30-day trial edition through *www.maximized.com/products/flashstats/*.

FlashStats is available for the following operating systems:

- Microsoft Windows 95 or Windows NT 3.51 (or later)
- Apple Mac OS—runs on any Macintosh; accelerated for Power Macintosh
- Sun Solaris 2.4 or later
- BSDI BSD/OS
- FreeBSD
- Linux (Intel)
- Linux (Alpha)
- Linux (MIPS)
- Digital UNIX (Alpha)
- SCO

Further, FlashStats 1.4 can use almost any custom log format.

If your home page (or full-blown Web site) is hosted on someone else's server and you want to run FlashStats, you have two options:

- Have your ISP install FlashStats on their servers so that you can run reports remotely.
- Ask your ISP to install FlashStats, or send a detailed e-mail about who your ISP is to maximize.com, and they'll be happy to contact your ISP for you.

Quick tips

✓ Look at your stat sheets regularly and keep using them as a base for improving your site.

✓ Look at your hit statistics long and hard before modifying your banner and links program. Counting hits can be very misleading.

> If you're going to get new traffic, you're going to need steady analysis of who is going to your site and why.

Summary

If you're going to get new traffic, you're going to need steady analysis of who is going to your site and why. Site statistics are not just a page of numbers, but a roadmap that can lead you on too growth if you study them long enough.

For more information on this topic, visit our Web site at www.businesstown.com

SECTION VI

Keeping Track

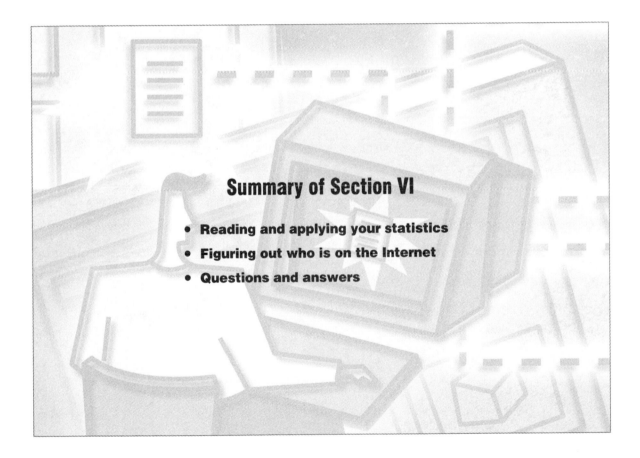

Summary of Section VI

- Reading and applying your statistics
- Figuring out who is on the Internet
- Questions and answers

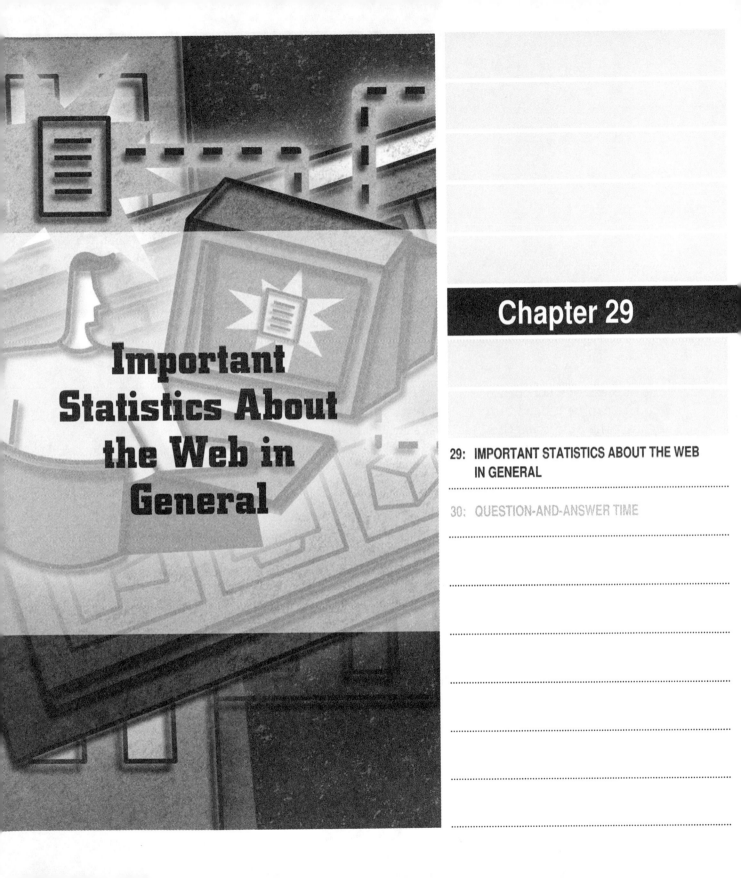

Important Statistics About the Web in General

Chapter 29

I s the Web going over the top, or is it overrated? There are a great many people who express both points of view. Many people would have you believe the Web is overrated as an advertising medium and as a business tool. They maintain that the hype surrounding electronic commerce is turning out to be just that— hype. As of this writing, only 20% of companies are now conducting commercial transactions online. They are simply not aware of what the Web can do to a bottom line. They tell us the Web must be a waste of time from a business perspective.

But remember, just like any other successful marketing communications program, the success of a corporate Web site can be judged only against the objectives the corporations set. A site whose objective was reducing customer service costs or driving more business into a company's retail sales outlets should not be judged a failure because no online transactions were conducted.

This is not to say that Web sites should not be required to manifest a strong ROI, but there are many other reasons, aside from sales, that people will enter a Web site. And, so, a broader view of Web site success is needed in order to provide appropriate accountability for the corporate investment.

Here are 10 steps that will provide agencies and organizations with a model for measuring and tracking their Web sites:

> The success of a corporate Web site can be judged only against the objectives the corporations set.

1. What is the Web site's objective? Just making money is too nebulous. That's like saying the purpose of a small flyer is to sell a million-dollar program. Clearly define the site's objectives. Leverage your existing intelligence.
2. What are all the variables that affect your objectives?
3. What data critical to these variables do you need to accumulate?
4. Can you create a viable working model from these variables?
5. Can, or should, you adjust your site design strategy to achieve objectives and collect data?
6. Can you ascribe values to the critical data and variables that affect your success?

7. Do the resulting ROI values make sense?
8. Can you forge a consensus among team members?
9. Can you apply the model?
10. Last and most important, constantly evaluate, revise, and apply your findings to strengthen your outcomes.

This basic evaluation will provide a means and appropriate criteria for making informed business decisions about further investments in your site. It will also provide you with a means of measuring the site's performance.

Adjust the values ascribed to key model variables based on observed results. In the process, you should continually increase the robustness of your model and, therefore, the accuracy of your ability to predict site results.

> Who plays more games on the Web, men or women? Surprise. Women, 37 to 32%!

Some interesting Web statistics

Who plays more games on the Web, men or women? Surprise. Women, 37 to 32%! Who uses the Web more for shopping? Men, 80 to 67%. Women are much more cautious than men when it comes to using credit cards.

Men aren't nearly as ready to capitalize on the power of e-mail. Sixty-five percent of women who use the Web report that they couldn't live without e-mail. Only 55% of men said the same. Women use e-mail to strengthen bonds with friends and family, and to expand their areas of acquaintance. Women tend to use the Web as a vehicle for reducing isolation. (So much for reports on the Web being a solitary experience.) Interestingly, a person who uses e-mail regularly is far more likely to visit or phone a friend than someone who doesn't use e-mail.

Not so surprising, men want stocks, scores, and other quantitative information. They want the information fast, on demand, and thoroughly explained. Women want more interactive information. Their interests are focused much more on health, religion, job researches, and online gaming.

If there is any significant segmentation criterion for usage of the Internet, it's age. Surveys have demonstrated that men and women, 30 years of age and younger, tend to act very much the same when it comes to the Internet. Both men and women download music with the same enthusiasm, search for information with the equal ease, and use their computer hardware with comparable capability.

Well, now, that does make sense. The big difference in Web usages seems to be whether one has grown up with technology. If we say the Web itself is 6 or 7 years old, then 30-year-olds today would have been 23 or 24 when it began. Even they didn't grow up with the technology or learn to turn to the Internet to satisfy their wants and needs.

What this means is Web sites must start catering to multiple audiences, offering everyone something uniquely interesting so that they will be compelled to stay put once they arrive. We can't focus on techno-geeks anymore. The Web is becoming a place where all walks of life are arriving by the truckload.

Americans born before 1964 are the fastest-growing population on the Web.

Age is no deterrent

Contrary to the widely accepted notion that older Americans are separated from the Internet and e-commerce by an insurmountable "digital divide," a survey released recently by Media Metrix (Nasdaq: MMXI) shows that Americans born before 1964 are the fastest-growing population on the Web.

This older group, which expanded its Internet presence by 20% last year, outpaced the 18-to-24-year-old demographic by about 1 percentage point. The survey also showed that older users went online more frequently than their younger counterparts, stayed on longer, and visited more Web sites. The older group is dominated by the Baby Boom generation, which includes those Americans born between 1946 and 1964.

The paradoxical generation

Interestingly, the results come on the heels of a recent report by the American Association of Retired Persons (AARP) showing that a lack of confidence in the Internet and technology in general is keeping Baby Boomers away from the Web. In fact, the Media Metrix report shows that 45- to 64-year-olds are more apt to invest in high-tech gadgets of all sorts, including fax and copy machines, large-screen televisions, and satellite dishes.

Of course, many of these purchases can be attributed to the fact that older Americans are generally more affluent than their younger counterparts and, therefore, have more disposable income, credit cards, and frequent flier miles. In one example, Media Metrix found that older users are more apt to buy a new car rather than lease or buy a used one.

According to the survey, the 45-to-64 age group went online an average of 6.3 days more than the 18-to-24-year-old "Internet Generation," stayed on more than two hours longer, and visited an average of 150 more unique pages a month.

On the other hand, older users were outdone in their Web use in most categories by the 25- to 34-year-olds, who were online more often, longer, and viewed more pages.

Successful Web business

E-tail success usually comes when a company outdoes its adversaries with a hard-hitting mix of product, price, and ease of use.

It also comes when a company figures out a way to service an underserved market. That's why the good news for e-tailers everywhere is that there is an age group that has not been fully served on the Web.

Generation which?

What age group is best at maneuvering through cyberspace? That's easy, Generation Y. These younger-than-X pups think that the Internet has always been around. They shop at Delia's and hang out at Pokemon World. They're savvy. They're smart. And, they're broke. You can get them to Disney.com, but they can't afford the Mickey Mouse watches.

E-tail success usually comes when a company outdoes its adversaries with a hard-hitting mix of product, price, and ease of use.

So whom do you turn to if you're an e-tailer? Next stop is ol' reliable, Generation X. They have money if they're professionals, but the retail crowd around their portals is thick.

Everybody wants a piece of that action.

So what about the Boomers? They're getting cyber-savvier, but they're not all the way there. The Boomers are the holdouts that broadband is supposed to capture. They've got bucks, and they want to be online, but they also have no time, and their kids are entering college. So they're broke, too.

> There are 87 million Gen A consumers compared with only 50 million 18- to 30-year-olds

The secret's out—it's Generation A

Who's left? Generation A, that's who. You can guess who Generation A is: the 50-plus generation. Ten million of them are now online, and that figure should double in the next two years. There are 87 million Gen A consumers compared with only 50 million 18- to 30-year-olds. What's more, they have 70% of America's financial assets and control 50% of our discretionary income. They even buy 25% of all toys.

And most of all, these people are beginning to get comfortable with e-tailing. "We are actually finding the 55- to 65-year-olds are highly comfortable buying online," said Gail Janensch, public relations director for research firm Greenfield Online. "Plus, these people have a great amount of disposable income."

Segment Gen A by sex and viewing habits

RelevantKnowledge measured the most popular sites among users age 50 and above (Tables 29.1 and 29.2). Traffic was measured for one month. As a whole, users age 50 and up surfed 19% longer than all other Web users combined.

Table 29.1   TOP SITES AMONG WOMEN AGE 50 AND UP

Rank	Site	Average Minutes Per Month
1	*previewtravel.com*	324
2	*hotmail.com*	142
3	*nasa.gov*	85
4	*msn.com*	45
5	*yahoo.com*	39
6	*marthastewart.com*	33
7	*cnn.com*	31
8	*earthlink.net*	30
9	*bluemountain.com*	30
10	*hallmarkconnections.com*	30

Table 29.2   TOP SITES AMONG MEN AGE 50 AND UP

Rank	Site	Average Minutes Per Month
1	*pointcast.net*	1205
2	*ebay.com*	414
3	*search.com*	146
4	*sportszone.com*	135
5	*hotmail.com*	124
6	*bigcharts.com*	100
7	*schwab.com*	91
8	*infobeat.com*	81
9	*imdb.com*	68
10	*zdnet.com*	65

Average minutes per month: The mean number of minutes per month that a demographic group accesses the site.

The sleeping giant

So what is it that has kept e-tailers from lunging after Generation A consumers the way they do the others? Do our Gen A-ers lack the flash and sizzle that Internet marketers and PR flacks need to justify their existence? Or do these Young Turks figure that technology has forever passed these people by?

Actually, the reasons do not even matter. Our largest industries, such as autos and vitamin supplements, have long known that seniors are a prosperous and loyal group. They will continue to harness the huge financial resources, and eventually, someone on the Internet will figure it out. Until then, these Gen A-ers will continue to do what they have been doing—spend money at somebody else's site.

> Most recently, the ethnic and minority groups in the United States are joining the excitement. And e-business is just beginning to realize this is a viable market segment to pursue online.

U.S. ethnic groups getting piece of e-commerce pie

Most recently, the ethnic and minority groups in the United States are joining the excitement. And e-business is just beginning to realize this is a viable market segment to pursue online.

Hispanic Market Weekly reported recently that 32% of PC-owning households in the United States are Latino, and 59% of those PC owners are on the Web. That's one heck of a large market—close to two million Spanish-speaking people in the United States alone—and to date they've been largely neglected. The University of Georgia's Terry College of Business reports that this U.S. Spanish-speaking market segment generates roughly $383 billion in buying power to e-commerce.

EPublicEye.com and La Opinión are just two of the sites that are targeting the population that the U.S. Census estimates is growing 10 times faster than all other ethnic groups, including whites. They argue that the Hispanic market is vastly underserved on the Web and have committed to rectify this deficiency.

The Hispanic population is just one of many ethnic groups whose time has come in cyberspace.

Courting diverse viewers

Other ethnic consumer groups are also attracting more attention as online merchants look for ways to increase their customer bases. Savvy e-commerce merchants are judiciously developing their Web sites to accommodate African-Americans, Asian-Americans, and Native Americans as well as Hispanics.

In fact we're realizing that the global market is far more extensive than the WASP population that lives in the United States. To do business effectively on the Web, e-commerce is stretching to meet new challenges. Cultural multiplicity magnifies the opportunities and the challenges inherent in communicating and doing business effectively on the Web. Even the smallest Web site is affected.

We're also discovering that the English that is spoken in the midwestern United States is not always the English that is spoken elsewhere. In fact, it's a very small dialect in the context of the global Internet community of English-speaking surfers. We're discovering that adaptability is important if we're to address the needs of those whose mother language is not English. The language we use every day may need to be broadened to accommodate the differences. And we are beginning to realize that in many cases we may need to include translations on our Web site.

Building your online presence is more than just putting up some HTML code. These are some of the factors that you will want to at least think about as you develop your presence on the Web. Again it goes back to our discussions of identifying your market and catering to their needs. It goes back to finding out where your market is. It might be much different from what you initially thought.

As you study your statistics, you may find that the vast majority of your traffic comes from places you had no idea existed. Capitalize on that knowledge. Learn about those sources for traffic. Make whatever adjustments are necessary to keep them coming back. And use those statistics to introduce yourself to the markets that are looking for your products or services.

> Building your online presence is more than just putting up some HTML code.

Follow-up e-mail saying, "I noticed you stopped by my site and was wondering if I might be of further service" can expand your opportunities. (That's not spam.) It's easier to keep the attention of those who have demonstrated an interest in what you have to offer than to try to grab strangers' attention on the Web.

Micro-target your marketing efforts

There are lots of ways to target your markets to specific demographic, psychographic, or geographic groups. Pogo.com is one of many sites that provide a broad lineup of family games. Their media advertising solutions like Superstitials, e-mail marketing, and Enliven expanding and transactional banners offer a strong promotional vehicle you might want to take a serious look at. Visit *www.pogo.com/advertise* for details.

Consider the "other" interests of your market

While you're closely studying your own statistics, get out there and find other statistics that might affect your potential for pulling traffic.

I found an interesting set of statistics the other day. It was compiled in December 1999 by Jupiter Communications/NFO Interactive at Macroview That's Entertainment. It reminds us that online users are as much captivated by entertainment that borders on reality's edge as they are interested in doing business. Surfers are not just out there scanning the Internet for you and your business or service. They're pursuing other interests as well. Amusements range from staring at dirty pictures to downloading MP3 files, chatting, swapping gossip and racy jokes via e-mail, browser window shopping, celebrity fawning, and watching streaming video clips. Table 29.3 shows how these activities stack up against each other among users who say they go online for any of these activities at least once a month.

> While you're closely studying your own statistics, get out there and find other statistics that might affect your potential for pulling traffic.

Table 29.3   What Users Do to Entertain Themselves Online

Online Activity	Percent Usage	Worldwide Users
E-mail	96%	188M
E-greetings	55	108
Instant message	51	100
Travel research	47	92
Online chat	45	88
Music sites	40	78
Play games	38	74
TV program sites	33	65
Sports sites	28	55
View video online	25	49
Download music	22	43
View adult content	22	43
Movie-related sites	18	35
Online dating services	7	14
Gamble	2	4

The numbers are based on the estimated number of worldwide users at the end of 1999–an estimate of 196 million users.

How can you incorporate these elements into your Web site?

Are your beginning to get some ideas? Consider how, at the Grammy Awards, Jennifer Lopez wowed the crowd with a very "sticky" dress. EMAZING seized that as an entertaining opportunity and enabled visitors to send Jennifer Lopez greeting cards to friends at *http://greetings.emazing.com/lopez.html.*

Sending electronic greeting cards has become so popular that NPD Online Research reported that as many as 66% of the users it surveyed planned to e-mail a Valentine's Day card in the year 2000, a nice jump from the 55% who intended to do so in 1999. The chief benefactor of all this online love was Blue Mountainart, which Excite@Home craftily snapped up last fall.

Sending electronic greeting cards has become so popular that NPD Online Research reported that as many as 66% of the users it surveyed planned to e-mail a Valentine's Day card in the year 2000, a nice jump from the 55% who intended to do so in 1999.

Table 29.4   AUDIENCE VIEWING TIMES

Rank	Domain	Unique Total Time Audience Spent	Per View Average Minutes
1.	bluemountain.com	14,515,462	17.2
2.	americangreetings.com	7,466,223	11.7
3.	disney.go.com	3,492,121	11.7
4.	greetings.yahoo.com	3,151,320	12.0
5.	egreetings.com	3,093,664	11.9
6.	uproar.com	3,062,605	33.6
7.	eonline.com	2,676,641	6.8
8.	mtv.com	2,558,192	9.5
9.	justsaywow.com	2,413,376	6.2
10.	ticketmaster.com	2,323,359	18.1
11.	games.yahoo.com	2,284,492	21.7
12.	windowsmedia.microsoft.com	2,269,348	3.0
13.	ticketmaster.com	2,160,705	11.4
14.	webshots.com	2,114,746	17.1
15.	ign.com	1,933,208	16.5
16.	broadcast.com	1,930,528	3.7
17.	nick.com	1,907,758	26.8
18.	entertainment.msn.com	1,787,100	4.0
19.	mp3.com	1,757,946	5.0
20.	iwin.com	1,639,237	24.1
21.	gamesville.com	1,455,874	90.9
22.	moviefone.com	1,332,279	5.7
23.	imdb.com	1,329,968	27.1
24.	discovery.com	1,305,530	11.7
25.	123greetings.com	1,266,077	12.5

Source: March 2000 Nielsen/NetRatings Inc.

Target your message

About(.com) offers extreme targeting like no one else—their more than 650 niche vertical sites allow you to talk directly to consumers in an environment they've selected. You might want to check with them at their e-mail address *adsales6@about-inc.com* to learn their options. Although some of their programs may cost money, they may also significantly improve your Web presence.

Sports is big

Besides celebrities, most entertainment-related marketing tie-ins involve some reference to sporting events. You might take lessons from the "big boys" and find a way to tie in your interest—and your audience's interest—in sports to build your Web site traffic.

Unicast used the Super Bowl to hype a "Superstitial Showdown," which, the company said, attracted nearly 250,000 visitors. InfoBeat partnered with Sandbox.com, a provider of interactive games, to produce "It's Madness!"–a college basketball tournament site that offers $10 million to the contestant who picks a perfect NCAA Basketball Tournament bracket. Go.com's ESPN.com reported that about 590,000 basketball fans, which the company said was the largest Internet tournament of all, were playing its Men's NCAA Tournament Challenge sponsored by Pizza Hut and Courtyard by Marriott. You can check out these sites yourself at the following addresses to see if there's a way for you to incorporate some of their tactics:

> *www.espn.com*
> *http://infobeat.itsmadness.com*
> *www.supershowdown.com*

> You might take lessons from the "big boys" and find a way to tie in your interest—and your audience's interest—in sports to build your Web site traffic.

Attract surfers while they're having fun

Online marketers who attract consumers while they're having fun find consumers are in a far better mindset and are much more receptive than business users who tend to be more pressed for time.

When ABCNEWS.com hosted a 20- to 30-minute chat with "millionaire wife" Darva Conger, some 58,000 questions were reportedly posted. Jupiter Communications Analyst David Card recently observed that "chat has always been more about entertainment than communication and eBay is more about fun than about actually buying things." That's why eBay logs an average visit length (AVL) of 100-plus minutes, which is tops among the big sites. Even eBay's average visit length is bested by sites that feature dating services (Matchmarket.com at 174 minutes) and peeping Toms (VoyeurWeb.com, 114 min.), according to a recent Media Metrix report.

Given the trend toward more 360-degree marketing, it's not surprising that leading media companies are circling the online wagons with cyber-entertainment properties. MTV's WebRIOT, for example, launched in November 1999, uses an interactive format to pit its 700,000 registered online users against studio contestants. Trashing real-world opponents, it's the ultimate commentary on edgy entertainment. Ideas? What can you do to capitalize on this newest marketing strategy?

> When ABCNEWS.com hosted a 20- to 30-minute chat with "millionaire wife" Darva Conger, some 58,000 questions were reportedly posted.

Surveys help identify ways to reach your market

I was just reading the latest *Business 2.0*, the best offline magazine about e-commerce. They quoted the results of a survey that asked how Web users find new Web sites. Here are their results:

Search engines	45.8%	Television	1.4%
Word-of-mouth	20.3%	E-mail	1.2%
Random surfing	19.9%	Banner/Web ads	1.0%
Magazines	4.4%	Other	0.9%
By accident	2.1%	Don't know	0.7%
Newspapers	1.4%	Radio	0.4%

Survey sources

How do you find surveys that will help you keep your finger on trends that are as volatile as those on the Internet? Here are some places that help. You'll surely find many others as you continue your market research:

Search IW

Daily newsletter

Sign up for the free Internet World Daily E-mail newsletter

Internet.com

BrowserWatch

E-Commerce Guide

InternetNews.com

Internet Product Watch

Internet Shopper

Internet World

JavaBoutique

Webopaedia

SearchEngineWatch

ServerWatch

Stroud's CWSApps

The List

WDVL

WebServer Compare.com

WebDeveloper.com

WebReference.com

Mecklermedia

Internet World Trade Shows

Advertising info

Corporate information

Quick tips

✓ Look at your stat sheets regularly and keep using them as a base for improving your site.

✓ Use the demographics on this page to target your site.

✓ Sign up for newsletters that can help you gain more insight into your market.

Summary

If you're going to get new traffic, you're going to need steady analysis of who is visiting your site and why. Site statistics are not just a page of numbers, but a roadmap that can lead you to growth if you study them long enough. There are also many sites that offer research on who is going where on the Web—and why. Search for them and use them to achieve your Web goals.

> If you're going to get new traffic, you're going to need steady analysis of who is visiting your site and why.

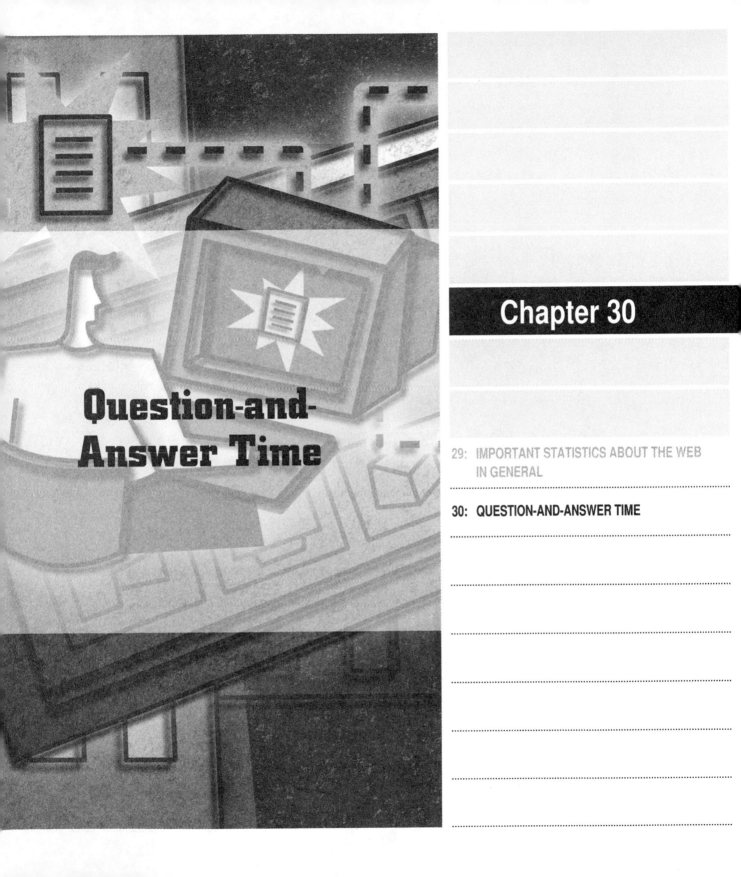

Question-and-Answer Time

Chapter 30

We discussed a great many things in this book and have tried to give real-world answers and examples wherever and whenever possible. Here are some real-world questions and answers to help you prepare and promote your new Web site. If your exact question or business is not specifically mentioned, try to analyze the answers and fit them into your particular needs.

What is e-marketing anyway?

Question: I've just started my career in marketing for an Internet firm. This sounds pretty basic, but what exactly does e-marketing and Web marketing mean?

Answer: We all get caught up in tightly wound definitions that can really hinder our growth if we take them too literally. But here's one that you can use. E-marketing (or cybermarketing or Web marketing) is a carefully planned, controlled, and continual effort at promoting a company or organization, its products or its services, through the most efficient use of electronic media, using the most practical, effective, thoroughly researched and up-to-date strategies.

Search engine services

Question: I found a company on the Web that is supposed to be able to promote my online business by submitting to over 1,000 search engines for $159. I'm trying to find out if they are for real or not. Should I do it?

Answer: There are two questions here. One is whether they are legitimate or not, the second is should you use an outside source. One way to find out if they are legitimate is to ask for a list of their clients and call them directly. But remember, they will give you only a list of satisfied clients. No one gives unsatisfactory recommendations. If you do call the companies they have dealt with, there are two key questions you must ask:

1. Would you use the company again?

> E-marketing (or cybermarketing or Web marketing) is a carefully planned, controlled, and continual effort at promoting a company or organization, its products or its services, through the most efficient use of electronic media.

2. After the initial submission, will the company keep submitting for you on a regular basis, register by hand with the directories, and follow up until you get strong search ratings?

You can also ask about the company in one of the many forums or newsgroups that are dedicated to Internet marketing

The second issue you have raised is whether you should use an outside source at all. About 950 of the search engines are totally unimportant. Many are spam engines. Once your site is submitted to them, all you will get is repeat e-mails.

Don't let the big numbers fool you. You don't need them. Concentrate on the major search engines in this book, because they will drive 80% of your hits. If you think you don't have the time to do the submissions properly, you can consider an outside source (after reading the book, you definitely have the knowledge). Don't forget that there are also many online companies that will submit your site free of charge.

Developing your Web site

Question: I have just launched a combination newsletter and search engine for business publications. I'd like to fill my site with business articles from service companies like legal firms, accounting firms, consultants, or others who have a specific knowledge of certain business areas. After submitting the firm's Web site to my search engine, companies can register their free publications and articles. Do you think this is a good idea?

> Decide what kind of budget you have. Are you going to sell the information in the reports or generate income through the sale of ads on your site?

Answer: It sounds as if it may be a good idea. Some of the questions you need to answer are how you plan to differentiate your site from everyone else's and decide what kind of budget you have. Are you going to sell the information in the reports or generate income through the sale of ads on your site? Are you going to charge your "experts" to be listed in return for a free link? How do you expect to build up the credibility of your experts? Who is your target market? Look at exp.com for a model of what you're trying to do, but don't forget, they started with major funding.

How to make banners

Question: I would like to make my own professional-looking banner. I'd like to know what programs to use and how to make them as small as possible.

Answer: The first thing you need to know is the standard banner sizes. Look at Chapter 16 on banners for examples. Small banners generally do not generally achieve as great a click-through as larger banners.

There are at least two good banner-making programs available. Both are available for 30-day free trials. BannermakerPro is good and quick to learn. Fireworks 3.0, from Macromedia, does animations or static banners with more pizzazz. It's easy to learn, and it's specific to Web graphics.

What's reciprocal about links?

Question: I have a game site that draws many visitors and would like to get reciprocal links by placing banners on my site. What is the best way to do this?

Answer: Bcentral.com (formerly Link Exchange) is the biggest banner operation. Bannerate.com has also been recommended to me. At Bannerate, you can choose your own banner exchange ratio. They claim to have automatic and human checks to make sure only quality sites with good banners participate. They also make periodic human checks of all members' sites. They claim they give 500 banner impressions for free just for trying them out.

You might also think of paying for banners. Banner ads cost 2 to 5 cents per view, $2 to $5 per visitor, and perhaps $50 to $100 per sale (depending upon your conversion rate). All marketing should be done on an ROI analysis. Figure out what is the most that you can spend per new visitor to your site. Even if it is 50 cents, you at least have an indicator to use when approaching places to advertise.

> Small banners generally do not generally achieve as great a click-through as larger banners.

Are premium banner services worth paying for?

Question: Is it worth the expense to go with the premium banner services, or shall I stick with just the free basic services? Which gives you the most bang for the buck? Our average sale is about $250.

Answer: If you purchase banners outright, you won't have to carry too many on our own site. Too many banners make your site clumsy looking and make your page longer to load. You can also spend a little to advertise on subsections of search engines specific to your industry. Consider even more expensive search engine sites that will put your ads on pages specific to where people will be searching for your product

     Check out 1001mediakits.com. There you can compare many sites where you could buy banner ad placements. They have many media kits where you can compare site strengths and demographics.

Domain names—who owns what and what cost?

Question: I registered a few domain names three months ago, and they still are on the registrar's site. Can I find out how many hits these names are getting?

> Too many banners make your site clumsy looking and make your page longer to load. You can also spend a little to advertise on subsections of search engines specific to your industry.

Answer: The company that you purchased the domain names from should have a log of what hits there were for each name. If you request that info from them, they may send it to you.

Question: How can domain registration fees be so inexpensive? Alldns.com gets what seems like a full dotcom name for $14.95 a year, half of what Network Solutions gets. A company called bulkregister.com says they can do it for $10.

Answer: If you register your domain through a hosting company, they are registering the domain as a service to you. You are paying for the registration service, not the name itself. So the domain name belongs to the host, not you. Depending on the policies of the host, you may or may not take the name with you to a new host.

Companies like bulkmaster.com are high-volume dealers who register names in bulk. They claim to provide business customers with fast, reliable, and secure registration services at the lowest prices available anywhere. The more names you register, the lower the cost per name. It works like an airline consolidator that can provide lower prices because they are buying in bulk.

Pros and cons of doorway pages

> *Content-based pages, with well-written headlines, keywords, and copy still capture the most interest from search engines.*

Question: What's the best way of optimizing gateway pages for the various major search engines?

Answer: Even in this computer age of doing everything automatically, the best way is to do it by hand. Despite the popularity of doorway pages, some search engines appear to be displeased, and some consider doorway pages spam. Content-based pages, with well-written headlines, keywords, and copy still capture the most interest from search engines. They lead to the best, most qualified hits.

Question: A couple of months back, we uploaded some doorway pages at the advice of an allegedly competent Internet marketing company. After investigating our lack of any kind of visibility on AltaVista, I found that we were expunged from their index. Here's what we got back from AltaVista:

"Thank you for taking the time to write to us about your site and the error message you received while trying to submit it. You have been blocked from submitting because we consider certain pages on your site, the machine/program generated pages, to be Spam (pages which lack content and are only there to draw the user further into your site)."

Should I eliminate doorway pages altogether for fear of offending other search engines?

Answer: Doorway pages can work if they are submitted properly and individually to the major search engines. Read each site's rules carefully. They will tell you exactly what to do to get submitted.

Counterintelligence

Question: I hate to sound covert and unethical here, but what is the best way to spy on competitors? Is there any software that will do the job? Are there free spying services? I want to know where my competitor's visitors are coming from and how often they change their site—all in the good name of Web site promotion.

Answer: There is a basic "rule" in journalism that if you steal from one source it's plagiarism, but if you steal from two or more, it's research. This doesn't actually pertain to your question, but I like the line. Some of the information you want you can get by checking and rechecking your competitor's sites. Many businesses have a "updated on" line on their Web site. You can also look at their source code.

Here's another way. Contact the company and pretend you want to advertise on their pages and need to know their key demographics. (Remember you did *not* get that tip in this book.) You can also check on a site called Spyonit.com. Check it out and use it often.

> There is a basic "rule" in journalism that if you steal from one source it's plagiarism, but if you steal from two or more, it's research.

Mass press releases

Question: I have recently started a Web site and have my press release all ready to go. My biggest concern is finding lists to send my press kit to. I want to send it to both online and offline resources. Do you have any ideas that may help me find sites that will be receptive to my press campaign? Also, do you know of a company that will get press releases out for me? They have to be cheap and good.

Answer: Two good sources are Tenagra (*www.tenagra.com*) and PRWeb.com. I believe, though, that it more important to develop your own lists and build lasting relationships with the editors.

You should also make sure your lists are highly targeted. If you blitz everyone, you'll feel like your getting your message across, but you might not be targeting the right people. A new Web site is not big news anymore (for the most part). It might be news to a reporter for a trade magazine in a field that doesn't have a great many Web sites. Make sure the information is newsy and newsworthy.

Pop-ups—the good, the bad, and the spam

Question: I have a very successful e-zine and I would like to use pop-up ads to get more visitors to subscribe. I have been told by some people it is considered spam. I have been told by others that it is perfectly OK. To pop-up or not to pop-up, that is the question.

Answer: Yes, you're right. Some people consider it spam. Some consider it a necessary part of doing business. There is a definite split in opinion on the subject. I personally hate them and never have subscribed to a pop-up ad. But there is strong evidence that pop-up ads can increase signups. I've also heard a lot of people complain about the intrusion of pop-ups. Try it out. If it works, do it. If you get too many complaints, jettison them.

But there is strong evidence that pop-up ads can increase signups.

New Internet business— what do I do first and next?

Question: A friend and I are starting a new ladies wear business over the Internet. Our domain name has been chosen and protected. We already have our name and Internet address protected, and we are in the process of choosing an Internet provider. What are the next steps we should take that would maximize our time and effort? What would get us going in the right direction before we even open our doors for business?

Answer: Obviously you have your goals and objectives in place. Since you haven't yet designed your Web site, make sure it reeks of promotion, and build your site around the keywords and graphics tips mentioned in Chapters 5 and 6.

When you're first starting out, you'll want to use a few low-cost or free Web site promotion tactics, especially if you are on a budget. Go to the newsgroups related to your field and start developing relationships with the posters. Run a search for your competitors and look at their keywords. Start exploring Web rings and cybermalls so you know which ones (if any) you should use.

Staying on top of trends

Question: I am familiar with WebTrends, and have used it in the past. Can anyone recommend other software that can give me the same, or more, data, and what about cost?

Answer: EMarketer.com is a free source that offers statistical information about the latest research, surveys, and reports. You can also buy a great many reports from them on various business aspects in the Internet marketplace.

Music and the Web

Question: I am thinking of creating a Web site for my band. We are interested in Web exposure. We don't want a niche but a wide audience.

Answer: You'll get much better results if you concentrate on a niche, say grunge rock or heavy metal (I don't know if I'm getting the terms right–I'm really old). The secret to starting out in Web marketing is to really home in on an audience that *wants* to know about the type of music you're playing. Who would your music appeal to? What age levels, and so on? Once you know that, you can successfully reach your target market segment.

EMarketer.com is a free source that offers statistical information about the latest research, surveys, and reports. You can also buy a great many reports from them on various business aspects in the Internet marketplace.

Legal, but profitable?

Question: I've just created a free membership-based service that helps people find an attorney who best suits their needs. Attorneys are charged a fee to have their info listed in the database. Attorneys also can participate in the online forum, and compete for business on our Legal Opportunity Board—a classified ad service in which prospective clients describe their needs. It works like the many "dating" Internet sites. The "ad" shows up as "brief description of the need, the city, and the state." All attorneys can see this info, but only paid-up attorneys will be e-mailed this person's name, address, phone, and e-mail address in order to contact them.

Answer: Optimize your search engine campaign. Eighty-five percent of your clients will come from there. Your main priority is to get ranked higher on search engines listings than your competitors are. Your search position will be of key importance, so watch those keywords carefully. Submit your site yourself. Go to all the major search engines and manually submit your site. Make sure that your site is up and running before you submit.

Other forms of online advertising such as banner ad campaigns or e-zines can be used. Consider doing a newsletter and send it out to all attorneys using an opt-in mail list.

Personally visit a few attorneys in your area and discuss your idea. You'll be surprised at how many people will help you if you don't try to sell anything to them. Perhaps you can offer a free listing to them to "seed" your new contacts.

Surf the net for similar sites. Ask Webmasters to link to you, and you will link to them. This will bring in targeted traffic. I know for my site I get tons of hits from students doing market research, but they are not my target audience.

> Optimize your search engine campaign. Eighty-five percent of your clients will come from there. Your main priority is to get ranked higher on search engines listings than your competitors are.

Research on the cheap

Question: I have three home "lifestyle" products that I've conceived of, designed, and found fairly cheap manufacturers for. I've got my domain name, my storefront, and my shopping cart program set.

My problem is that I don't know which products will sell. I don't know who my target market is, beyond Middle America. I can't really trust either myself or my friends to know what's going to sell. How do I get the opinions the people I want to sell to—without hiring a professional polling firm?

Answer: Congratulations, you have 90% of the work done because you realize that consumers are going to drive the market, and you know that you don't know everything. Many, if not most, companies start out with a lot less preparation and are hindered by "I know it all" mentalities.

Start an opt-in e-mail list as soon as possible. An opt-in e-mail list will give you a repeated, persuasive contact with your likely customers. It will also be an excellent source for feedback and will function as a free focus group.

Check out ListBot Gold ($99 per year). You can:

- Communicate directly with your potential customers by sending them e-mail messages with research questions, product announcements, or special offers.
- Store an archive of your messages to analyze your results.
- Send e-mails quickly and professionally to communicate with your customers.
- Create a customer database to learn about your customers.
- Collect vital demographic information.
- Create your own customized and targeted demographic questions.
- Have people sign up directly from your Web site to get your polls, product ideas, and be put on the mailing list.

> An opt-in e-mail list will give you a repeated, persuasive contact with your likely customers.

Making newsletters newsy

Question: I plan to develop a newsletter for my products. Do you have any quick hints you can give me?

Answer: Don't focus your newsletter on products. Instead, offer advice or something else that will satisfy a need on the part of the readers. You'll be surprised at how many people will love it and send it to their friends. Remember to constantly encourage feedback!

Question: I have been put in charge of articles and information for a newsletter for two of our clients. One is involved with nutritional products, and the other is in computers, computer hardware, and accessories. Could you tell me where I get the content or ideas of what to put in this newsletter?

Answer: Search newsgroups online to see what information people are looking for, and give them that information in your newsletter. There is a ton of free information available online. You should have no problem finding articles to include. Research other newsletters to see how they handle subject matter and what their graphic format is.

Here's an e-mail I recently received. Though it is far from an ideally crafted letter (much too many points covered), the middle of the letter requests articles from me.

> I would like to introduce our company to you. We are Bratek Inc. (not their real name) and I have attached several of our most recent press releases since this is the easiest way to explain what our company is about and the continued success we are experiencing. We offer our customers on-line B2B services for the Grocery, Apparel, Footwear and Jewelry industries.
>
> In addition to selling business solutions on our site, a part of the service that we provide our customers is industry specific on-line publishing. With the launch of our grocery vertical, we are looking for freelance writers to provide informational content that pertains to our grocer customer's business. We have seen your name in several trade publications

> Don't focus your newsletter on products. Instead, offer advice or something else that will satisfy a need on the part of the readers.

and are interested in exploring a partnership with you. Please take some time and visit our Web site *http://www.retail.com* to get a better understanding of the quality of content which we provide.

If you wish to discuss pursuing a partnership with us, please contact me at 612/632-8108. I look forward to hearing from you soon. Thank you for taking the time to read my message.

Making money on taxes

Question: My client wants to e-market a tax-advantaged college savings investment product. For a variety of reasons, the biggest tax break comes to residents of one small state. We want to focus on those residents of that particular state, who have money to save for their children or grandchildren, and for whom an income tax break would be appealing. What are the best channels and means to e-market?

Answer: Ah yes, target marketing to the max. Nice job of focusing. Check *http://local.yahoo.com* and see what sites there are that are specific to that state and approach them. See if these sites have the mailing lists that you can use.

You might also want to run banner ads on those sites. Think about writing an article specific to that state and explaining the benefits. Include solid info, a good SIG, and a link back to your site. You might also want to use a pop-up to get key contact information. Offer the article to those sites. (I don't like pop-ups but they have their place.)

> Think about writing an article specific to that state and explaining the benefits.

E-mail stats

Question: What percentage of opt-in e-mail gets through compared to bulk mail? Yes, I know bulk mail is considered spamming, but I'm just looking for numbers.

Answer: If you've developed your opt-in mail list by yourself, just about 100% gets through. If you send unsolicited bulk e-mail, that depends. Once you get caught, there's a good chance that one-third of the Internet may be closed off to you entirely. Here's an example of what happened to me. Someone on my server sent a few spams to America Online. Because of this, AOL banned all e-mail from and to my server, which obviously caused a great many problems for me.

An opt-in mail list means that every person who receives the e-mail asked to receive it, and understood what he or she was getting.

What is permission marketing?

Question: What is permission marketing? I have heard the phrase often lately. Does it mean I have to have the prospect's permission every time I send him or her e-mail?

Be personal.

Answer: Pick up Seth Godin's book, *Permission Marketing: Turning Strangers Into Friends, and Friends into Customers.* The three key rules are:

1. Be anticipated.
2. Be personal.
3. Be relevant.

The concept behind permission marketing is relatively simple: Offer consumers the opportunity to volunteer to receive marketing materials via e-mail, and the "takers" will be much more likely to pay attention to the message. Add an incentive of sorts to the mix, and you've laid the framework to build a loyal following for a long-term, interactive Web-based marketing campaign.

It's not only about getting permission, but being wanted

Permission marketing is about building long-term relationships with your customers, which is the best way to get traffic. This is not only useful for e-marketing, but for all marketing. This is a blatant plug, but you might want to read my book, *Marketing Straight to the*

Heart (Amacom). It tells how to build long-terms relationships with customers in any business.

There are three major rules to building relationships and getting permission to contact them time and time again: (1) Make it easy, (2) build trust, and (3) serve.

Web site failures

Question: I'm thinking of developing a Web site for baby products, and before I start, I'd like to know the biggest mistakes Web marketers make in developing their site.

Answer: In the scads of Web sites I have researched in the development of this book, I have found two problems.

1. Lack of focus. Most sites are much too cluttered. The visitor doesn't know what the site is really all about. If you sell something, clear the site of anything that doesn't have to do with that objective. Get rid of too many links and irrelevant content. Don't use hit counters, too many off-target graphics, and anything that doesn't add to what you're trying to do.
2. Sites that read like brochures. Me. Me. Me. It's *not* about you. It's about the customer. People have lost sight of why they are designing a Web site or never had sight of it in the first place. People need to focus on why and how they should design a Web site. Until they do, they're simply wasting Web space and money.

> There are three major rules to building relationships and getting permission to contact them time and time again: (1) Make it easy, (2) build trust, and (3) serve.

For more information on this topic, visit our Web site at www.businesstown.com

Glossary

Advertising network

A collection of Web sites that share banner or advertising. It can deliver various combinations of targeted placements because they can put your banner on numerous sites.

Agents

They can be brokers of Web advertising space or a spider for a search engine.

Affinity group

A group of people with common interests. Used to target ads.

ALT

An HTML tag that, when viewed by text-only browsers, inserts text in place of an image. They are widely used in newsgroups.

America Online

The world's largest Internet and service provider. AOL is a fast and easy way to get Internet access. And with over 10 million subscribers, a fast way to get your message across to members.

Auto-responder

Similar to the way fax-back services operate, an auto-responder is a program that will automatically generate a response when an e-mail comes in. Auto-responders are extremely useful for handling information requests and for generating order acknowledgments.

Backbone

A high-speed connection within a network that connects shorter, usually slower circuits. Also used in reference to a system that acts as a "hub" for activity.

Bandwidth

Although it has a number of technical definitions, "bandwidth" has come to be a simple shorthand term for "Internet airtime." Web designers use the term to mean download time, or the time the reader needs to wait to be able to view a site. There is even a Society for Bandwidth Conservation, which is a forum for graphics designers to share tips on how to make Web pages load faster.

Banners

The most popular form of advertising on the Web. These are usually narrow graphics, sometimes logos, sometimes about 1½ inches high and about 8 inches long. The main purpose of a banner is to get someone to click on it although some companies just use banners for billboard advertising. The very popular sites, like Yahoo!, and other directories and search engines actually sell banner space on their pages. There are some popular banner exchange programs that trade banner space among smaller sites.

Bleeding edge

A slang term that means the newest in multimedia technologies—things that Web designers are not quite sure are going to make it to the mainstream.

Bookmark

An address book entry for a Web site. Some browsers call this a favorite place. Most browsers contain a simple address book where the reader can store the addresses of their favorite places. Click on the name of the place, and the browser automatically goes there. When someone bookmarks your site, it means he or she is probably going to come back.

Browser

The essential tool of the Web. The browser is the software program that runs on your computer and lets you see Web pages. Internet Explorer and Netscape are the two most common browsers. Both work essentially the same way. Both Explorer and Netscape have slightly different formats and standards, so you need to keep them both in mind when designing your site.

Cache

A cache is a file on your reader's computer that stores Web pages from his or her last visit to a particular Web site. Then, if the reader wants to go to the same site again, instead of waiting for a page to download, the reader's computer can simply use the copy from the cache, sometimes saving as much as 10 or 20 seconds. The user has complete control of how big the cache is and how often it is emptied.

Click

A click of the mouse that brings you to a Web site or performs some other kind of computer action.

Click-through

A click-through is when someone clicks on a banner or link and leaps to your Web site or Web page.

Clickable maps

These are graphical images visitors to your page can click on to jump to other locations or see other images.

Client

The user of a network service (you are probably a client of the people who host your Web site). The word *client* is also used to describe a computer that relies upon another for some or all of its resources.

Compression

This is a way to make graphics faster to load. Various compression formats can encode the same data in a form that uses up less memory and can be transmitted more quickly.

Cookie

Part of a special file used to store information from one Web page to another. A cookie details your visitor's habits, wants, and needs. They are a strong promotional tool when you apply them to learn your customers' preferences. If you use cookies correctly, you can personalize your message for each visitor.

Content

All the information you have on your Web site. Think of a Web site as a documentary, educational TV show, or something on one of the home shopping networks. Content can be graphical, lists of Web addresses to other sites of interest to the reader, or just words. Many consumer surveys on the Web show that what makes readers come back to a Web page is content, not a pretty layout.

Copy

The printed words on a Web site.

CPM

Cost per thousand impressions. The price you pay to buy 1,000 banner looks.

CGI

Common gateway interfaces. Sorry to get technical here, but these are computer programs that allow for two-way communication and interactivity. For example, when you are using forms in your Web site, requesting information from potential customers, CGI takes the data from the browser and translates it into a useful format for you to use.

Demographics

Characteristics of a certain group of people. These can include variables such as age, sex, income levels, and psychological data. Very important in targeting your Web site.

Directories

Although they are similar to search engines, directories usually have real people going over submissions by hand. Directories take a longer time than automated search engines to index a site, and often don't revise a site description once it's indexed. They are collections of data, typically grouped by subject matter.

DNS

Domain name system. The method used to convert Internet names to their corresponding Internet numbers.

Domain name

A unique identifier, or a way of subdividing the Internet, which enables any Internet-connected computer to locate another. The domain name itself (such as mycompany.com) actually represents a number, or Internet protocol (IP) number (such as 204.119.240.10).

E-mail

Electronic mail is the messages delivered via networks to a specific person or mailbox. You can send not only messages, but also files, artwork, or spreadsheets. E-mail is used both as a noun and as a verb.

E-mail bombs

Because distribution on the Internet is so inexpensive, it's tempting to think of using it like direct mail—to broadcast general advertisements to thousands of people. E-mail is a wonderful way to distribute information about your company and products, provided you're working with a qualified list of people that *want* to receive the information. Sending unwanted e-mail, or posting ads to noncommercial areas of newsgroups, may generate some sales, but it will also alienate many more potential customers than it gets.

FAQs

Frequently asked questions. Many people are asking the same questions, on any given topic. Therefore, people or companies compile a list of these questions and the appropriate answers. They are often listed on home pages and Web sites as FAQs.

Firewall

A security barrier set up between a company's internal systems and outside systems. Firewalls can be designed to keep hostile visitors out, as a way of protecting the company's internal information, or they can be designed to keep company employees in, usually as a means of discouraging people from playing games or playing on the Web on company time. If a customer calls you and says he can get to your site just fine from home, but can't reach it from the office or from school, the problem is often a firewall.

Freeware

Software that is distributed free of charge. It often has poor documentation and customer service, but it is free.

Frequency

The number of times your ad is shown to one person. You may have to reach these same people 10 or more times to get them to respond.

FTP

File transfer protocol. Many FTP servers allow you to download files without having an account by using "anonymous" or "ftp" for a user name and your e-mail address as a password. This is a major means of distributing software and info on the Internet. To make a complicated definition really short, it usually refers to a program that allows you to transfer data between connected computers.

Flame

A nasty note, or hostile letter, either written to a public forum or sent privately. A flame war is an exchange of these types of notes between two or more people. You can inadvertently start a flame war by typing your postings to newsgroups in all capital letters. Typing in all capital letters is thought of as yelling. You can start a flame war when you post something that is perceived as an advertisement to an area that is regarded as noncommercial. This will generate a lot of hostile response, and can be very damaging to a company's reputation.

Frame

Frames are a way of dividing a browser window into two or more parts. This allows the reader to scroll through one part, while leaving another part untouched. Although frames are used for a number of purposes, one of the most common is for a navigation bar.

GIF (Graphics Interchange Format)

A standard color image format commonly encountered on the Internet.

Graphics

This term refers to digitized images, either photographs or artwork, as opposed to text.

GUI

Graphical user interface, or GUI (pronounced "goo-ey"). Many computer programs and operating systems are using a system of graphics and icons. When you take the mouse and point and click on the graphic, you can access the appropriate data.

Hacker

This was not always a bad thing. Originally, this term referred to really good programmers and computer experts and connoted respect. The word is now used (especially by the media) to refer to people who deliberately try to penetrate the security of other computers.

Hit

One visit from a reader. Different statistical packages count hits differently, which is one reason people are so confused about how hits are counted. For example, if you have a page that has some text and 10 tiny graphics, the way the Web works, the reader's system will have to ask your site for 11 things: the main page, plus the 10 graphics. But some statistical packages will count that as 11 hits. Even worse, some packages continue to count hits if the reader reloads the page.

Hits are important because they're the same as the circulation of your site. But depending on how you count, you may be overestimating or underestimating your readership. Hits should be counted on the basis of one per page, not one per graphic. Like any circulation estimates, hits require interpretation and analysis.

Hit counter

Usually a graphical image (but sometimes a hidden file), and often similar to an automobile's odometer. It displays the number of hits a page receives.

Home page

Usually the first page or welcome page of any Web site. It introduces the person or organization to anyone on the Web. It provides links to other pages at the site.

GLOSSARY

Host

The service organization that carries your Web site. Every Web site requires two computers: the sender's host or server, and the reader's browser. The host is a sender that sends the Web site to your reader. The browser is the receiver, which displays it on the reader's computer. Servers are senders, browsers are receivers. Although you can host your own Web site, it requires an additional level of technical expertise and a great deal more money. Running your own server is probably best justified when you run an intranet—when you use the server to communicate with your own employees.

HTML

Hypertext markup language. This comprises the standardized set of commands that allows you to format and link documents, graphics, and the like on the Web. Web browsers read this language and encode it so you can view documents and surf the Internet. It refers to a technique for creating links. The links in this file are usually connected to text (in which case, it's called hypertext) or graphics, and can, when activated by the click of a mouse or stroke of a key, display another document or graphic. It's relatively easy to learn.

Hypertext

Text that, when clicked on, jumps the reader to somewhere else. This makes research fast and easy. It may not make it efficient, since you don't really know where you're going until you get there, and several clicks later, you may not remember just how to get back to an earlier item. In most browsers, hypertext is shown underlined.

Impression

The opportunity to see a banner. Whenever a page loads and you see the banner, that is called an impression.

Information tracking

As Web sites became more complex and traffic harder to get, information tracking is becoming more important. It tells you where your visitors spend time, how they got to your site, and how long they spend on each page of your site. Cookies put info into the reader's browser so that the browser itself can remember some information. Then the browser can, on request, pass all that information up to the server at one time.

Internet

A concentration of many individual TCP/IP campus, state, regional, and national networks (into one single logical network all sharing a common addressing scheme). No matter how it's technically defined, this book is about the Internet.

Internet service provider

These are the telephone services that help people get online. When it comes to the Internet, your computer plus your modem is your "phone"—your access account will come from an Internet service provider (ISP).

InterNIC

The Inter-Networking Information Center is the organization that regulates and authorizes domain names in the United States. InterNIC is an entity formed by the National Science Foundation, Network Solutions, Inc., and AT&T to provide management functions for the Internet, such as domain name registration.

IP address

Internet protocol addresses are unique numbers that represent your Web site address.

Interstitial ad

Ads that pop up between what the viewer is looking at and before he gets to a new page.

Intranet

The setting up of an Internet for internal communications within an organization. There is often no connection to the WWW.

Java

A programming language that allows applets (small programs) to be downloaded and executed in your computer when it is triggered in some way.

JPEG

Joint Photographics Expert Group. A standard (compressed) format for color images common on the Internet. JPEGs tend to be smaller files than GIFs.

Juno

Juno provides free e-mail service to anyone with a personal computer and a modem (no Internet connection is required). To take advantage of it, you must install their software on your computer and put up with the on-screen advertising that makes the service possible.

Keywords

These are words or phrases you use to get the search engines to index your site and are of key importance to many search engines. They are a clear demonstration of how the Web has grown. Every site administrator knows what they'd like keywords to do: they'd like to be able to tell the search engines how to catalog their site so that readers can find it.

Each search engine has its own method of cataloging, and none of them are as simple as yellow pages categories. Many search engines can handle only one-word keywords, but that is changing since search engines are now reading phrases rather than just words.

Link

Usually a hypertext entry that lets the reader jump to a new location. Specifically, it means a Web address, or URL, which, when clicked on, transfers the reader to that location. The disadvantage to links is they encourage people to leave your site—and they may not come back.

Listserv

A program for the management of electronic mailing lists that allows the user to (1) join lists (or subscribe), (2) quit lists (or unsubscribe), or (3) send messages to mailing lists. Most lists are offered at no cost. Listservs can be great for research, too, since you can effectively target your audience.

Mailing list

A discussion group, distributed via e-mail from a central computer, maintaining the list of people involved in the discussion.

Mailto

A hypertext link that produces a screen that permits a visitor to send e-mail directly from your Web page, without having to open other software.

Metatags

Words hidden in your coding to get some search engines to index you. "Descriptions" and "keywords" are the only categories of metatags.

Majordomo

Another program for managing mailing lists, similar in functionality to Listserv.

Mirror site

Files at ftp sites are often made available at additional sites, called mirror sites, to better serve users.

Newbie

A term for new Internet users, especially with regard to Usenet and newsgroups. Newbies should not be scorned. We were all newbies at one time.

Newsgroup

A Usenet discussion group or bulletin board, usually devoted to a particular subject.

Navigation bar

If you're used to Windows, you know that at the top of the screen there is often a menu bar—a list of choices for you to pick from. This menu usually stays available to you at the top of the screen, even as you go from place to place. A navigation bar is a kind of menu of a site that stays available so the reader can move easily from place to place.

Online brochure

Also called brochureware. A Web site that is the online equivalent of a paper brochure. This is essentially a description of a business, product, or service, with an e-mail link to allow customers to get more information.

Open Web

Web sites and Web addresses that are available to anyone with Internet access. For example, some providers, like AOL, have information that is available only to America Online members.

Page view

When a person requests your page through a browser. Page views are often used to track the effectiveness of your banners and are a more reliable way of counting your traffic than hits.

Push

A marketing strategy that sends information directly to a user's browser rather than waiting for him or her to search the Web.

Psychographics

Emotional and psychological graphics that are used for targeting and segmentation. These can include attitudes, opinions, purchasing behavior, and lifestyle issues.

Rating services

The most common reason for a Web site rating is to identify sites with adult content that might not be suitable for children. Many different services are available. Almost all allow you to register your site for free. Once registered, your Web site must include a rating indicator. Rating services can help you develop traffic. You may want to add the word's "suitable for children" if you're trying to reach teachers who may be using school systems to reach the Web.

Reach

The total number of people who see a given ad.

Reciprocal links

This is a trade deal where you place links on another Web site and that site places their links on yours. Reciprocal links are links between two sites—sort of "I'll tell my readers about you if you'll tell your readers about me." A banner exchange is a form of reciprocal linking. Links can be contractually bound, or they may be exchanged informally.

Robot

See spider.

Screen resolution

The measurement of the detail you want on your computer screen. At 800×600, you can get almost twice as much detail on the screen as you can at 640×480. You need to be aware of who your audience is, and what kinds of systems they are likely to have. If your site is finely detailed and geared to a 800×600 resolution, it might not show up well on screens with a smaller resolution, say, 640x480.

Search engines

The automated indexers of the Web. They keep huge files with short entries of millions of Web sites. You type in a query, and the search engines do their best to make a list of all the catalog entries that might be what you're looking for.

Secure server

A secure server uses a special code to make sensitive information difficult to read for anyone not authorized to access it. Most companies that accept credit cards over the Web do so through a secured server. You might also want to secure other sensitive types of information. If you don't want to bother with adding a secure server to your site, you can rent space in a cybermall that provides secure shopping.

Session

A completed visit from a surfer. A session can start anywhere on your site and can last from minutes to hours.

Shopping cart

A program that lets visitors to your site make selections from more than one page before sending in their order. Your customers can "put things into the shopping cart" but not have to actually pay for them until they check out.

SMTP

Simple mail transfer protocol. The Internet standard protocol for transferring electronic mail messages from one computer to another. SMTP specifies how two mail systems interact and the format of control messages they exchange to transfer mail.

Signature

The small, usually four- to six-line, message at the bottom of a piece of e-mail or a Usenet article. It should include all contact information and a small blurb.

Spiders

Also called robots, these are automated programs that explore the Web, looking for information. The most common kinds of spiders are the ones that collect Web addresses for the search engines to catalog.

Shareware

Software that is distributed for a small fee or sometimes simply a postcard to the author (on the honor system). There is a large shareware community that is philosophically opposed to selling software for profit.

Sound files

These are digitized files that, when activated, play voice or music. The most common formats for sound files used on the Internet are .avi, .mov, .mpg, .qt (audio/video files), .au, .mid, .ra, and .wav (audio files).

Spam

Unsolicited e-mail advertising. Spam is considered poor business etiquette and can result in the loss of your server.

Streaming

A process for playing audio or video files over the Internet. Streamed files can begin to play while the file is downloading.

Summarize

To encapsulate a number of responses into one coherent, usable message. Often done on controlled mailing lists or active newsgroups to help reduce bandwidth.

Valid HTML

This is HTML that has been "validated" (checked for errors and corrected) by a computer program. Validation ensures that any properly functioning browser will be able to retrieve and display the page without errors.

URL

Universal resource locator. The mechanism used by the WWW system to find a particular page, image, or sound; basically, an address for the page. For example, the URL for my home page is *www.barryfeig.com*.

Usenet

A text-based mechanism that supports discussion groups, called newsgroups, that allow users from anywhere on the Internet to participate. Though a service rather than a network, it is the most popular of the Internet's many services.

User

A term similar in spirit to "consumer" or "public" that generically refers to someone who uses a computer, network, or piece of software.

Web server

This is the host computer that houses your home page and Web site. It serves many functions, allowing full-time access to your site. For example, it houses software to facilitate CGI forms, e-mail, and domain names.

WWW

World Wide Web. This is the same as the Open Web. Most people use the terms *Web* and *World Wide Web* interchangeably. With the exception of a few Web sites, it refers to a single Web address, whether available from an intranet or on the Open Web. Also called "the Web," it is a system that allows users to graphically browse through documents on sites throughout the Internet.

Web marketing

This refers to any type of Internet-based promotion, including Web sites, targeted e-mail, Internet bulletin boards, sites where customers can dial-in and download files. The term doesn't have a strict meaning, but people use it to cover any computer-based marketing.

Web site

A collection of one or more Web pages. A Web page is a single file that can be displayed on the Web. Some Web pages are just a few lines of text. Some can contain whole volumes of information. A rule of thumb is that if you can get to all the information by using just the scrolling arrows, it's all one Web page. If you have to "click here" or use your mouse to get to additional information, it's a new page.

Word processor

This is a program like Microsoft Word, WordPerfect, or Word Express (my favorite). It lets you format your work using bold, italics, page headers, indexes, and much more. Each word processor works a little differently, and despite what the manufacturers say, they all work about the same.

Index

multimedia
    when to avoid, 31–32
    when to use, 32–33, 34
multimedia-tasking, 275
music, 337

N

name, *see* domain name
navigation, of site, 51–52, 53,
    253–254
NetMind, 85
netWatch, 85–86
Netwhistle.com, 63
networking
    B2B and, 267–269, 270
    see also affiliate programs; links
"new", 60
newbies, 16
newsgroups
    advertising on, 278
    basics of, 114–117
    hierarchies of, 119–120
    market research with, 82
    posting to, 105, 125–126
    power of, 141
    reciprocal links and, 174
    reviewing threads on, 123–125
    rules for promotion on, 117–118
    signature line for, 121–122
    subscribing to, 122–123
newsletters, 150–151
    advantages of, 151–152
    advertising and, 278
    B2B and, 266
    content for, 152–153,
        340–341
    list of links to, 159
    subscribers for, 153–155
newspapers, specialty, 277

niche marketing
    reinforcement and, 42–43
    segmentation and, 39–42
Noga, Lee, 233

O

objectives, defining, 14–15
occupation, as a niche, 41
OfficeMax, 258
On Writing (King), 60
opinion columns, 231–232
opt-in mailings, 293–294
opt-in marketing, 152, 158, 339

P

page impressions, 304
Pareto principle, 76
partner, for cross-promotion, 184–185
partnerships, 292–293
performance-based marketing, *see*
    affiliate programs
permission marketing, 342–343
phone service, offering free, 164
Pogo.com, 322
pop-up advertisements, 292, 336
pop-up captions, 52
pornography sites, 248
portal, 240–241
position analysis tool, 217
positioning, of site, *see* focus, of site
posting, to newsgroups, 125
preplanning
    checklist for, 10–11
    importance of, 9–10
press kit, 132
press releases
    format of, 134
    ideas for, 131–133, 134–135

kinds of, 133
    purpose of, 130–131, 141
    where to send, 139, 335–336
Pressaccess.com, 139
privacy
    cookies and, 229
    creating policy for, 188
Prodigy, 226
promotion
    planning for, 14–24
    preplanning for, 9–11
    ten commandments of, 8
promotional message, 92–93
    AIDA formula for, 93–94
    buying premade, 97–98
    creating alone, 95–97
    share of heart and, 94–95
PRWeb, 139, 335
publicity, *see* media relations
push marketing, 243–244

Q

questionnaires, *see* surveys

R

readability, 60–61
reciprocal links, 172, 174–175, 307,
    332
Recycler.com, 234
Refer-it.com, 189, 190
referrals
    B2B and, 266, 268
    from site visitors, 21
Register.com game, 16
registration
    of domain name, 19–20, 46–48,
        333–334
    of trademark, 44

A Note from the Author

Thank you for reading this book. It will always be a work in progress. If you have any ideas for future editions, or if you have a particular— or unusual—strategy that worked for you, please contact me at:

Barry Feig's Center for Product Success
772B Hwy 165
Placitas, NM 87043
You can call me at 505-771-FEIG (3344)
My e-mail address is *feig@barryfeig.com*

I'm looking forward to hearing from you.

STREETWISE® BOOKS

Newest Arrivals!

Crash Course MBA
$19.95 (CAN $29.95)
ISBN 1-59337-210-8

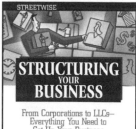

Structuring Your Business
$19.95 (CAN $29.95)
ISBN 1-59337-177-2

Also Available in the *Streetwise*® Series:

24 Hour MBA
$19.95 (CAN $29.95)
ISBN 1-58062-256-9

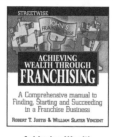

**Achieving Wealth
Through Franchising**
$19.95 (CAN $29.95)
ISBN 1-58062-503-7

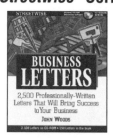

**Business Letters
with CD-ROM**
$29.95 (CAN $47.95)
ISBN 1-58062-133-3

Business Valuation
$19.95 (CAN $31.95)
ISBN 1-58062-952-0

Complete Business Plan
$19.95 (CAN $29.95)
ISBN 1-55850-845-7

**Complete Business Plan
with Software**
$29.95 (CAN $47.95)
ISBN 1-58062-798-6

Complete Publicity Plans
$19.95 (CAN $29.95)
ISBN 1-58062-771-4

**Customer-Focused
Selling**
$19.95 (CAN $29.95)
ISBN 1-55850-725-6

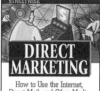

Direct Marketing
$19.95 (CAN $29.95)
ISBN 1-58062-439-1

**Do-It-Yourself
Advertising**
$19.95 (CAN $29.95)
ISBN 1-55850-727-2

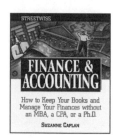

Finance & Accounting
$19.95 (CAN $29.95)
ISBN 1-58062-196-1

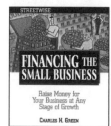

**Financing the Small
Business**
$19.95 (CAN $29.95)
ISBN 1-58062-765-X

**Human Resources
Management**
$19.95 (CAN $29.95)
ISBN 1-58062-699-8

Independent Consulting
$19.95 (CAN $29.95)
ISBN 1-55850-728-0

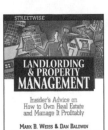

**Landlording & Property
Management**
$19.95 (CAN $29.95)
ISBN 1-58062-766-8

Low-Cost Marketing
$19.95 (CAN $31.95)
ISBN 1-58062-858-3

**Low-Cost Web Site
Promotion**
$19.95 (CAN $29.95)
ISBN 1-58062-501-0

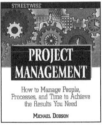

Managing a Nonprofit
$19.95 (CAN $29.95)
ISBN 1-58062-698-X

Managing People
$19.95 (CAN $29.95)
ISBN 1-55850-726-4

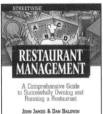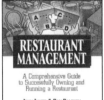

Marketing Plan
$19.95 (CAN $29.95)
ISBN 1-58062-268-2

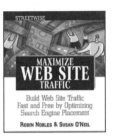

**Maximize Web
Site Traffic**
$19.95 (CAN $29.95)
ISBN 1-58062-369-7

**Motivating & Rewarding
Employees**
$19.95 (CAN $29.95)
ISBN 1-58062-130-9

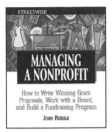

Project Management
$19.95 (CAN $29.95)
ISBN 1-58062-770-6

**Relationship Marketing
on the Internet**
$17.95 (CAN $27.95)
ISBN 1-58062-255-0

**Restaurant
Management**
$19.95 (CAN $29.95)
ISBN 1-58062-781-1

Retirement Planning
$19.95 (CAN $29.95)
ISBN 1-58062-772-2

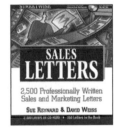

**Sales Letters
with CD-ROM**
$29.95 (CAN $44.95)
ISBN 1-58062-440-5

Selling Your Business
$19.95 (CAN $29.95)
ISBN 1-58062-602-5

Small Business Start-Up
$19.95 (CAN $29.95)
ISBN 1-55850-581-4

Time Management
$19.95 (CAN $29.95)
ISBN 1-58062-131-7

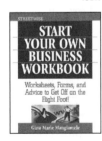

**Start Your Own
Business Workbook**
$9.95 (CAN $15.95)
ISBN 1-58062-506-1

Available wherever books are sold.
For more information, or to order, call 800-872-5627 or visit www.*adamsmedia.com*
Adams Media, an F+W Publications Company, 57 Littlefield Street, Avon, MA 02322

Marketing Guru Launches New Marketing Wise Web Site Offering Free Marketing Tips and Info

Marketing guru Barry Feig, president of Barry Feig's Center for Product Success announced his appearance on the Web with free columns that offer unique insights about marketing and consumer purchase motivation. His new site, located at *www.barryfeig.com,* brings his singular approach to marketing and positioning new products to the online business community. This innovation has won international recognition for Barry Feig and his clients. For the first time, Barry Feig offers his internationally acclaimed approach to marketing, complete with published books and articles to aid businesses in focusing their products and services on success.

"The virtual arm of my business has expanded my availability to reach those who need my services most. The Web site offers power and visibility that were not previously available," said Feig.

Barryfeig.com offers insights into the heretofore confusing and mysterious processes involved in developing and marketing products that achieve uncommon success.

Feig said that the single biggest mistake that businesses make in developing their products is assuming that they know what their customers want. "We've seen it over and over again," said Feig. "Businesses come up with what looks like an exciting new product and they fall in love with it assuming that the whole world will agree with them. But it just doesn't work that way. The buying public holds the key to what products will survive in the market today and which will fail."

"We're leading the way by providing a service that capitalizes on the strengths of the Internet, while adhering to the best in marketing principles."

On the site, there is a special free section that features new product articles, insights, and tips written by Feig, which have been featured in the world's leading marketing magazines. Marketers and entrepreneurs can learn:

- How to speed up the product development process by $2/3$.
- The secret visual that marketers can employ to create an emotional bond with consumers.
- How to generate new product and positioning ideas quickly and efficiently.
- Why most marketers go wrong when they introduce or market a new product.
- A breakthrough marketing concept called "Share of Heart" and how it can revitalize even shopworn products.

Barry Feig's books are considered the benchmark publications in new product development and brand and product positioning. They are influential not only in the United States but around the world. *Marketing Straight to the Heart* (Amacom) has been translated and published in China and Germany as well as in the United States *The New Products Workshop, Hand-on Methods for Developing Winners* (McGraw-Hill) was voted one of the top 30 business books of the year. *Winning Marketing Strategies* was published last year by Prentice-Hall.

Feig has offered world-class marketing services to a large roster of clients for more than 20 years. His work on products like Glad Locks bags, Kellogg's Smart Start, American Express Gift Cheques, and Arm & Hammer Dryer Sheets has helped generate billions of dollars in sales.